6. Enter your class ID code to join a class.

IF YOU HAVE A CLASS CODE FROM YOUR TEACHER

a. Enter your class code and click [Next]

b. Once you have joined a class, you will be able to use the Discussion Board and Email tools.

c. To enter this code later, choose **Join a Class**.

IF YOU DO NOT HAVE A CLASS CODE

a. If you do not have a class ID code, click [Skip]

b. You do not need a class ID code to use *iQ Online*.

c. To enter this code later, choose **Join a Class**.

7. Review registration information and click Log In. Then choose your book. Click **Activities** to begin using *iQ Online*.

IMPORTANT

- After you register, the next time you want to use *iQ Online*, go to www.iQOnlinePractice.com and log in with your email address and password.
- The online content can be used for 12 months from the date you register.
- For help, please contact customer service: eltsupport@oup.com.

WHAT IS iQ ONLINE ?

All new activities provide essential skills **practice** and support.

Vocabulary and Grammar **games** immerse you in the language and provide even more practice.

Authentic, engaging **videos** generate new ideas and opinions on the Unit Question.

Go to the Media Center to download or stream all **student book audio**.

Use the **Discussion Board** to discuss the Unit Question and more.

Email encourages communication with your teacher and classmates.

Automatic grading gives immediate feedback and tracks progress.

Progress Reports show what you have mastered and where you still need more practice.

OXFORD
UNIVERSITY PRESS

198 Madison Avenue
New York, NY 10016 USA

Great Clarendon Street, Oxford, OX2 6DP, United Kingdom

Oxford University Press is a department of the University of Oxford.
It furthers the University's objective of excellence in research, scholarship,
and education by publishing worldwide. Oxford is a registered trade
mark of Oxford University Press in the UK and in certain other countries

Adult Content Director: Stephanie Karras
Publisher: Sharon Sargent
Managing Editor: Mariel DeKranis
Development Editor: Eric Zuarino
Head of Digital, Design, and Production: Bridget O'Lavin
Executive Art and Design Manager: Maj-Britt Hagsted
Design Project Manager: Debbie Lofaso
Content Production Manager: Julie Armstrong
Image Manager: Trisha Masterson
Image Editor: Liaht Ziskind
Production Coordinator: Brad Tucker

ISBN: 978 0 19 481950 3 Student Book 5 with iQ Online pack
ISBN: 978 0 19 481951 0 Student Book 5 as pack component
ISBN: 978 0 19 481802 5 iQ Online student website

Printed in China
This book is printed on paper from certified and well-managed sources.

ACKNOWLEDGEMENTS
*The authors and publisher are grateful to those who have given permission to reproduce the
following extracts and adaptations of copyright material:* p. 6 "The History of the
Maori Language," from "History of the Maori language – Te Wiki o Te Reo
Maori," New Zealand Ministry for Culture and Heritage, http://www.nzhistory.
net.nz. Used by permission.; p. 16 "When Languages Die" from *When Languages
Die: The Extinction of the World's Languages and the Erosion of Human Knowledge* by
K. David Harrison, 2007, pp. 15–16, 53–55. Used by permission of Oxford
University Press, USA.; p. 23 "Knowledge" adapted from *Oxford Learner's
Thesaurus: A dictionary of synonyms* by Diana Lea. © Oxford University Press 2008.
Reproduced by permission of Oxford University Press.; p. 38 From "Laid-Back
Labor: The $140 Homemade Scarf" by Stephen J. Dubner and Steven D. Levitt
as appeared in *The New York Times*, May 6, 2007. Copyright © 2007 Stephen J.
Dunbar and Steven D. Levitt. Used by permission of William Morris Endeavor
Entertainment, LLC.; p. 47 From "Tae Kwon Do for Health: Train Smart Now
or Pay the Price Later!" by Grandmaster Kim Soo, International Chayon-Ryu
Martial Association, *Black Belt* Magazine, September 2011. Used by permission
of author and Black Belt Magazine.; p. 69 "Infographics Lie: Here's How"
adapted from "Infographics Lie: Here's How to Spot the B.S." by Randy Olson,
posted on Fast Company, January 6, 2014, © 2014 Mansueto Ventures, LLC. All
rights reserved. Used by permission and protected by the Copyright Laws of the
United States. The printing, copying, redistribution, or retransmission of this
Content without express written permission is prohibited.; p. 76 "Phototruth
or Photofiction?" from *Phototruth or Photofiction? Ethics and Media Imagery in the
Digital Age* by Thomas H. Wheeler. Copyright © 2002. Reproduced by
permission of Taylor and Francis Group, LLC, in the format Textbook via
Copyright Clearance Center and the author. Used by permission.; p. 98 From

"Near Arctic, Seed Vault Is a Fort Knox of Food" by Elisabeth Rosenthal, *The New
York Times*, February 29, 2008. © 2008 The New York Times. All rights reserved.
Used by permission and protected by the Copyright Laws of the United States.
The printing, copying, redistribution, or retransmission of the Material
without express written permission is prohibited.; p. 107 "Building the perfect
spaceman: Inside NASA's training facility that turns mortals into astronauts,
and one into spaceship commander" by Kate Lunau, from *Maclean's*, October 2,
2012, www.macleans.ca. Used by permission.; p. 132 From "The New Oases" as
appeared in *The Economist*. © The Economist Newspaper Limited, London April
12, 2008. Reproduced by permission.; p. 140 From "A Path to Road Safety with
No Signposts" by Sarah Lyall, *The New York Times*, January 22, 2005. © 2005 The
New York Times. All rights reserved. Used by permission and protected by the
Copyright Laws of the United States. The printing, copying, redistribution, or
retransmission of the Material without express written permission is prohibited.;
p. 139 "The New Third Places" from "Where Everybody Knows Your Name" by
Mary Newsom, September 24 2009, http://citiwire.net. Copyright owned by The
Charlotte Observer. Reprinted with permission from The Charlotte Observer.;
p. 163 "Garbage of Eden" from "Garbage of Eden: want to be at one with
nature? Take a stroll round Singapore's island of trash," by Eric Bland, *New
Scientist*, April 14, 2007. © Reed Business Information – UK. All rights reserved.
Distributed by Tribune Content Agency, LLC. Used by permission.; p. 171 "The
Glorious Feeling of Fixing Something Yourself" by Christina Cooke, *The Atlantic*,
January 10, 2014 © 2014 The Atlantic Media Co., as first published in The
Atlantic Magazine. All rights reserved. Distributed by Tribune Content Agency,
LLC. Used by permission.; p. 194 From "Set in Our Ways: Why Change Is So
Hard" by Nikolas Westerhoff, *Scientific American Mind*, December 17, 2008,
http://www.sciam.com. Copyright © 2008 by Scientific American, Inc. All rights
reserved. Reproduced with permission.; p. 204 From "Cancer be damned, kids
wanna tan," by Danylo Hawaleshka from *Maclean's*, June 27, 2005. www.
macleans.ca. Used by permission.; p. 214 "Children as Young as 11 Use Sunbed
Salons in Northern England," from "Children as Young as 11 Use Sunbed
Salons," by Sam Jones, *The Guardian*, December 14, 2005, http://www.guardian.
co.uk. Copyright Guardian News & Media Ltd., 2005. Used by permission.;
p. 228 From "A Healthy Lifestyle Can Reduce Fatigue, Boost Energy," by David A.
Norrie, January 7, 2009, http://www.sptimes.com. Used by permission of the
author.; p. 238 "A Jolt of Caffeine, by the Can," from "A Jolt of Caffeine, by the
Can; Caution: Energy Drink Profits May be Addictive" by Melanie Warner, *The
New York Times*, November 23, 2005. © 2005 The New York Times. All rights
reserved. Used by permission and protected by the Copyright Laws of the
United States. The printing, copying, redistribution, or retransmission of the
Material without express written permission is prohibited.

Illustrations by: p. 4 Stacy Merlin; p. 66 Karen Minot; pp. 70–71, 5W Infographics;
74–75, 5W Infographics; p. 89 Marc Kolle; p. 96 Stacy Merlin; p. 128 Stacy
Merlin; p. 160 Stacy Merlin; p. 165 Karen Minot; p. 226 Karen Minot.

*We would also like to thank the following for permission to reproduce the following
photographs:* Cover: Yongyut Kumsri/Shutterstock; Video Vocabulary (used
throughout the book): Oleksiy Mark/Shutterstock; p. 2 Michael S. Yamashita/Getty
Images; p. 3 Underwood & Underwood/Corbis, Frédéric Soreau/Photononstop/
Corbis, Radharc Images/Alamy, Robert Harding Picture Library Ltd/Alamy; p. 4 2/
Ocean/Corbis UK Ltd. (Bowing), Radius Images/Corbis UK Ltd. (Shoes); p. 16
Jeremy Fahringer/K. David Harrison, Ph.D.; p. 30 Mark Hunt/Rex Features; p. 34
Rhona Wise/epa/Corbis; p. 35 Christopher Furlong/Getty Images, Sandratsky
Dmitriy/shutterstock; p. 36 Catchlight Visual Services/Alamy (#1), Westend61/
Oxford University Press (#2), Jordan Siemens/Getty Images (#3), Rick Gomez/
Masterfile Royalty Free (#4), David Young-Wolff/Alamy (#5), Blend Images/Alamy
(#6), Tetra Images/Corbis UK Ltd. (#8), Andres Rodriguez/Alamy (#9); p. 38 betty
finney/Alamy; p. 47 Panorama Media/Age Fotostock; p. 65 Paul Hackett/Reuters/
Corbis; p. 66 ADS/Alamy (Photograph), Imagezoo/Corbis UK Ltd. (Cartoon),
3LH-B&W ART FILE/Getty Images (Drawing); p. 77 GAHAN, GORDON/National
Geographic Creative/National Geographic Society; p. 82 Blend Images/Alamy;
p. 94 Ton Koene/Visuals Unlimited/Corbis; p. 95 Park Jin-hee Xinhua News Agency/
Newscom, Vicki Beaver/Alamy; p. 98 National Geographic Image Collection/Alamy
(All); p. 99 Bon Appetit/Alamy; p. 107 NASA; p. 114 NASA; p. 127 Tony C French/
Getty Images; p. 133 Associated Press/Press Association Images; p. 135 Andria
Patino/Alamy; p136 David Sailors/Corbis UK Ltd. (MIT); p. 136 Ambient Images
Inc./Alamy (Bryant Park); p. 140 Jerry Michalski; p. 152 Anne-Marie Palmer/
Alamy; p. 159 Randy Duchaine/Alamy; p. 161 Corbis/Oxford University Press;
p. 163 Roslan Rahman/AFP/ Getty Images; p. 170 2005 AFP/Getty Images; pp. 171,
172 Christina Cooke; p. 191 Tim Pannell/Corbis; p. 192 Emil Pozar/Age Fotostock
(#1), Soren Hald/Getty Images (#2), Digital Vision./Getty Images (#3), Lasse
Kristensen/Alamy (#4); p. 194 StockShot/Alamy; p. 195 John Peters/Getty Images;
p. 204 NASA Photo/Alamy; p. 214 deepblue4you/iStockphoto; p. 224 Dennis Cox/
AGE Fotostock; p. 225 wavebreakmedia/Shutterstock, fotostokers/Shutterstock;
p. 228 MIXA /Alamy; p. 246 Kanjanee Chaisin/Shutterstock; Back Cover: mozcann/
iStockphoto.

SHAPING learning TOGETHER

We would like to acknowledge the teachers from all over the world who participated in the development process and review of the Q series.

Special thanks to our *Q: Skills for Success* Second Edition Topic Advisory Board

Shaker Ali Al-Mohammad, Buraimi University College, Oman; **Dr. Asmaa A. Ebrahim**, University of Sharjah, U.A.E.; **Rachel Batchilder**, College of the North Atlantic, Qatar; **Anil Bayir**, Izmir University, Turkey; **Flora Mcvay Bozkurt**, Maltepe University, Turkey; **Paul Bradley**, University of the Thai Chamber of Commerce Bangkok, Thailand; **Joan Birrell-Bertrand**, University of Manitoba, MB, Canada; **Karen E. Caldwell**, Zayed University, U.A.E.; **Nicole Hammond Carrasquel**, University of Central Florida, FL, U.S.; **Kevin Countryman**, Seneca College of Applied Arts & Technology, ON, Canada; **Julie Crocker**, Arcadia University, NS, Canada; **Marc L. Cummings**, Jefferson Community and Technical College, KY, U.S.; **Rachel DeSanto**, Hillsborough Community College Dale Mabry Campus, FL, U.S.; **Nilüfer Ertürkmen**, Ege University, Turkey; **Sue Fine**, Ras Al Khaimah Women's College (HCT), U.A.E.; **Amina Al Hashami**, Nizwa College of Applied Sciences, Oman; **Stephan Johnson**, Nagoya Shoka Daigaku, Japan; **Sean Kim**, Avalon, South Korea; **Gregory King**, Chubu Daigaku, Japan; **Seran Küçük**, Maltepe University, Turkey; **Jonee De Leon**, VUS, Vietnam; **Carol Lowther**, Palomar College, CA, U.S.; **Erin Harris-MacLead**, St. Mary's University, NS, Canada; **Angela Nagy**, Maltepe University, Turkey; **Huynh Thi Ai Nguyen**, Vietnam; **Daniel L. Paller**, Kinjo Gakuin University, Japan; **Jangyo Parsons**, Kookmin University, South Korea; **Laila Al Qadhi**, Kuwait University, Kuwait; **Josh Rosenberger**, English Language Institute University of Montana, MT, U.S.; **Nancy Schoenfeld**, Kuwait University, Kuwait; **Jenay Seymour**, Hongik University, South Korea; **Moon-young Son**, South Korea; **Matthew Taylor**, Kinjo Gakuin Daigaku, Japan; **Burcu Tezcan-Unal**, Zayed University, U.A.E.; **Troy Tucker**, Edison State College-Lee Campus, FL, U.S.; **Kris Vicca**, Feng Chia University, Taichung; **Jisook Woo**, Incheon University, South Korea; **Dunya Yenidunya**, Ege University, Turkey

UNITED STATES Marcarena Aguilar, North Harris College, TX; **Rebecca Andrade**, California State University North Ridge, CA; **Lesley Andrews**, Boston University, MA; **Deborah Anholt**, Lewis and Clark College, OR; **Robert Anzelde**, Oakton Community College, IL; **Arlys Arnold**, University of Minnesota, MN; **Marcia Arthur**, Renton Technical College, WA; **Renee Ashmeade**, Passaic County Community College, NJ; **Anne Bachmann**, Clackamas Community College, OR; **Lida Baker**, UCLA, CA; **Ron Balsamo**, Santa Rosa Junior College, CA; **Lori Barkley**, Portland State University, OR; **Eileen Barlow**, SUNY Albany, NY; **Sue Bartch**, Cuyahoga Community College, OH; **Lora Bates**, Oakton High School, VA; **Barbara Batra**, Nassau County Community College, NY; **Nancy Baum**, University of Texas at Arlington, TX; **Rebecca Beck**, Irvine Valley College, CA; **Linda Berendsen**, Oakton Community College, IL; **Jennifer Binckes Lee**, Howard Community College, MD; **Grace Bishop**, Houston Community College, TX; **Jean W. Bodman**, Union County College, NJ; **Virginia Bouchard**, George Mason University, VA; **Kimberley Briesch Sumner**, University of Southern California, CA; **Kevin Brown**, University of California, Irvine, CA; **Laura Brown**, Glendale Community College, CA; **Britta Burton**, Mission College, CA; **Allison L. Callahan**, Harold Washington College, IL; **Gabriela Cambiasso**, Harold Washington College, IL; **Jackie Campbell**, Capistrano Unified School District, CA; **Adele C. Camus**, George Mason University, VA; **Laura Chason**, Savannah College, GA; **Kerry Linder Catana**, Language Studies International, NY; **An Cheng**, Oklahoma State University, OK; **Carole Collins**, North Hampton Community College, PA; **Betty R. Compton**, Intercultural Communications College, HI; **Pamela Couch**, Boston University, MA; **Fernanda Crowe**, Intrax International Institute, CA; **Vicki Curtis**, Santa Cruz, CA; **Margo Czinski**, Washtenaw Community College, MI; **David Dahnke**, Lone Star College, TX; **Gillian M. Dale**, CA; **L. Dalgish**, Concordia College, MN; **Christopher Davis**, John Jay College, NY; **Sherry Davis**, Irvine University, CA; **Natalia de Cuba**, Nassau County Community College, NY; **Sonia Delgadillo**, Sierra College, CA; **Esmeralda Diriye**, Cypress College & Cal Poly, CA; **Marta O. Dmytrenko-Ahrabian**, Wayne State University, MI; **Javier Dominguez**, Central High School, SC; **Jo Ellen Downey-Greer**, Lansing Community College, MI; **Jennifer Duclos**, Boston University, MA; **Yvonne Duncan**, City College of San Francisco, CA; **Paul Dydman**, USC Language Academy, CA; **Anna Eddy**, University of Michigan-Flint, MI; **Zohan El-Gamal**, Glendale Community College, CA; **Jennie Farnell**, University of Connecticut, CT; **Susan Fedors**, Howard Community College, MD; **Valerie Fiechter**, Mission College, CA; **Ashley Fifer**, Nassau County Community College, NY; **Matthew Florence**, Intrax International Institute, CA; **Kathleen Flynn**, Glendale College, CA; **Elizabeth Fonsea**, Nassau County Community College, NY; **Eve Fonseca**, St. Louis Community College, MO; **Elizabeth Foss**, Washtenaw Community College, MI; **Duff C. Galda**, Pima Community College, AZ; **Christiane Galvani**, Houston Community College, TX; **Gretchen Gerber**, Howard Community College, MD; **Ray Gonzalez**, Montgomery College, MD; **Janet Goodwin**, University of California, Los Angeles, CA; **Alyona Gorokhova**, Grossmont College, CA; **John Graney**, Santa Fe College, FL; **Kathleen Green**, Central High School, AZ; **Nancy Hamadou**, Pima Community College-West Campus, AZ; **Webb Hamilton**, De Anza College, San Jose City College, CA; **Janet Harclerode**, Santa Monica Community College, CA; **Sandra Hartmann**, Language and Culture Center, TX; **Kathy Haven**, Mission College, CA; **Roberta Hendrick**, Cuyahoga Community College, OH; **Ginny Heringer**, Pasadena City College, CA; **Adam Henricksen**, University of Maryland, MD; **Carolyn Ho**, Lone Star College-CyFair, TX; **Peter Hoffman**, LaGuardia Community College, NY; **Linda Holden**, College of Lake County, IL; **Jana Holt**, Lake Washington Technical College, WA; **Antonio Iccarino**, Boston University, MA; **Gail Ibele**, University of Wisconsin, WI; **Nina Ito**, American Language Institute, CSU Long Beach, CA; **Linda Jensen**, UCLA, CA; **Lisa Jurkowitz**, Pima Community College, CA; **Mandy Kama**, Georgetown University, Washington, DC; **Stephanie Kasuboski**, Cuyahoga Community College, OH; **Chigusa Katoku**, Mission College, CA; **Sandra Kawamura**, Sacramento City College, CA; **Gail Kellersberger**, University of Houston-Downtown, TX; **Jane Kelly**, Durham Technical Community College, NC; **Maryanne Kildare**, Nassau County Community College, NY; **Julie Park Kim**, George Mason University, VA; **Kindra Kinyon**, Los Angeles Trade-Technical College, CA; **Matt Kline**, El Camino College, CA; **Lisa Kovacs-Morgan**, University of California, San Diego, CA; **Claudia Kupiec**, DePaul University, IL; **Renee La Rue**, Lone Star College-Montgomery, TX; **Janet Langon**, Glendale College, CA; **Lawrence Lawson**, Palomar College, CA; **Rachele Lawton**, The Community College of Baltimore County, MD; **Alice Lee**, Richland College, TX; **Esther S. Lee**, CSUF & Mt. SAC, CA; **Cherie Lenz-Hackett**, University of Washington, WA; **Joy Leventhal**, Cuyahoga Community College, OH; **Alice Lin**, UCI Extension, CA; **Monica Lopez**, Cerritos College, CA; **Dustin Lovell**, FLS International Marymount College, CA; **Carol Lowther**, Palomar College, CA; **Candace Lynch-Thompson**, North Orange County Community College District, CA; **Thi Thi Ma**, City College of San Francisco, CA; **Steve Mac Isaac**, USC Long Academy, CA; **Denise Maduli-Williams**, City College of San Francisco, CA; **Eileen Mahoney**, Camelback High School, AZ; **Naomi Mardock**, MCC-Omaha, NE; **Brigitte Maronde**, Harold Washington College, IL; **Marilyn Marquis**, Laposita College CA; **Doris Martin**, Glendale Community College; Pasadena City College, CA; **Keith Maurice**, University of Texas at Arlington, TX; **Nancy Mayer**, University of Missouri-St. Louis, MO; **Aziah McNamara**, Kansas State University, KS; **Billie McQuillan**, Education Heights, MN; **Karen Merritt**, Glendale Union High School District, AZ; **Holly Milkowart**, Johnson County Community College, KS; **Eric Moyer**, Intrax International Institute, CA; **Gino Muzzatti**, Santa Rosa Junior College, CA; **Sandra Navarro**, Glendale Community College, CA; **Than Nyeinkhin**, ELAC, PCC, CA; **William Nedrow**, Triton College, IL; **Eric Nelson**, University of Minnesota, MN; **Than Nyeinkhin**, ELAC, PCC, CA; **Fernanda Ortiz**, Center for English as a Second Language at the University of Arizona, AZ; **Rhony Ory**, Ygnacio Valley High School, CA; **Paul Parent**, Montgomery College, MD; **Dr. Sumeeta Patnaik**, Marshall University, WV; **Oscar Pedroso**, Miami Dade College, FL; **Robin Persiani**, Sierra College, CA; **Patricia Prenz-Belkin**, Hostos Community College, NY; **Suzanne Powell**, University of Louisville, KY; **Jim Ranalli**, Iowa State University, IA; **Toni R. Randall**, Santa Monica College, CA; **Vidya Rangachari**, Mission College, CA; **Elizabeth Rasmussen**, Northern Virginia Community College, VA; **Lara Ravitch**, Truman College, IL;

Deborah Repasz, San Jacinto College, TX; **Marisa Recinos**, English Language Center, Brigham Young University, UT; **Andrey Reznikov**, Black Hills State University, SD; **Alison Rice**, Hunter College, NY; **Jennifer Robles**, Ventura Unified School District, CA; **Priscilla Rocha**, Clark County School District, NV; **Dzidra Rodins**, DePaul University, IL; **Maria Rodriguez**, Central High School, AZ; **Josh Rosenberger**, English Language Institute University of Montana, MT; **Alice Rosso**, Bucks County Community College, PA; **Rita Rozzi**, Xavier University, OH; **Maria Ruiz**, Victor Valley College, CA; **Kimberly Russell**, Clark College, WA; **Stacy Sabraw**, Michigan State University, MI; **Irene Sakk**, Northwestern University, IL; **Deborah Sandstrom**, University of Illinois at Chicago, IL; **Jenni Santamaria**, ABC Adult, CA; **Shaeley Santiago**, Ames High School, IA; **Peg Sarosy**, San Francisco State University, CA; **Alice Savage**, North Harris College, TX; **Donna Schaeffer**, University of Washington, WA; **Karen Marsh Schaeffer**, University of Utah, UT; **Carol Schinger**, Northern Virginia Community College, VA; **Robert Scott**, Kansas State University, KS; **Suell Scott**, Sheridan Technical Center, FL; **Shira Seaman**, Global English Academy, NY; **Richard Seltzer**, Glendale Community College, CA; **Harlan Sexton**, CUNY Queensborough Community College, NY; **Kathy Sherak**, San Francisco State University, CA; **German Silva**, Miami Dade College, FL; **Ray Smith**, Maryland English Institute, University of Maryland, MD; **Shira Smith**, NICE Program University of Hawaii, HI; **Tara Smith**, Felician College, NJ; **Monica Snow**, California State University, Fullerton, CA; **Elaine Soffer**, Nassau County Community College, NY; **Andrea Spector**, Santa Monica Community College, CA; **Jacqueline Sport**, LBWCC Luverne Center, AL; **Karen Stanely**, Central Piedmont Community College, NC; **Susan Stern**, Irvine Valley College, CA; **Ayse Stromsdorfer**, Soldan I.S.H.S., MO; **Yilin Sun**, South Seattle Community College, WA; **Thomas Swietlik**, Intrax International Institute, IL; **Nicholas Taggert**, University of Dayton, OH; **Judith Tanka**, UCLA Extension–American Language Center, CA; **Amy Taylor**, The University of Alabama Tuscaloosa, AL; **Andrea Taylor**, San Francisco State, CA; **Priscilla Taylor**, University of Southern California, CA; **Ilene Teixeira**, Fairfax County Public Schools, VA; **Shirl H. Terrell**, Collin College, TX; **Marya Teutsch-Dwyer**, St. Cloud State University, MN; **Stephen Thergesen**, ELS Language Centers, CO; **Christine Tierney**, Houston Community College, TX; **Arlene Turini**, North Moore High School, NC; **Cara Tuzzolino**, Nassau County Community College, NY; **Suzanne Van Der Valk**, Iowa State University, IA; **Nathan D. Vasarhely**, Ygnacio Valley High School, CA; **Naomi S. Verratti**, Howard Community College, MD; **Hollyahna Vettori**, Santa Rosa Junior College, CA; **Julie Vorholt**, Lewis & Clark College, OR; **Danielle Wagner**, FLS International Marymount College, CA; **Lynn Walker**, Coastline College, CA; **Laura Walsh**, City College of San Francisco, CA; **Andrew J. Watson**, The English Bakery; **Donald Weasenforth**, Collin College, TX; **Juliane Widner**, Sheepshead Bay High School, NY; **Lynne Wilkins**, Mills College, CA; **Pamela Williams**, Ventura College, CA; **Jeff Wilson**, Irvine Valley College, CA; **James Wilson**, Consomnes River College, CA; **Katie Windahl**, Cuyahoga Community College, OH; **Dolores "Lorrie" Winter**, California State University at Fullerton, CA; **Jody Yamamoto**, Kapi'olani Community College, HI; **Ellen L. Yaniv**, Boston University, MA; **Norman Yoshida**, Lewis & Clark College, OR; **Joanna Zadra**, American River College, CA; **Florence Zysman**, Santiago Canyon College, CA;

CANADA Patricia Birch, Brandon University, MB; **Jolanta Caputa**, College of New Caledonia, BC; **Katherine Coburn**, UBC's ELI, BC; **Erin Harris-Macleod**, St. Mary's University, NS; **Tami Moffatt**, English Language Institute, BC; **Jim Papple**, Brock University, ON; **Robin Peace**, Confederation College, BC;

ASIA Rabiatu Abubakar, Eton Language Centre, Malaysia; **Wiwik Andreani**, Bina Nusantara University, Indonesia; **Frank Bailey**, Baiko Gakuin University, Japan; **Mike Baker**, Kosei Junior High School, Japan; **Leonard Barrow**, Kanto Junior College, Japan; **Herman Bartelen**, Japan; **Siren Betty**, Fooyin University, Kaohsiung; **Thomas E. Bieri**, Nagoya College, Japan; **Natalie Brezden**, Global English House, Japan; **MK Brooks**, Mukogawa Women's University, Japan; **Truong Ngoc Buu**, The Youth Language School, Vietnam; **Charles Cabell**, Toyo University, Japan; **Fred Carruth**, Matsumoto University, Japan; **Frances Causer**, Seijo University, Japan; **Jeffrey Chalk**, SNU, South Korea; **Deborah Chang**, Wenzao Ursuline College of Languages, Kaohsiung; **David Chatham**, Ritsumeikan University, Japan; **Andrew Chih Hong Chen**, National Sun Yat-sen University, Kaohsiung; **Christina Chen**, Yu-Tsai Bilingual Elementary School, Taipei; **Hui-chen Chen**, Shi-Lin High School of Commerce, Taipei; **Seungmoon Choe**, K2M Language Institute, South Korea; **Jason Jeffree Cole**, Coto College, Japan; **Le Minh Cong**, Vungtau Tourism Vocational College, Vietnam; **Todd Cooper**, Toyama National College of Technology, Japan; **Marie Cosgrove**, Daito Bunka

University, Japan; **Randall Cotten**, Gifu City Women's College, Japan; **Tony Cripps**, Ritsumeikan University, Japan; **Andy Cubalit**, CHS, Thailand; **Daniel Cussen**, Takushoku University, Japan; **Le Dan**, Ho Chi Minh City Electric Power College, Vietnam; **Simon Daykin**, Banghwa-dong Community Centre, South Korea; **Aimee Denham**, ILA, Vietnam; **Bryan Dickson**, David's English Center, Taipei; **Nathan Ducker**, Japan University, Japan; **Ian Duncan**, Simul International Corporate Training, Japan; **Nguyen Thi Kieu Dung**, Thang Long University, Vietnam; **Truong Quang Dung**, Tien Giang University, Vietnam; **Nguyen Thi Thuy Duong**, Vietnamese American Vocational Training College, Vietnam; **Wong Tuck Ee**, Raja Tun Azlan Science Secondary School, Malaysia; **Emilia Effendy**, International Islamic University Malaysia, Malaysia; **Bettizza Escueta**, KMUTT, Thailand; **Robert Eva**, Kaisei Girls High School, Japan; **Jim George**, Luna International Language School, Japan; **Jurgen Germeys**, Silk Road Language Center, South Korea; **Wong Ai Gnoh**, SMJK Chung Hwa Confucian, Malaysia; **Sarah Go**, Seoul Women's University, South Korea; **Peter Goosselink**, Hokkai High School, Japan; **Robert Gorden**, SNU, South Korea; **Wendy M. Gough**, St. Mary College/Nunoike Gaigo Senmon Gakko, Japan; **Tim Grose**, Sapporo Gakuin University, Japan; **Pham Thu Ha**, Le Van Tam Primary School, Vietnam; **Ann-Marie Hadzima**, Taipei; **Troy Hammond**, Tokyo Gakugei University International Secondary School, Japan; **Robiatul 'Adawiah Binti Hamzah**, SMK Putrajaya Precinct 8(1), Malaysia; **Tran Thi Thuy Hang**, Ho Chi Minh City Banking University, Vietnam; **To Thi Hong Hanh**, CEFALT, Vietnam; **George Hays**, Tokyo Kokusai Daigaku, Japan; **Janis Hearn**, Hongik University, South Korea; **Chantel Hemmi**, Jochi Daigaku, Japan; **David Hindman**, Sejong University, South Korea; **Nahn Cam Hoa**, Ho Chi Minh City University of Technology, Vietnam; **Jana Holt**, Korea University, South Korea; **Jason Hollowell**, Nihon University, Japan; **F. N. (Zoe) Hsu**, National Tainan University, Yong Kang; **Kuei-ping Hsu**, National Tsing Hua University, Hsinchu City; **Wenhua Hsu**, I-Shou University, Kaohsiung; **Luu Nguyen Quoc Hung**, Cantho University, Vietnam; **Cecile Hwang**, Changwon National University, South Korea; **Ainol Haryati Ibrahim**, Universiti Malaysia Pahang, Malaysia; **Robert Jeens**, Yonsei University, South Korea; **Linda M. Joyce**, Kyushu Sangyo University, Japan; **Dr. Nisai Kaewsanchai**, English Square Kanchanaburi, Thailand; **Aniza Kamarulzaman**, Sabah Science Secondary School, Malaysia; **Ikuko Kashiwabara**, Osaka Electro-Communication University, Japan; **Gurmit Kaur**, INTI College, Malaysia; **Nick Keane**, Japan; **Ward Ketcheson**, Aomori University, Japan; **Nicholas Kemp**, Kyushu International University, Japan; **Montchatry Ketmuni**, Rajamangala University of Technology, Thailand; **Dinh Viet Khanh**, Vietnam; **Seonok Kim**, Kangsu Jongro Language School, South Korea; **Suyeon Kim**, Anyang University, South Korea; **Kelly P. Kimura**, Soka University, Japan; **Masakazu Kimura**, Katoh Gakuen Gyoshu High School, Japan; **Gregory King**, Chubu Daigaku, Japan; **Stan Kirk**, Konan University, Japan; **Donald Knight**, Nan Hua/Fu Li Junior High Schools, Hsinchu; **Kari J. Kostiainen**, Nagoya City University, Japan; **Pattri Kuanpulpol**, Silpakorn University, Thailand; **Ha Thi Lan**, Thai Binh Teacher Training College, Vietnam; **Eric Edwin Larson**, Miyazaki Prefectural Nursing University, Japan; **David Laurence**, Chubu Daigaku, Japan; **Richard S. Lavin**, Prefectural University of Kumamoto, Japan; **Shirley Leane**, Chugoku Junior College, Japan; **I-Hsiu Lee**, Yunlin; **Nari Lee**, Park Jung PLS, South Korea; **Tae Lee**, Yonsei University, South Korea; **Lys Yongsoon Lee**, Reading Town Geumcheon, South Korea; **Mallory Leece**, Sun Moon University, South Korea; **Dang Hong Lien**, Tan Lam Upper Secondary School, Vietnam; **Huang Li-Han**, Rebecca Education Institute, Taipei; **Sovannarith Lim**, Royal University of Phnom Penh, Cambodia; **Ginger Lin**, National Kaohsiung Hospitality College, Kaohsiung; **Noel Lineker**, New Zealand/Japan; **Tran Dang Khanh Linh**, Nha Trang Teachers' Training College, Vietnam; **Daphne Liu**, Buliton English School, Taipei; **S. F. Josephine Liu**, Tien-Mu Elementary School, Taipei; **Caroline Luo**, Tunghai University, Taichung; **Jeng-Jia Luo**, Tunghai University, Taichung; **Laura MacGregor**, Gakushuin University, Japan; **Amir Madani**, Visuttharangsi School, Thailand; **Elena Maeda**, Sacred Heart Professional Training College, Japan; **Vu Thi Thanh Mai**, Hoang Gia Education Center, Vietnam; **Kimura Masakazu**, Kato Gakuen Gyoshu High School, Japan; **Susumu Matsuhashi**, Net Link English School, Japan; **James McCrostie**, Daito Bunka University, Japan; **Joel McKee**, Inha University, South Korea; **Colin McKenzie**, Wachirawit Primary School, Thailand; **Terumi Miyazoe**, Tokyo Denki Daigaku, Japan; **William K. Moore**, Hiroshima Kokusai Gakuin University, Japan; **Kevin Mueller**, Tokyo Kokusai Daigaku, Japan; **Hudson Murrell**, Baiko Gakuin University, Japan; **Frances Namba**, Senri International School of Kwansei Gakuin, Japan; **Keiichi Narita**, Niigata University, Japan; **Kim Chung Nguyen**, Ho Chi Minh University of

Industry, Vietnam; **Do Thi Thanh Nhan**, Hanoi University, Vietnam; **Dale Kazuo Nishi**, Aoyama English Conversation School, Japan; **Huynh Thi Ai Nguyen**, Vietnam; **Dongshin Oh**, YBM PLS, South Korea; **Keiko Okada**, Dokkyo Daigaku, Japan; **Louise Ohashi**, Shukutoku University, Japan; **Yongjun Park**, Sangji University, South Korea; **Donald Patnaude**, Ajarn Donald's English Language Services, Thailand; **Virginia Peng**, Ritsumeikan University, Japan; **Suangkanok Piboonthamnont**, Rajamangala University of Technology, Thailand; **Simon Pitcher**, Business English Teaching Services, Japan; **John C. Probert**, New Education Worldwide, Thailand; **Do Thi Hoa Quyen**, Ton Duc Thang University, Vietnam; **John P. Racine**, Dokkyo University, Japan; **Kevin Ramsden**, Kyoto University of Foreign Studies, Japan; **Luis Rappaport**, Cung Thieu Nha Ha Noi, Vietnam; **Lisa Reshad**, Konan Daigaku Hyogo, Japan; **Peter Riley**, Taisho University, Japan; **Thomas N. Robb**, Kyoto Sangyo University, Japan; **Rory Rosszell**, Meiji Daigaku, Japan; **Maria Feti Rosyani**, Universitas Kristen Indonesia, Indonesia; **Greg Rouault**, Konan University, Japan; **Chris Ruddenklau**, Kindai University, Japan; **Hans-Gustav Schwartz**, Thailand; **Mary-Jane Scott**, Soongsil University, South Korea; **Dara Sheahan**, Seoul National University, South Korea; **James Sherlock**, A.P.W. Angthong, Thailand; **Prof. Shieh**, Minghsin University of Science & Technology, Xinfeng; **Yuko Shimizu**, Ritsumeikan University, Japan; **Suzila Mohd Shukor**, Universiti Sains Malaysia, Malaysia; **Stephen E. Smith**, Mahidol University, Thailand; **Moon-young Son**, South Korea; **Seunghee Son**, Anyang University, South Korea; **Mi-young Song**, Kyungwon University, South Korea; **Lisa Sood**, VUS, BIS, Vietnam; **Jason Stewart**, Taejon International Language School, South Korea; **Brian A. Stokes**, Korea University, South Korea; **Mulder Su**, Shih-Chien University, Kaohsiung; **Yoomi Suh**, English Plus, South Korea; **Yun-Fang Sun**, Wenzao Ursuline College of Languages, Kaohsiung; **Richard Swingle**, Kansai Gaidai University, Japan; **Sanford Taborn**, Kinjo Gakuin Daigaku, Japan; **Mamoru Takahashi**, Akita Prefectural University, Japan; **Tran Hoang Tan**, School of International Training, Vietnam; **Takako Tanaka**, Doshisha University, Japan; **Jeffrey Taschner**, American University Alumni Language Center, Thailand; **Matthew Taylor**, Kinjo Gakuin Daigaku, Japan; **Michael Taylor**, International Pioneers School, Thailand; **Kampanart Thammaphati**, Wattana Wittaya Academy, Thailand; **Tran Duong The**, Sao Mai Language Center, Vietnam; **Tran Dinh Tho**, Duc Tri Secondary School, Vietnam; **Huynh Thi Anh Thu**, Nhatrang College of Culture Arts and Tourism, Vietnam; **Peter Timmins**, Peter's English School, Japan; **Fumie Togano**, Hosei Daini High School, Japan; **F. Sigmund Topor**, Keio University Language School, Japan; **Tu Trieu**, Rise VN, Vietnam; **Yen-Cheng Tseng**, Chang-Jung Christian University, Tainan; **Pei-Hsuan Tu**, National Cheng Kung University, Tainan City; **Hajime Uematsu**, Hirosaki University, Japan; **Rachel Um**, Mok-dong Oedae English School, South Korea; **David Underhill**, EEExpress, Japan; **Ben Underwood**, Kugenuma High School, Japan; **Siriluck Usaha**, Sripatum University, Thailand; **Tyas Budi Utami**, Indonesia; **Nguyen Thi Van**, Far East International School, Vietnam; **Stephan Van Eycken**, Kosei Gakuen Girls High School, Japan; **Zisa Velasquez**, Taihu International School/Semarang International School, China/Indonesia; **Jeffery Walter**, Sangji University, South Korea; **Bill White**, Kinki University, Japan; **Yohanes De Deo Widyastoko**, Xaverius Senior High School, Indonesia; **Dylan Williams**, SNU, South Korea; **Jisuk Woo**, Ichean University, South Korea; **Greg Chung-Hsien Wu**, Providence University, Taichung; **Xun Xiaoming**, BLCU, China; **Hui-Lien Yeh**, Chai Nan University of Pharmacy and Science, Tainan; **Sittiporn Yodnil**, Huachiew Chalermprakiet University, Thailand; **Shamshul Helmy Zambahari**, Universiti Teknologi Malaysia, Malaysia; **Ming-Yuli**, Chang Jung Christian University, Tainan; **Aimin Fadhlee bin Mahmud Zuhodi**, Kuala Terengganu Science School, Malaysia;

TURKEY Shirley F. Akis, American Culture Association/Fomara; **Gül Akkoç**, Boğaziçi University; **Seval Akmeşe**, Haliç University; **Ayşenur Akyol**, Ege University; **Ayşe Umut Aribaş**, Beykent University; **Gökhan Asan**, Kapadokya Vocational College; **Hakan Asan**, Kapadokya Vocational College; **Julia Asan**, Kapadokya Vocational College; **Azarvan Atac**, Piri Reis University; **Nur Babat**, Kapadokya Vocational College; **Feyza Balakbabalar**, Kadir Has University; **Gözde Balikçi**, Beykent University; **Deniz Balım**, Haliç University; **Asli Başdoğan**, Kadir Has University; **Ayla Bayram**, Kapadokya Vocational College; **Pinar Bilgiç**, Kadir Has University; **Kenan Bozkurt**, Kapadokya Vocational College; **Yonca Bozkurt**, Ege University; **Frank Carr**, Piri Reis; **Mengü Noyan Çengel**, Ege University; **Elif Doğan**, Ege University; **Natalia Donmez**, 29 Mayis Üniversite; **Nalan Emirsoy**, Kadir Has University; **Ayşe Engin**, Kadir Has University; **Ayhan Gedikbaş**, Ege University; **Gülşah Gençer**, Beykent University; **Seyit Ömer Gök**, Gediz University; **Tuğba Gök**, Gediz University; **İlkay Gökçe**, Ege University; **Zeynep Birinci Guler**, Maltepe University; **Neslihan Güler**, Kadir Has University; **Sircan Gümüş**, Kadir Has University; **Nesrin Gündoğu**, T.C. Piri Reis University; **Tanju Gurpinar**, Piri Reis University; **Selin Gurturk**, Piri Reis University; **Neslihan Gurutku**, Piri Reis University; **Roger Hewitt**, Maltepe University; **Nilüfer İbrahimoğlu**, Beykent University; **Nevin Kaftelen**, Kadir Has University; **Sultan Kalin**, Kapadokya Vocational College; **Sema Kaplan Karabina**, Anadolu University; **Eray Kara**, Giresun University; **Beylü Karayazgan**, Ege University; **Darren Kelso**, Piri Reis University; **Trudy Kittle**, Kapadokya Vocational College; **Şaziye Konaç**, Kadir Has University; **Güneş Korkmaz**, Kapadokya Vocational College; **Robert Ledbury**, Izmir University of Economics; **Ashley Lucas**, Maltepe University; **Bülent Nedium Uça**, Dogus University; **Murat Nurlu**, Ege University; **Mollie Owens**, Kadir Has University; **Oya Özağaç**, Boğaziçi University; **Funda Özcan**, Ege University; **İlkay Özdemir**, Ege University; **Ülkü Öztürk**, Gediz University; **Cassondra Puls**, Anadolu University; **Yelda Sarikaya**, Cappadocia Vocational College; **Müge Şekercioğlu**, Ege University; **Melis Senol**, Canakkale Onsekiz Mart University, The School of Foreign Languages; **Patricia Sümer**, Kadir Has University; **Rex Surface**, Beykent University; **Mustafa Torun**, Kapadokya Vocational College; **Tansel Üstünloğlu**, Ege University; **Fatih Yücel**, Beykent University; **Şule Yüksel**, Ege University;

THE MIDDLE EAST Amina Saif Mohammed Al Hashamia, Nizwa College of Applied Sciences, Oman; **Jennifer Baran**, Kuwait University, Kuwait; **Phillip Chappells**, GEMS Modern Academy, U.A.E.; **Sharon Ruth Devaneson**, Ibri College of Technology, Oman; **Hanaa El-Deeb**, Canadian International College, Egypt; **Yvonne Eaton**, Community College of Qatar, Qatar; **Brian Gay**, Sultan Qaboos University, Oman; **Gail Al Hafidh**, Sharjah Women's College (HCT), U.A.E.; **Jonathan Hastings**, American Language Center, Jordan; **Laurie Susan Hilu**, English Language Centre, University of Bahrain, Bahrain; **Abraham Irannezhad**, Mehre Aval, Iran; **Kevin Kempe**, CNA-Q, Qatar; **Jill Newby James**, University of Nizwa; **Mary Kay Klein**, American University of Sharjah, U.A.E.; **Sian Khoury**, Fujairah Women's College (HCT), U.A.E.; **Hussein Dehghan Manshadi**, Farhang Pajooh & Jaam-e-Jam Language School, Iran; **Jessica March**, American University of Sharjah, U.A.E.; **Neil McBeath**, Sultan Qaboos University, Oman; **Sandy McDonagh**, Abu Dhabi Men's College (HCT), U.A.E.; **Rob Miles**, Sharjah Women's College (HCT), U.A.E.; **Michael Kevin Neumann**, Al Ain Men's College (HCT), U.A.E.;

LATIN AMERICA Aldana Aguirre, Argentina; **Claudia Almeida**, Coordenação de Idiomas, Brazil; **Cláudia Arias**, Brazil; **Maria de los Angeles Barba**, FES Acatlan UNAM, Mexico; **Lilia Barrios**, Universidad Autónoma de Tamaulipas, Mexico; **Adán Beristain**, UAEM, Mexico; **Ricardo Böck**, Manoel Ribas, Brazil; **Edson Braga**, CNA, Brazil; **Marli Buttelli**, Mater et Magistra, Brazil; **Alessandra Campos**, Inova Centro de Linguas, Brazil; **Priscila Catta Preta Ribeiro**, Brazil; **Gustavo Cestari**, Access International School, Brazil; **Walter D'Alessandro**, Virginia Language Center, Brazil; **Lilian De Gennaro**, Argentina; **Mônica De Stefani**, Quality Centro de Idiomas, Brazil; **Julio Alejandro Flores**, BUAP, Mexico; **Mirian Freire**, CNA Vila Guilherme, Brazil; **Francisco Garcia**, Colegio Lestonnac de San Angel, Mexico; **Miriam Giovanardi**, Brazil; **Darlene Gonzalez Miy**, ITESM CCV, Mexico; **Maria Laura Grimaldi**, Argentina; **Luz Dary Guzmán**, IMPAHU, Colombia; **Carmen Koppe**, Brazil; **Monica Krutzler**, Brazil; **Marcus Murilo Lacerda**, Seven Idiomas, Brazil; **Nancy Lake**, CEL-LEP, Brazil; **Cris Lazzerini**, Brazil; **Sandra Luna**, Argentina; **Ricardo Luvisan**, Brazil; **Jorge Murilo Menezes**, ACBEU, Brazil; **Monica Navarro**, Instituto Cultural A. C., Mexico; **Joacyr Oliveira**, Faculdades Metropolitanas Unidas and Summit School for Teachers, Brazil; **Ayrton Cesar Oliveira de Araujo**, E&A English Classes, Brazil; **Ana Laura Oriente**, Seven Idiomas, Brazil; **Adelia Peña Clavel**, CELE UNAM, Mexico; **Beatriz Pereira**, Summit School, Brazil; **Miguel Perez**, Instituto Cultural, Mexico; **Cristiane Perone**, Associação Cultura Inglesa, Brazil; **Pamela Claudia Pogré**, Colegio Integral Caballito / Universidad de Flores, Argentina; **Dalva Prates**, Brazil; **Marianne Rampaso**, Iowa Idiomas, Brazil; **Daniela Rutolo**, Instituto Superior Cultural Británico, Argentina; **Maione Sampaio**, Maione Carrijo Consultoria em Inglês Ltda, Brazil; **Elaine Santesso**, TS Escola de Idiomas, Brazil; **Camila Francisco Santos**, UNS Idiomas, Brazil; **Lucia Silva**, Cooplem Idiomas, Brazil; **Maria Adela Sorzio**, Instituto Superior Santa Cecilia, Argentina; **Elcio Souza**, Unibero, Brazil; **Willie Thomas**, Rainbow Idiomas, Brazil; **Sandra Villegas**, Instituto Humberto de Paolis, Argentina; **John Whelan**, La Universidad Nacional Autonoma de Mexico, Mexico

CONTENTS

UNIT 1

Linguistics

READING	▶	distinguishing main ideas from details
VOCABULARY	▶	using a thesaurus
WRITING	▶	writing an extended definition
GRAMMAR	▶	contrast and concession connectors

UNIT QUESTION

What happens when a language disappears?

A Discuss these questions with your classmates.

1. Which languages can you speak? Which one is spoken by the most people? What other languages would you like to learn? Why?

2. Do you think your identity is connected to the language that you speak? Why or why not?

3. Look at the photo. How do people preserve their language? What might cause a language to disappear?

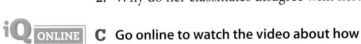

UNIT
OBJECTIVE ▶▶▶▶ Read an article from a government website and a book excerpt. Gather information and ideas to develop an extended definition of a word or concept from another language or culture.

🔊 **B** Listen to *The Q Classroom* online. Then answer these questions.

1. Why does Sophy think that languages are never lost?

2. Why do her classmates disagree with her?

iQ ONLINE **C** Go online to watch the video about how language works in the brain. Then check your comprehension.

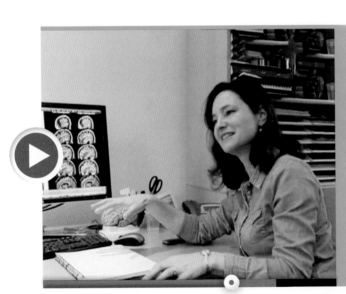

integral *(adj.)* being an essential part of something

MRI *(n.)* magnetic resonance imaging, a method of using a strong magnetic field to produce an image of the inside of a person's body

psycholinguist *(n.)* a scientist who studies how the mind processes and produces language

superimpose *(v.)* to put one image on top of another so that the two can be seen combined

VIDEO VOCABULARY

iQ ONLINE **D** Go to the Online Discussion Board to discuss the Unit Question with your classmates.

Please Watch Out For Steps

请注意梯层

足元にお気を
つけ下さい。

PHOTO
ENFORCED

SURVEILLANCE
PAR
CINÉMOMÈTRE

ᐅᖅ ᑲᓐᒃ
STOP

ᓐᒃᒪᒡ ᐊᕐᓄᐊᒍ ᐊᕙᒋᖕᒃ
FOUR WAY

3

E Work with a partner. Read the customs from various countries. Decide where each custom belongs in the chart and write its letter. Then add your own examples.

CUSTOMS QUIZ

a. In Bulgaria, shaking your head back and forth means "yes," and up and down means "no."

b. In South Korea, it is polite to leave some rice at the bottom of your bowl.

c. In France, people kiss on the cheek—sometimes three or four times—to greet each other.

d. In the US, it can be threatening to stand closer than 18 inches to someone you don't know very well.

e. In Japan, it is rude to wear your shoes inside someone's house.

Feature of Culture	Custom/Behavior	Your Example
1. Greetings	c	*A firm handshake is considered professional in the United States.*
2. Styles of dress		
3. Personal space		
4. Gestures		
5. Politeness		

F Discuss these questions with a partner.

1. Do you think that any of the various customs listed in Activity E are related to language? Which ones? Why or why not?

2. How does your behavior change when you speak a different language?

READING

READING 1 | **History of the Maori Language**

You are going to read a page from the New Zealand government's History Online website that describes the history of the Maori language. The Maori are the indigenous people (original inhabitants) of New Zealand. Use the article to gather information and ideas for your Unit Assignment.

PREVIEW THE READING

A. **PREVIEW** Skim the Web page. Answer these questions.

1. Who is the Web page written for?

2. Where in the text do you expect to find the main ideas?

B. **QUICK WRITE** How can indigenous (native) languages be protected? Write for 5–10 minutes in response. Remember to use this section for your Unit Assignment.

C. **VOCABULARY** Check (✓) the words you know. Then work with a partner to locate each word in the reading. Use clues to help define the words you don't know. Check your definitions in the dictionary.

assimilate *(v.)*	**oblige** *(v.)*
confine *(v.)*	**persist** *(v.)*
divorced from *(phr.)*	**predominant** *(adj.)*
ethnicity *(n.)*	**revival** *(n.)*
initiative *(n.)* 🔑	**suppress** *(v.)*
integral *(adj.)*	**target** *(v.)* 🔑

🔑 Oxford 3000™ words

 D. Go online to listen and practice your pronunciation.

WORK WITH THE READING

A. Read the Web page and gather information on what happens when a language disappears.

History of the Maori Language

Decline and revival

1   In the last 200 years, the history of the Maori language (*te reo Maori*) has been one of ups and downs. At the beginning of the 19th century, it was the **predominant** language spoken in *Aotearoa* (the Maori name for New Zealand). As more English speakers arrived in New Zealand, the Maori language was increasingly confined to Maori communities. By the mid-20th century, there were concerns that the language was dying out. Major **initiatives** launched from the 1980s have brought about a **revival** of the Maori language. In the early 21st century, more than 130,000 people of Maori **ethnicity** could speak and understand Maori, one of the three official languages of New Zealand.

Maori: A common means of communication

2   For the first half century or so of the European settlement of New Zealand, the Maori language was a common way of communicating. Early settlers[1] had to learn to speak the language if they wished to trade with Maori because settlers were dependent on Maori for many things at this time.

3   Up to the 1870s, it was not unusual for government officials, missionaries,

Aotearoa (New Zealand)

and prominent *Pakeha*[2] to speak Maori. Their children often grew up with Maori children and were among the most fluent European speakers and writers of Maori. Particularly in rural areas, the interaction between Maori and Pakeha was constant.

Korero Pakeha ("Speak English!")

4   Pakeha were in the majority by the early 1860s, and English became the dominant language of New Zealand. Increasingly, the Maori language **was confined** to Maori communities that existed separately from the Pakeha majority.

5   The Maori language was not understood as an essential expression and envelope[3] of Maori culture, important for the Maori

---

[1] **settler:** a person who goes to live in a new country
[2] *Pakeha*: Maori word for people who were originally from Europe and also for the English language. Today it refers to any non-Maori.

[3] **envelope:** a container, used metaphorically to suggest that a language might contain information about a culture

in maintaining their pride and identity as a people. Maori was now officially discouraged. Many Maori themselves questioned its relevance in a Pakeha-dominated world where the most important value seemed to be to get ahead as an individual.

6   The Maori language was **suppressed** in schools, either formally or informally, so that Maori youngsters could **assimilate** with the wider community. Some older Maori still recall being punished for speaking their language. Many Maori parents encouraged their children to learn English and even to turn away from other aspects of Maori custom. Increasing numbers of Maori people learned English because they needed it in the workplace or places of recreation such as the football field. "Korero Pakeha" (Speak English) was seen as essential for Maori people.

A language lives

7   Despite the emphasis on speaking English, the Maori language **persisted**. Until the Second World War[4] most Maori spoke Maori as their first language. They worshipped[5] in Maori, and Maori was the language of the marae[6]. Political meetings were conducted in Maori, and there were Maori newspapers and literature. More importantly, it was the language of the home, and parents could pass on the language to their children.

The lure of the city

8   The Second World War brought about momentous[7] changes for Maori society. There was plenty of work available in towns and cities due to the war, and Maori moved into urban areas in greater numbers. Before the war, about 75 percent of Maori lived in rural areas. Two decades later, approximately 60 percent lived in urban centers.

9   English was the language of urban New Zealand—at work, in school, and in leisure activities. Maori children went to city schools where Maori was unheard of in teaching programs. The new, enforced contact of large numbers of Maori and Pakeha caused much strain and stress, and the language was one of the things to suffer.

10   The number of Maori speakers began to decline rapidly. By the 1980s, less than 20 percent of Maori knew enough of their traditional language to be regarded as native speakers. Even for those people, Maori was ceasing to be the language of everyday use in the home. Some urbanized Maori people became **divorced from** their language and culture. Others maintained contact with their original communities, returning for important *hui* (meetings) and *tangihanga* (funerals) or allowing the *kaumatua* (elders) at home to adopt or care for their children.

Seeds of change

11   From the 1970s, many Maori people reasserted[8] their identity as Maori. An emphasis on the language as an **integral** part of Maori culture was central to this. Maori leaders were increasingly recognizing the dangers of the loss of Maori language. New groups emerged that were committed to strengthening Maori culture and the language.

---

[4] **Second World War:** also called World War II (1939–1945)
[5] **worship:** to pray
[6] *marae*: Maori word for a meetinghouse or a place for formal discussions
[7] **momentous:** very important or serious

[8] **reassert:** to make other people recognize again your right or authority after a period when this has been in doubt

12   Major Maori language recovery programs began in the 1980s. Many were **targeted** at young people and the education system, such as a system of primary schooling[9] in a Maori-language environment.

Legislating for change

13   Efforts to secure the survival of the Maori language stepped up in 1985. In that year the Waitangi Tribunal[10] heard the Te Reo Maori claim, which asserted that the Maori language was a *taonga* (a treasure) that the government was **obliged** to protect under the Treaty of Waitangi. The Waitangi Tribunal agreed with the Maori and recommended a number of laws and policies. In 1987, Maori was made an official language of New Zealand.

14   There are now many institutions working to recover the language. Even so, the decline of the Maori language has only just been arrested[11]. There is a resurgence[12] of Maori, but to survive as a language, it needs enough fluent speakers of all ages as well as the respect and support of the wider English-speaking and multi-ethnic New Zealand community.

---

[9] **primary school:** elementary school, starting at about age 5 and continuing until age 12 to 14
[10] **Waitangi Tribunal:** a court created to honor the Waitangi Treaty of 1840 between Great Britain and the Maori people. Under the treaty, the Maori accepted British rule, and the British agreed to treat the Maori fairly.
[11] **arrested:** stopped
[12] **resurgence:** the return and growth

Vocabulary
Skill Review

When you see a new word, look at the words and sentences around it. This can help you find the meaning in context.

B. VOCABULARY **Complete the sentences with the vocabulary from Reading 1. You may need to change the form of the word or phrase to make the sentence grammatically correct.**

assimilate *(v.)*	ethnicity *(n.)*	oblige *(v.)*	revival *(n.)*
confine *(v.)*	initiative *(n.)*	persist *(v.)*	suppress *(v.)*
divorced from *(phr.)*	integral *(adj.)*	predominant *(adj.)*	target *(v.)*

1. Words or phrases that are out of style sometimes experience a
   _____ and become popular again.

2. The language spoken by most of the people in a country is the
   _____ language of the country.

3. It is hard to _____ a language to a certain community and
   never allow it to be spoken outside that place.

4. A government _____ can help to create new laws, for
   language programs in schools, for example.

5. Many people are proud of their _____, that is, their racial and cultural background.

6. Some people in the United States want to _____ the use of languages other than English in public schools.

7. Learning a new language is one way that people can blend in with, or _____ into, a new society.

8. It takes a long time to learn a new language, so you must _____ by taking classes and practicing speaking.

9. Some people think language lessons should _____ very young children because they learn new languages so fast.

10. Immigrants often worry that they will forget their customs and become _____ their culture.

11. A person's language is such a central and _____ part of her culture that she should try to preserve it.

12. Some parents do not believe their children should _____ to learn a language other than the one they speak at home.

iQ ONLINE **C. Go online for more practice with the vocabulary.**

D. Complete the timeline with information from Reading 1.

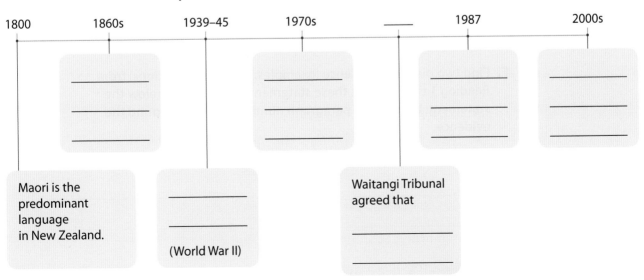

| 1800 | 1860s | 1939–45 | 1970s | _____ | 1987 | 2000s |

_____
_____
_____

_____
_____
_____

_____
_____
_____

_____
_____
_____

Maori is the predominant language in New Zealand.

_____
_____
(World War II)

Waitangi Tribunal agreed that
_____
_____
_____

E. Match each subheading with the correct main idea.

Subheadings	Main ideas
____ 1. Decline and revival	a. After English became the dominant language, Maori was suppressed and many Maori had to learn English.
____ 2. Maori: A common means of communication	b. The Maori language has had periods of use and disuse over the last two centuries, but it is currently undergoing a revival.
____ 3. *Korero Pakeha* ("Speak English!")	c. After the Second World War, the majority of Maori lived in cities, and some lost their knowledge of their traditional language and customs.
____ 4. A language lives	d. At first, Europeans used Maori to communicate with the local people.
____ 5. The lure of the city	e. The Maori language survived in public and private places.
____ 6. Seeds of change	f. In 1987, Maori became an official language of New Zealand, but more speakers and more support are necessary for its survival.
____ 7. Legislating for change	g. More recently, the Maori have begun to reassert their identity as Maori by learning and speaking the Maori language.

F. Find two pieces of evidence (examples, facts, or quotations) from Reading 1 that support these statements. Write them below the statement. Include the paragraph number where you found the evidence.

1. Europeans who lived in New Zealand before the 1870s learned Maori.

   a. _____

   b. _____

2. Both the Maori and the Pakeha were responsible for the increase in the use of English after 1860.

   a. _____

   b. _____

3. The Maori language survived until the mid-20th century because most Maori lived in rural areas where Maori was still an important language for communication.

   a. _____

   b. _____

4. As the 20th century progressed, there were fewer native speakers of Maori, but some Maori in the cities maintained a basic knowledge of their language.

   a. _____

   b. _____

5. Starting in the 1970s, the Maori realized that they needed to save their language in order to maintain their cultural identity.

   a. _____

   b. _____

6. The Waitangi Tribunal helped to make Maori an official language and raise its status in New Zealand.

   a. _____

   b. _____

G. List reasons why the Maori maintained their traditional language. Then list reasons why the Maori learned to speak English. Write the paragraph number in which you found the information next to each reason.

Maori language	English language
Used in religious ceremonies (Para. 7)	Needed in the workplace (Para. 6)

H. Read the statements. Write *T* (true) or *F* (false). Then correct each false statement to make it true. Write the number of the paragraph where you found the answer.

____ 1. The Maori language has been in steady decline since the arrival of Europeans in New Zealand. Paragraph: ____

____ 2. The Maori people have always maintained their native language with pride. Paragraph: ____

____ 3. In the early 20th century, the Maori language survived in both public and private settings. Paragraph: ____

____ 4. Maori people were forced to move to the cities during and after the Second World War. Paragraph: ____

____ 5. Although some city Maori lost contact with their language, others maintained links to their traditions. Paragraph: ____

____ 6. The resurgence of Maori since the Waitangi Tribunal guarantees the survival of the Maori language. Paragraph: ____

 I. Go online to read *Languages in Switzerland* and check your comprehension.

WRITE WHAT YOU THINK

A. Discuss these questions in a group.

1. Do you think the efforts to save the Maori language will continue to be successful? Why or why not?

2. Is it important for society to try to save languages that are in danger of disappearing? Should governments create laws to encourage the protection of endangered languages?

3. What would be the advantages and disadvantages of having a common language of worldwide communication alongside native languages? How would local languages be affected? Would all languages be affected in the same way? Who would benefit and lose most from this situation?

B. Choose one question and write a paragraph in response. Look back at your Quick Write on page 5 as you think about what you learned.

Main ideas are the major points that support the focus of a piece of writing. If you can find the main ideas and distinguish them from the supporting details, you will understand the purpose and focus of the writing. In most texts, you can find main ideas by doing the following:

- paying attention to repeated vocabulary, which may be key words
- looking for words in the headline or title of the text
- reading subheadings and the captions of any graphs or illustrations
- watching for words that introduce conclusions and main ideas, such as *therefore, as a result, so, (more/most) importantly, finally*, and *to conclude*
- focusing on words in bold, italics, or different colors

The position of the main ideas may depend on the **genre**, or **type of text**, because there are different ways of organizing information.

Academic writing is divided into paragraphs that usually contain one main idea. The main idea is often stated near the beginning of the paragraph and summarized at the end, so read the first and last sentences of each paragraph carefully. Remember that all the main ideas in the text are usually connected to the central focus, argument, or thesis of the paper. This is often stated near the end of the introduction.

News articles, whether in print or on the Web, have to catch readers' attention and then keep them reading. They frequently use headlines and subheadings to give main ideas.

Business communication has to be brief, efficient, and persuasive, so main ideas are often stated early and repeated at the end of the text. Bullet points, bold text, and repetition are often used to draw the readers' attention.

A. Read the excerpts. Identify the genre of the writing. Then write the main idea in a sentence.

1.

> When people move to a new culture, they usually experience a series of different feelings as they adjust to their new surroundings. A new culture is not necessarily another country or a place where another language is spoken. Therefore, this adjustment can occur in any situation where a person's normal rules of behavior no longer work. The process of adapting to these differences has four stages and is called culture shock.

Genre: _____

Main idea: _____

_____

2.

> **Solution: *Say It Again* Language Learning Program**
> The company is interested in investing in a language learning program. There are two suitable programs available: ***Say It Again*** and ***Language Now***. We recommend ***Say It Again*** for these reasons:
> * cost—19 percent less
> * technical support—included in price
>
> ***Say It Again*** will meet our needs at a lower cost and with better service.

Genre: _____

Main idea: _____

_____

3.

> **Language Researcher Faces Challenges**
> Dr. Wilde's research is certainly exciting. It could change the way we think about the original inhabitants of New Zealand. But it is not without difficulty. "Of course, the greatest challenge will be getting the local chiefs to talk to me," Wilde admitted. "Without their cooperation, my project can't go forward." Gaining the trust of the local population is just one of the many challenges facing Dr. Wilde in his research.

Genre: _____

Main idea: _____

_____

4.

> Languages change through two processes: internal change and language contact. Internal change occurs slowly over time as words or phrases shift in meaning or grammatical structure. For instance, the Old English *a nadder*, meaning "a snake," gradually became *an adder*, the modern word, when the *n* became attached to the article. The second source of change is external, and it occurs when another, usually more powerful, language comes into contact with it.

Genre: _____

Main idea: _____

_____

5.

> **New Zealand in the 1830s**
>
> New Zealand was largely a Maori world in the 1830s. There were perhaps 100,000 Maori, divided into major *iwi*, or tribes. Relations between groups could be tense, and conflict was common. Maori traditions and social structures prevailed, but more Europeans arrived in New Zealand throughout the decade. There were about 200 in the North Island in the early 1830s. By 1839, there may have been 2,000 throughout the country (including around 1,400 in the North Island), attracted by trade and settlement.

Genre: _____

Main idea: _____

_____

B. How would you find the main ideas in the following types of writing? Discuss your answers with a partner.

1. an email   3. an advertisement

2. a business letter   4. a newspaper editorial

 **C.** Go online for more practice distinguishing main ideas from details.

READING 2 | When Languages Die

UNIT OBJECTIVE ▶▶▶

You are going to read an excerpt from the book *When Languages Die*, by linguistics professor K. David Harrison. In it, Dr. Harrison examines the traditional knowledge that is lost when a language becomes extinct (that is, when nobody speaks it anymore). Use the article to gather information and ideas for your Unit Assignment.

PREVIEW THE READING

A. **PREVIEW** What knowledge do you think can be lost when languages die? Make three predictions.

B. QUICK WRITE Where in the world do you think languages are in danger of dying? Why do you think this is happening? Write for 5–10 minutes in response. Remember to use this section for your Unit Assignment.

C. VOCABULARY Work with a partner to find these words in the reading. Circle clues in the text that help you understand the meaning of each word. Then use a dictionary to define any unknown words.

abandon *(v.)* 🔑	**indigenous** *(adj.)*	**scenario** *(n.)*
cure *(n.)* 🔑	**in jeopardy** *(phr.)*	**shift** *(n.)* 🔑
exploit *(v.)*	**in the face of** *(phr.)*	**substitute** *(v.)* 🔑
habitat *(n.)*	**retain** *(v.)* 🔑	**wake-up call** *(n. phr.)*

🔑 Oxford 3000™ words

D. Go online to listen and practice your pronunciation.

WORK WITH THE READING

A. Read the book excerpt and gather information on what happens when a language disappears.

When Languages Die

1   What exactly do we stand to lose when languages vanish? It has become a cliché[1] to talk about a **cure** for cancer that may be found in the Amazon rain forest, perhaps from a medicinal plant known only to local shamans[2] (Plotkin 1993). But pharmaceutical companies have spared no efforts to get at this knowledge, and in many cases, have **exploited** it to develop useful drugs. An estimated $85 billion in profits per year is made on medicines made from plants that were first known to **indigenous** peoples for their healing properties (Posey 1990).

2   An astonishing 87 percent of the world's plant and animal species have not yet been

K. David Harrison

identified, named, described, or classified by modern science (Hawksworth & Kalin-Arroyo 1995). Therefore, we need to look to indigenous cultures to fill in our vast knowledge gap about the natural world. But can they **retain** their knowledge **in the face of** global linguistic homogenization[3]?

---

[1] **cliché:** a phrase or saying that has been used so many times that it no longer has any real meaning or interest
[2] **shamans:** traditional healers or medicine men
[3] **homogenization:** a process in which everything becomes the same

3   Much—if not most—of what we know about the natural world lies completely outside of science textbooks, libraries, and databases, existing only in unwritten languages in people's memories. It is only one generation away from extinction and always **in jeopardy** of not being passed on. This immense knowledge base remains largely unexplored and uncataloged. We can only hope to access it if the people who possess and nurture it can be encouraged to continue to do so.

4   If people feel their knowledge is worth keeping, they will keep it. If they are told, or come to believe, that it is useless in the modern world, they may well **abandon** it. Traditional knowledge is not always easily transferred from small, endangered languages to large, global ones. How can that be true if any idea is expressible in any language? Couldn't Solomon Islanders talk about the behavior patterns of fish in English just as easily as in Marovo, their native language? I argue that when small communities abandon their languages and switch to English or Spanish, there is also massive disruption of the transfer of traditional knowledge across generations. This arises in part from the way knowledge is packaged in a particular language.

5   Consider Western !Xoon, a small language of Namibia (the exclamation mark is a click sound). In !Xoon, clouds are called "rain houses." By learning the word for *cloud*, a !Xoon-speaking child automatically gets (for free) the extra information that clouds contain and are the source of rain. An English child learning the word *cloud* gets no information about rain and has to learn on her own that rain comes from clouds.

6   Languages package and structure knowledge in particular ways. You cannot merely **substitute** labels or names from another language and hold onto all of the implicit[4], hidden knowledge that resides in a taxonomy, or naming system. Still, each language and indigenous people is unique, and language **shift** takes place at different speeds and under very different conditions. Can we then predict how much traditional knowledge will successfully be transferred and how much will be lost?

7   Some scientists have tried to do just that. The Bari language (1,500–2,500 speakers) of Venezuela was studied by linguists who asked how much knowledge of the plant world was being lost and how much retained. The Bari live in a close relationship with the rain forest and have learned to use many of its plants for food, material goods, medicine, and construction of houses. One scientist found that the loss of Bari traditional knowledge corresponded with decreasing use of forest resources and a shift from the traditional hunter-gatherer lifestyle, along with a shift to speaking Spanish. His conservative estimate of the rate of knowledge loss should be a **wake-up call** to all: "I estimate that the real loss of ethnobotanical[5] knowledge from one generation to the next may be on the order of 40 to 60 percent." (Lizarralde 2001).

8   This is a dire[6] **scenario**: Bari people who have limited connection with the forest have lost up to 45 percent of traditional plant names. Similar patterns of knowledge erosion[7] may be observed among indigenous peoples all around the world as they undergo a cultural shift away from traditional lifestyles and languages.

---

[4] **implicit:** suggested without being directly expressed
[5] **ethnobotanical:** describing customs and beliefs about plants and agriculture held by a group of people

[6] **dire:** very serious; terrible
[7] **erosion:** the process of gradually destroying or weakening something over a period of time

9　　Some researchers offer hope for the persistence and resilience[8] of very basic forms of traditional knowledge. A study by anthropologist Scott Atran (1998) tested residents of Michigan on their knowledge of local animals. He concluded that elements of folk knowledge persist even when people have been schooled in modern scientific classification.

10　　Though folk knowledge may persist in modern cultures, we are also losing traditional knowledge at an alarming rate. This loss is accompanied by a severe reduction in number of species and range of **habitats**. Perhaps future technologies hold enough promise that humanity will be able to survive without making use of this accumulated ecological knowledge. Perhaps we will grow plants in greenhouses and breed animals in laboratories and feed ourselves via genetic engineering. Perhaps there are no new medicines to be found in the rain forests. All such arguments appeal to ignorance: we do not know what we stand to lose as languages and technologies vanish because much or even most of it remains undocumented. So it is a gamble to think that we will never use it in the future. Do we really want to place so much trust in future science and pay so little attention to our inherited science?

[8] **resilience:** the ability of something to return to its original strength

---

Tip for Success

In Reading 2, the name(s) and year in parentheses form a citation. Citations tell you that an idea comes from another source. You can look in the publication's references list for full information about the source.

References

Atran, Scott (1998). Folk biology and the anthropology of science: Cognitive universals and cultural particulars. *Behavioral and Brain Sciences* 21: 547–609.

Hawksworth, D.L., and M.T. Kalin-Arroyo (1995). Magnitude and distribution of biodiversity. In V.H. Heywood (ed.), *Global Biodiversity Assessment*. Cambridge: Cambridge University Press, pp. 107–192.

Lizarralde, Manuel (2001). Biodiversity and loss of indigenous languages and knowledge in South America. In L. Maffi (ed.), *On Biocultural Diversity*. Washington, D.C.: Smithsonian, pp. 265–281.

Plotkin, Mark (1993). *Tales of a Shaman's Apprentice*. New York: Viking.

Posey, Darrell A. (1990). Intellectual property rights and just compensation for indigenous knowledge. *Anthropology Today* 6(4): 13–16.

B. **VOCABULARY** Here are some words and phrases from Reading 2. Read the sentences. Then write each bold word or phrase next to the correct definition. You may need to change verbs to their base form and nouns to the singular form.

1. Some researchers hope that plants from the Amazon rain forest can provide a **cure** for cancer.

2. To develop new drugs, some drug makers have **exploited** the knowledge that people of the Amazon have about native plants.

3. The **indigenous** people of the Amazon know more about its native plants than researchers from other countries do.

4. People can still **retain** some traditional knowledge even if they give up some of their old ways of doing things.

5. It can be hard for people to resist doing what others ask, but sometimes we must be strong **in the face of** pressure.

6. Old ways of doing things are **in jeopardy** when the only people who know those traditions grow old and die.

7. People may **abandon** their native languages if they think they are useless.

8. You cannot simply **substitute** words from one language into another.

9. Many groups have made a **shift** away from the traditional hunter-gatherer lifestyle.

10. Many scientists believe that recent changes should be a **wake-up call** that gets the attention of people all over the world.

11. If we take the most negative view of the future, we can picture a disastrous **scenario**.

12. The loss of large parts of the rain forest has reduced the **habitats** of many native Amazon species.

a. _____ (phr.) in a dangerous position or situation and likely to be lost or harmed

b. _____ (n.) a description of how things might happen in the future

c. _____ (n.) a medicine or medical treatment for an illness

d. _____ (n.) a place where a particular type of animal or plant is normally found

e. _____ (phr.) despite (problems, difficulties, etc.)

f. _____ (n. phr.) an event that makes people realize that there is a problem they need to do something about

g. _____ (v.) to leave a thing or place; to stop supporting or believing in something

h. _____ (v.) to use in place of

i. _____ (v.) to use something in order to gain as much from it as possible

j. _____ (v.) to keep

k. _____ (n.) a change in position or direction

l. _____ (adj.) belonging to a particular place rather than coming to it from somewhere else

C. Go online for more practice with the vocabulary.

D. Each statement summarizes the main idea of a paragraph in Reading 2. Write the paragraph number next to the summarizing statement.

_7_ 1. As the Bari people become divorced from their surroundings and their language, they lose a lot of traditional knowledge.

____ 2. Some traditional knowledge survives even in modern societies in the United States.

____ 3. Scientists could find new treatments for serious diseases from plants that only indigenous people know about.

____ 4. Information can be lost in translations from indigenous languages.

____ 5. We should not trust science to replace the knowledge that is being lost in indigenous communities.

____ 6. Indigenous people know more about many plant and animal species than scientists.

____ 7. This pattern of knowledge loss exists all over the world.

____ 8. If information is lost in translation, it may be impossible to measure how much traditional knowledge is being lost.

____ 9. Traditional knowledge is in danger of disappearing if we do not encourage the people who hold it to preserve it.

____ 10. In some languages, words contain extra information about the things they describe.

E. Scan Reading 2 and write the correct numbers.

1. Number of speakers of Bari: _____1,500–2,500_____

2. Proportion of the world's plants and animals that are unknown to modern science: _____

3. Amount of profits made per year on medicines based on indigenous knowledge: _____

4. Lizarralde's estimate of the loss of knowledge about plants and animals in Venezuela: _____

5. The year of Scott Atran's study in Michigan: _____

F. Why does the author include these examples and statistics? Circle the answer that best connects each example or statistic to the main idea.

1. An estimated $85 billion in profits per year is gained on medicines made from plants that were first known to indigenous peoples for their healing properties. (Paragraph 1)
   a. to show that drug companies make too much money
   b. to show that indigenous knowledge is valuable
   c. to show that drug companies treat indigenous cultures badly

2. An astonishing 87 percent of the world's plant and animal species have not yet been identified, named, described, or classified by modern science. (Paragraph 2)
   a. to support the importance of traditional knowledge for modern science
   b. to criticize scientists for not studying more plants and animals
   c. to explain that the author is surprised about the number of unidentified species

3. Couldn't Solomon Islanders talk about the behavior patterns of fish in English just as easily as in Marovo, their native language? (Paragraph 4)
   a. to suggest that it is impossible to talk about the behavior of fish in English
   b. to suggest that Marovo can be translated into English without any loss
   c. to suggest that English words might not carry the same information as words in Marovo

4. In !Xoon, clouds are called "rain houses." (Paragraph 5)
   a. to make fun of the !Xoon word for *clouds*
   b. to show how a language packages information in a word
   c. to suggest that !Xoon is more useful than English

5. Bari people who have limited connection with the forest have lost up to 45 percent of traditional plant names. (Paragraph 8)
   a. to emphasize how cultural changes can lead to the loss of traditional knowledge
   b. to demonstrate that 55 percent of traditional plant names have been retained
   c. to criticize the Bari people for forgetting traditional plant names

G. Write answers to these questions in your own words, using information from Reading 2. Provide the paragraph numbers where you found the information.

1. What is "global linguistic homogenization"? Paragraph: ____

2. Why is global linguistic homogenization a threat to indigenous knowledge?

Paragraph: ____

_____

3. What is the difference between the !Xoon and English words for cloud?

Paragraph: ____

_____

4. What does Dr. Harrison mean by the "transfer" of traditional knowledge, and why is it important? Paragraphs: ____

_____

5. What was the purpose of the research conducted with the Bari people in Venezuela? Paragraph: ____

_____

6. Why does Dr. Harrison describe Atran's research in Michigan as hopeful?

Paragraph: ____

_____

7. Which arguments does Dr. Harrison believe are "appeals to ignorance"?

Paragraph: ____

_____

8. Why does he believe such arguments are ignorant? Paragraph: ____

_____

WRITE WHAT YOU THINK

A. Discuss these questions in a group. Look back at your Quick Write on page 16 as you think about what you have learned.

1. Have you ever tried to translate directly between two languages or used an online translation program? How accurate was the translation?

2. Can you think of examples of words or idioms that lose meaning when translated into English? How can you express the same ideas in English?

3. Dr. Harrison clearly does not believe that science can replace all the indigenous knowledge that is being lost. Do you agree with him? Support your opinion with examples from the text or your experience.

B. Think about the unit video, Reading 1, and Reading 2 as you discuss these questions. Then choose one question and write a paragraph in response.

1. The professor at the end of the video says that language "is an integral part of our human nature." Does this claim affect your understanding of language loss?

2. What can be done to save languages such as Bari that are in danger of extinction? Would the strategies that worked for the Maori language work in other cultures?

3. Is bilingualism an option for endangered languages? Can a language such as English or Spanish exist alongside native languages?

Vocabulary Skill | Using a thesaurus

A thesaurus is a reference book that gives you **synonyms**, words with similar meanings, and **antonyms**, words with opposite meanings. Learning synonyms and antonyms is a good way to build your vocabulary, and it allows you to use more variety in your writing and speaking. You should always be sure to check the meaning and use of new words carefully. The *Oxford Learner's Thesaurus* lists collocations and appropriate contexts for using each synonym correctly.

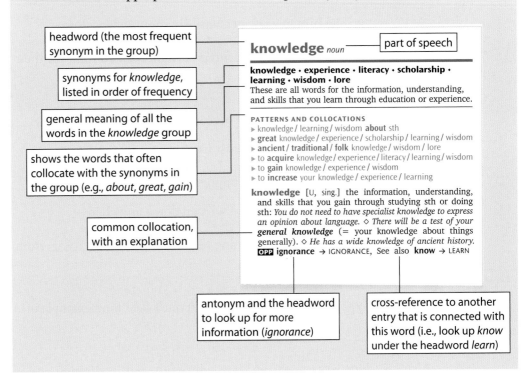

Adapted from *Oxford Learner's Thesaurus: A dictionary of synonyms* by Diana Lea © Oxford University Press 2008.

A. Complete each sentence with a word from the remainder of the thesaurus entry for *knowledge*. Use a different word in each sentence. Discuss your choices with a partner.

knowledge *noun*

knowledge · experience · literacy · scholarship · learning · wisdom · lore
These are all words for the information, understanding, and skills that you learn through education or experience.

PATTERNS AND COLLOCATIONS
▶ knowledge / learning / wisdom **about** sth
▶ **great** knowledge / experience / scholarship / learning / wisdom
▶ **ancient / traditional / folk** knowledge / wisdom / lore
▶ to **acquire** knowledge / experience / literacy / learning / wisdom
▶ to **gain** knowledge / experience / wisdom
▶ to **increase** your knowledge / experience / learning

knowledge [U, sing.] the information, understanding, and skills that you gain through studying sth or doing sth: *You do not need to have specialist knowledge to express an opinion about language.* ◇ *There will be a test of your* **general knowledge** (= your knowledge about things generally). ◇ *He has a wide knowledge of ancient history.* **OPP ignorance** → IGNORANCE, See also **know** → LEARN

experience [U] the knowledge and ability that you have gained through doing sth for a period of time; the process of gaining this: *I have over ten years' teaching experience.* ◇ *Do you have any* **previous experience** *of this type of work?* ◇ *She didn't get paid much, but it was all* **good experience.** ◇ *We all* **learn by experience.** **OPP inexperience** → IGNORANCE

literacy [U] the ability to read and write: *The government is running a campaign to promote* **adult literacy** (= the ability of adults to read and write). **OPP illiteracy**

scholarship [U] the serious study of an academic subject and the knowledge and methods involved: *Oxford became one of the great centers of medieval scholarship.*

learning [U] knowledge that you get from reading and studying: *He is a teacher of great intellect and learning.* See also **learned** → INTELLECTUAL 2

wisdom [U] the knowledge that a society or culture has gained over a long period of time: *We need to combine ancient wisdom and modern knowledge.* See also **wise** → WISE

lore [U] knowledge and information related to a particular subject, especially when this is not written down; the stories and traditions of a particular group of people: *an expert in ancient Celtic lore*

Adapted from *Oxford Learner's Thesaurus: A dictionary of synonyms* by Diana Lea © Oxford University Press 2008.

1. K. David Harrison's _____ of living with indigenous people enables him to write persuasively about their cultures.

2. Modern medicine is turning to traditional cultures for their _____ .

3. The indigenous people of Australia retain traditional _____ about the land and its history.

4. Studying textbooks is important, but this type of _____ can ignore facts that are not written down anywhere.

5. Young people are learning Maori _____ from elders to preserve their culture.

6. Writing a book or article about one's field is an example of _____ .

7. One way to save the knowledge of the Bari is through _____ campaigns so that it can be written and retained.

Tip for Success

No two words have exactly the same meaning and use. Check the exact meaning of new words in a dictionary or thesaurus before you use them.

B. Write an appropriate synonym for each underlined word. Use your thesaurus or dictionary.

1. _____ : Indigenous people in many countries have faced similar <u>problems</u>.

2. _____ : The <u>shift</u> from native languages to Spanish can be seen across Central and South America.

3. _____ : Multiculturalism is the <u>idea</u> that people of different cultures and ethnicities can live and learn together.

4. _____ : One <u>opinion</u> about multiculturalism is that it puts national unity in jeopardy.

5. _____ : Linguists <u>say</u> that half of the world's languages are dying.

6. _____ : Until recently, native cultures <u>kept</u> knowledge by passing it from one generation to the next.

 C. Go online for more practice with using a thesaurus.

WRITING

 **UNIT OBJECTIVE** ▶▶▶▶ At the end of this unit, you will write an extended definition of a word or concept from a different language. You will use specific information from the readings, the unit video, and your own ideas.

Writing Skill | Writing an extended definition

New words or concepts that are complex are often introduced in an **extended definition**. An extended definition is an **analysis** of a concept. It helps the reader understand by focusing on different features of the concept. Extended definitions frequently answer these questions:

Culture shock	
What is it?	Culture shock is a feeling of confusion and anxiety that somebody may feel when he lives in or visits another country.
What is it not?	It is not unusual, and it is not an illness. It is a normal part of the experience of living abroad.
What is it similar/dissimilar to?	If you have ever felt uncomfortable or lost in a new place, such as a new school where you don't know anyone, you have come close to understanding culture shock.
What does it consist of?	Culture shock is divided into four stages, from the initial excitement to complete adjustment. The four stages are . . .
What are its characteristics?	Culture shock can lead to feelings of depression, isolation, and confusion, but ultimately it leaves the traveler with a deeper understanding of his old and new cultures.
What are some examples?	For example, when I lived in France, I was embarrassed to speak. If I used a word incorrectly, I thought people would laugh at me. I felt very alone.
How does it work? How is it used?	Culture shock affects everyone differently, and people go through the stages at different speeds. Most people do reach a comfortable level of adjustment eventually.
Why is it important?	It is important to understand culture shock so that you are not surprised when you encounter these feelings.

A. Read this extended definition of language. Underline and number (1–5) the information that answers the questions below.

What Is Language?

Language is one of the distinguishing capacities of human beings. The dictionary defines *language* as the system of communication in speech and writing that is used by people of a particular country or area, but in reality, language is much more than communication. A particular language comprises not only grammar and vocabulary, but also aspects of its speakers' culture, their traditional knowledge, their rules of behavior, and their forms of social interaction. For instance, the vocabulary of the Marovo language reflects the Solomon Islanders' understanding of fish behavior. In Japanese, the complex system of honorifics (suffixes added to names that indicate the relationship between speaker and listener) expresses the complex social roles that are important in that country. This deeper definition of language helps explain why translation is often so difficult and why so much human knowledge is lost when a language dies.

1. What is language?

2. What is language not?

3. What does language consist of?

4. What are some examples of language?

5. Why is language important?

Writing Tip

When you write an academic essay, indent the first line of each paragraph, use left-justified formatting, and double-space your text. Do not skip an extra line between paragraphs.

B. WRITING MODEL Read a longer extended definition contrasting a concept that is not quite the same in two languages. Then complete the chart with information from the model.

Wit or Humor?

Laughter appears to be a universal human reaction, but what makes us laugh is deeply cultural. As an Englishman living in France, I have learned that even though our countries are separated by a narrow stretch of water, our senses of humor are a million miles apart. Even the words fail to translate adequately: English "humor" is certainly not the same as French *esprit*.

The French word *esprit* is often translated in English as *wit*, a rarely used word that is hard for many people to understand. When English speakers use humor, they are trying to make others laugh with them. When the French employ *esprit*, they are often asking listeners to laugh at someone else. That is, a funny person in English demonstrates an ability to share humor, whereas being funny in France in certain social situations might mean making fun of someone else. *Esprit* can, therefore, be mocking or even, some would say, a little mean.

An example that contrasts these two cultural concepts will help explain the difference. The French movie *Ridicule* shows us the dark side of a culture in which social status depends on the ability to make jokes about other people. The jokes may be funny, but they are also hurtful. Such jokes are examples of *esprit*: witty, but perhaps not humorous. Towards the end of the movie, one of the main characters is standing with an English friend on a cliff above the English Channel. A gust of wind blows the Frenchman's hat into the water. The Englishman smiles and observes, "Better your hat than your head!" After a pause, his French friend laughs. "Ah! That's the English sense of humor!" The Frenchman struggles to understand humor whose purpose is not to mock, but to enjoy the strangeness of life. Although *Ridicule* is set in the 17th century, and French society has certainly changed since then, the spirit of *esprit* lives on today in many ways.

Just as the French *esprit* has no exact English equivalent, it is very hard to translate *humor* into French. When the French watch British comedies, they often cannot see what is supposed to be funny. The British have a love of silliness that is unfamiliar in France. For instance, one of the most popular types of theater in England is the traditional pantomime. A pantomime is usually a well-known children's story adapted for the stage. A lot of physical humor is added: the actors pretend to hit each other, they put cream pies in other characters' faces, and they get confused in ways which audiences find very funny. The children laugh at the silliness, while adults recognize other jokes that are meant for them. Unsurprisingly, there is no such thing as a French pantomime.

I live through these cultural differences in comedy on a daily basis. When I tell jokes and make fun of myself, my French friends wonder why I lack self-confidence. Often I am the only person in the room who does not laugh at a display of great *esprit*. However, despite these moments of culture shock, I would hate to see English humor or French *esprit* change. Both cultures have developed their different styles of comedy over many centuries, and laughter plays an important role in both countries. Humor and wit release tension and create social connections. They are responses to difficult situations and ways to tell the truth even when it is painful or unpopular.

	English	French
1. What is the word?	humor	esprit
2. What does it mean when people use this concept?		
3. What are some examples?		
4. Why is it important in the culture?		
5. Why is it confusing to people from the other culture?		

C. Read the two writing models in Activities A and B again and discuss these questions with a partner.

1. What is the purpose of the first sentence of both definitions?

2. How are the two definitions organized?

3. What words do the writers use to connect ideas in each definition?

4. How do the writers conclude their definitions?

D. Go online for more practice with writing an extended definition.

Grammar	Contrast and concession connectors

Contrast and concession connectors join ideas with different meanings. In a *concession*, you acknowledge an opposing idea and then show that it is less important than your idea.

The coordinating conjunctions *but* and *yet* are used to join two contrasting independent clauses of equal importance. *Yet* is stronger than *but* and introduces an unexpected contrast or concession with the first clause. Use a comma between the clauses.

> The Maori language was dying, **but** recent initiatives are now saving it.
> Traditional knowledge could save lives, **yet** modern medicine often ignores it.

The subordinators *although*, *though*, or *even though* are used in a dependent clause when the main clause is an unexpected contrast or a concession to the idea in the dependent clause. *Even though* is stronger than *although* and *though*. *While* introduces a direct contrast or opposition to the idea in the main clause.

> **Although** Europeans learned Maori at first, the English language soon dominated.
> The Maori have retained their language **while** the Bari are losing theirs.

Transitions are adverbs and phrases that show the relationship between the ideas in one sentence and the ideas in the next. A period or semicolon is necessary to separate the independent clauses. *However*, the most common transition, can be used to show differences of various kinds.

> The Maori language was dying. **However**, recent initiatives are saving it.

On the other hand introduces opposite but not contradictory ideas or qualities of one topic, often with a positive versus negative contrast.

> The Maori have successfully saved their language. The Bari, **on the other hand**, are losing theirs.

A. Circle the best connector to complete each sentence.

1. (But / Although) some words in French look like English words, they have different meanings.

2. Sign language consists of hand signals instead of words. (However / On the other hand), it is a fully functional language.

American Sign Language

3. Many Latin words survive in English (but / even though) Latin has not been spoken for centuries.

4. In many countries, an indigenous language is used for daily communication (while / even though) another language is used for official business.

5. The word *algebra* looks like a Latin or Greek word, (yet / however) it comes from Arabic.

6. Some immigrants retain their native languages, (but / however) more lose theirs.

7. Speaking two languages is sometimes seen as a disadvantage for young children, (but / yet) most linguists believe that the opposite is true.

8. (Although / Yet) some governments officially protect native languages, their survival is not guaranteed.

B. Combine each pair of sentences into one. Use the connector in parentheses.

1. (although) The children did not all speak the same language. They learned to communicate.

   Although the children did not all speak the same language, they learned

   to communicate.

2. (while) There are more than 6,000 languages in the world. The United Nations operates with only 6 official languages.

   _____

   _____

3. (yet) The translation was accurate. The book was extremely difficult to understand.

   _____

   _____

4. (however) Researchers have studied most of the world's languages. New languages are still being discovered.

_____

_____

iQ ONLINE **C.** Go online for more practice with contrast and concession connectors.

D. Go online for the grammar expansion.

Unit Assignment Write an extended definition

UNIT OBJECTIVE ▶▶▶▶ In this assignment, you will write an extended definition of a word or concept from a different language that cannot be translated exactly into English. As you prepare your extended definition, think about the Unit Question, "What happens when a language disappears?" Use information from Reading 1, Reading 2, the unit video, and your work in this unit to support your ideas. Refer to the Self-Assessment checklist on page 32.

iQ ONLINE Go to the Online Writing Tutor for a writing model and alternate Unit Assignments.

PLAN AND WRITE

A. BRAINSTORM Think of one or two words, phrases, or concepts from a language you know that lose their meaning when translated. Then follow these steps.

1. Write about the words, phrases, or concepts for ten minutes without stopping. Then read your freewriting and underline the best ideas to develop.

2. Choose one word, phrase, or concept from your freewriting in Step 1. Check (✔) at least four questions you can answer to define it. Make notes.

☐ What is it?   ☐ What are its characteristics?

☐ What is it not?   ☐ What are some examples?

☐ What is it similar to?   ☐ How does it work?

☐ What is it different from?   ☐ How is it used?

☐ What does it consist of?   ☐ Why is it important?

_____

_____

_____

B. PLAN Follow these steps to plan your extended definition.

1. Go to the Online Resources to download and complete the graphic organizer and outline for your extended definition.

2. Decide how many paragraphs you need and what information you are going to write in each paragraph.

C. WRITE Use your PLAN notes to write your extended definition. Go to *iQ Online* to use the Online Writing Tutor.

1. Write your extended definition.

2. Look at the Self-Assessment checklist to guide your writing.

REVISE AND EDIT

A. PEER REVIEW Read your partner's extended definition. Then go online and use the Peer Review worksheet. Discuss the review with your partner.

B. REWRITE Based on your partner's review, revise, and rewrite your extended definition.

C. EDIT Complete the Self-Assessment checklist as you prepare to write the final draft of your extended definition. Be prepared to hand in your work or discuss it in class.

SELF-ASSESSMENT		
Yes	**No**	
☐	☐	Have you adequately defined the concept so that readers will have a clear understanding of how it is used?
☐	☐	Have you used a variety of sentence types and lengths?
☐	☐	Are main ideas arranged appropriately and supported with convincing details?
☐	☐	Do you use appropriate contrast and concession connectors?
☐	☐	Have you checked new words and collocations in a dictionary or thesaurus?
☐	☐	Does the extended definition include vocabulary from the unit?
☐	☐	Did you check the extended definition for punctuation, spelling, and grammar?

D. REFLECT Go to the Online Discussion Board to discuss these questions.

1. What is something new you learned in this unit?

2. Look back at the Unit Question—What happens when a language disappears? Is your answer different now than when you started the unit? If yes, how is it different? Why?

TRACK YOUR SUCCESS

Circle the words and phrases you have learned in this unit.

Nouns
cure 🔑
ethnicity AWL
habitat
initiative 🔑 AWL
revival
scenario AWL
shift 🔑 AWL

Verbs
abandon 🔑 AWL
assimilate
confine AWL
exploit AWL
oblige
persist AWL
retain 🔑 AWL
substitute 🔑 AWL
suppress
target 🔑 AWL

Adjectives
indigenous
integral AWL
predominant AWL

Phrases
divorced from
in jeopardy
in the face of
wake-up call

🔑 Oxford 3000™ words

AWL Academic Word List

Check (✓) the skills you learned. If you need more work on a skill, refer to the page(s) in parentheses.

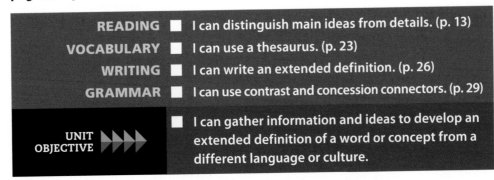

READING	☐ I can distinguish main ideas from details. (p. 13)
VOCABULARY	☐ I can use a thesaurus. (p. 23)
WRITING	☐ I can write an extended definition. (p. 26)
GRAMMAR	☐ I can use contrast and concession connectors. (p. 29)
UNIT OBJECTIVE ▶▶▶▶	☐ I can gather information and ideas to develop an extended definition of a word or concept from a different language or culture.

READING	▶	identifying contrasting ideas
VOCABULARY	▶	reporting verbs
WRITING	▶	using evidence to support an argument
GRAMMAR	▶	noun clauses

UNIT QUESTION

What is the difference between work and fun?

A Discuss these questions with your classmates.

1. What do you do for fun? Are your leisure activities the same as your parents' or grandparents' were at your age?

2. Can you think of a job that you would find fun? What would make work fun?

3. Look at the photos. What makes these jobs fun? What might make these jobs stressful?

◉ B Listen to *The Q Classroom* online and discuss these questions.

1. What activities do the students consider fun?

2. What activities do the students consider work?

3. Do you agree with the students' responses? Why or why not?

C Go online to watch the video about gardening as a leisure activity. Then check your comprehension.

compositions *(n.)* pieces of art

jammed *(adj.)* very full; crowded

landscaper *(n.)* someone who improves the appearance of an area of land by changing the design and planting trees, flowers, etc.

liven up *(phr.)* to make something more interesting or exciting

splurge *(v.)* to spend a lot of money on something that you do not really need

VIDEO VOCABULARY

D Go to the Online Discussion Board to discuss the Unit Question with your classmates.

E Look at the pictures. Would you describe the activities as fun or work? Circle your answers. Then discuss your answers in a group.

1. fun / work

2. fun / work

3. fun / work

4. fun / work

5. fun / work

6. fun / work

7. fun / work

8. fun / work

9. fun / work

F Discuss these questions in a group.

1. Think of your favorite sports. What are the benefits of being a professional athlete in these sports? What are the drawbacks?

2. All of the following are Olympic events. Which do you consider to be sports? Why or why not?

| tae kwon do | snowboarding | target shooting | show jumping on a horse |

READING 1 | Laid-Back Labor: The $140 Homemade Scarf

UNIT OBJECTIVE ►►►► You are going to read an article from the column "Freakonomics" in *The New York Times Magazine*. It was written by Stephen Dubner and Steven Levitt, the authors of the popular series of *Freakonomics* books, and it discusses how to define work and fun. Use the article to gather information and ideas for your Unit Assignment.

PREVIEW THE READING

A. **PREVIEW** Do you think people work more now than in the past? After you read the article, come back and check your prediction.

☐ Yes

☐ No

B. **QUICK WRITE** Do you have a hobby that people might pay you to do? Write for 5–10 minutes in response. Remember to use this section for your Unit Assignment.

C. **VOCABULARY** Check (✓) the words or phrases you know. Then work with a partner to locate each word or phrases in the reading. Use clues to help define the words or phrases you don't know. Check your definitions in the dictionary.

boom *(n.)*	**leisure** *(n.)*
consensus *(n.)*	**menial** *(adj.)*
engage in *(phr. v.)*	**respectively** *(adv.)*
gray area *(phr.)*	**the going rate** *(phr.)*
incentive *(n.)*	**the odds are** *(phr.)*
labor *(n.)* 🔑	**thriving** *(adj.)*

🔑 Oxford 3000™ words

 D. Go online to listen and practice your pronunciation.

WORK WITH THE READING

●) **A.** Read the article and gather information on the differences between work and fun.

FREAKONOMICS
Laid-Back Labor: The $140 Homemade Scarf
By Stephen J. Dubner and Steven D. Levitt

1   During the late 19th century, piano manufacturing was one of New York City's largest industries. Every right-minded American family, it seemed, wanted to fill its home with music. The advent of the player piano[1]—a music-making machine that required zero talent—drove the **boom** even further. By the 1920s, some 300,000 pianos were being sold in the United States each year, roughly two-thirds of them player pianos.

2   But a pair of newer technologies, the radio and the phonograph[2], soon began to drive the piano into a deep disfavor that continues to this day. Last year, Americans bought only 76,966 pianos. That's a decrease of 75 percent over a period in which the population more than doubled. As much as people may love music, most of them apparently don't feel the need to make it for themselves. According to Census Bureau[3] statistics, only 7.3 percent of American adults have played a musical instrument in the past 12 months.

knitting for fun

3   Compare this with the 17.5 percent of adults who currently **engage in** what the Census Bureau calls "cooking for fun." Or consider that 41 percent of households have flower gardens, 25 percent raise vegetables, and 13 percent grow fruit trees—even though just 1 percent of Americans live on a farm today, down from 30 percent in 1920. On a more personal note: one of the authors of this column has a sister who runs a **thriving** yarn[4] store, while the other is married to a knitting devotee who might buy $40 worth of yarn for a single scarf and then spend ten hours knitting it. Even if her **labor** is valued at only $10 an hour, the scarf costs at least $140—or roughly $100 more than a similar machine-made scarf might cost.

Knitting: a way to relax

4   Isn't it puzzling that so many middle-aged Americans are spending so much of their time and money performing **menial** labor when they don't have to? Just as the radio and phonograph proved to be powerful substitutes for the piano, the forces of technology have greatly eased the burden of feeding and clothing ourselves. So what's with all the knitting, gardening, and "cooking for fun"? Why do some forms of menial labor survive as hobbies while others have been killed off? (For instance, we can't think of a single person who, since the invention of the washing machine, practices "laundry for fun.")

5   Economists have been trying for decades to measure how much **leisure** time people have and how they spend it, but there has been precious little **consensus**. This is in part because

[1] **player piano:** a piano that can play automatically
[2] **phonograph:** a record player (old-fashioned)
[3] **Census Bureau:** the US government agency that collects information about the population
[4] **yarn:** thick thread (usually made of wool or cotton) that is used for knitting

it's hard to say what constitutes leisure and in part because measurements of leisure over the years have not been very consistent.

6   Economists typically separate our daily activities into three categories: market work (which produces income), home production (unpaid chores), and pure leisure. How, then, are we to categorize knitting, gardening, and cooking? While preparing meals at home can certainly be much cheaper than dining out and therefore viewed as home production, what about the "cooking for fun" factor?

7   In an attempt to address such **gray areas**, the economists Valerie A. Ramey and Neville Francis classified certain home activities as labor and others as leisure. In their recent paper "A Century of Work and Leisure," they employed a 1985 time-use survey in which people ranked their enjoyment of various activities on a scale of 0 to 10. Knitting, gardening, and cooking were in the middle of the scale, with a 7.7, 7.1, and 6.6, **respectively**. These ranked well behind some favorite activities—such as playing sports and fishing (which scored 9.2 and 9.1)—but firmly ahead of paying bills, cleaning the house and, yes, doing the laundry (5.2, 4.9, and 4.8).

8   But here's where it gets tricky. Ramey and Francis decided that anything at or above a 7.3 is leisure, while anything below is home production. (Knitting, therefore, makes the grade as leisure; gardening and cooking do not.) This leads them to calculate that we spend less time doing market work today than we did in 1900 but more time in home production. Men, it seems,

have contributed mightily to this upsurge: in 1920, employed men spent only 2 or 3 hours a week on home production, but they averaged 11 hours by 1965 and 16 hours by 2004.

9   But how many of those home-production hours are in fact leisure hours? This, it seems, is the real question here: What makes a certain activity work for one person and leisure for another?

10   With no disrespect toward Ramey and Francis, how about this for an alternative definition: Whether or not you're getting paid, it's work if someone else tells you to do it and leisure if you choose to do it yourself. If you are the sort of person who likes to mow[5] your own lawn even though you can afford to pay someone to do it, consider how you'd react if your neighbor offered to pay you **the going rate** to mow his lawn. **The odds are** that you wouldn't accept his job offer.

11   And so a great many people who can afford not to perform menial labor choose to do so, because—well, why? An evolutionary biologist might say that embedded in our genes is a drive to feed and clothe ourselves and tame our surroundings. An economist, meanwhile, might argue that we respond to **incentives** that go well beyond the financial; and that, fortunately, we are left free to choose which tasks we want to do ourselves.

12   Of course, these choices may say something about who we are and where we come from. One of us, for instance (the economist, who lives in Chicago), grew up comfortably in a midwestern city and has fond memories

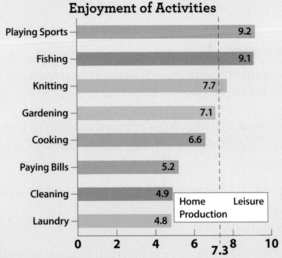

Enjoyment of Activities

Activity	Score
Playing Sports	9.2
Fishing	9.1
Knitting	7.7
Gardening	7.1
Cooking	6.6
Paying Bills	5.2
Cleaning	4.9
Laundry	4.8

Home Production — 7.3 — Leisure

---

[5] **mow**: to cut grass using a machine or tool with a special blade or blades

of visiting his grandparents' small farm. This author recently bought an indoor hydroponic[6] plant grower. It cost about $150 and to date has produced approximately 14 tomatoes—which, once you factor in the cost of seeds, electricity, and even a small wage for the labor, puts the average price of a single tomato at roughly $20.

13   The other one of us (the journalist, who lives in New York) grew up on a small farm and was regularly engaged in all sorts of sowing, mucking, and reaping.[7] He, therefore, has little desire to grow his own food—but he is happy to spend hours shopping for and preparing a special dinner for family and friends. Such dinners, even if the labor were valued at only $10 an hour, are more expensive than a similar takeout meal.

14   Maybe someday the New York guy will get to cook a meal with some of the Chicago guy's cherry tomatoes. It might become one of the most expensive meals in recent memory—and, surely, worth every penny.

From "Laid-Back Labor: The $140 Homemade Scarf" by Stephen J. Dubner and Steven D. Levitt, *The New York Times*, May 6, 2007. © 2007 Stephen J. Dubner and Steven D. Levitt. Used by permission.

[6] **hydroponic:** growing in water or sand, rather than in soil
[7] **sowing, mucking, and reaping:** farm chores

B. **VOCABULARY** Here are some words and phrases from Reading 1. Read the sentences. Circle the answer that best matches the meaning of each bold word or phrase.

Vocabulary Skill Review

In Unit 1, you learned how to use a thesaurus. Can you find good synonyms for some of the vocabulary words in Activity B?

1. When an activity becomes popular, companies that make equipment for the activity often have a **boom** in their sales.
   a. increase   b. problem   c. benefit

2. People who **engage in** gardening often form groups to share their plants and gardening tools with each other.
   a. have to do   b. enjoy   c. participate in

3. My sister's knitting store is **thriving** because every knitter in town buys supplies there.
   a. popular   b. successful   c. unusual

4. He didn't consider making his own furniture to be **labor** because he enjoyed it so much.
   a. hard work   b. a waste of time c. unnecessary work

5. Gardening, cooking, and knitting used to be considered **menial** tasks, but they are now expensive hobbies for many people.
   a. physical or difficult   b. boring or unskilled   c. useless or hopeless

6. Although we know how many hours Americans work each week, we still don't know how much **leisure** time they have.
   a. occupied   b. spare   c. uninterrupted

7. People pursue so many different hobbies that there is little **consensus** about the best way to spend free time.
   a. agreement   b. cooperation   c. argument

8. Some economists say there is a **gray area** between work and hobbies because it can be difficult to identify when a hobby becomes work.
   a. unclear difference   b. opposition   c. empty space

9. Fewer Americans live on farms today compared to 1920: 1 percent and 30 percent, **respectively**.
   a. honestly   b. most likely   c. in that order

10. I didn't know **the going rate** for professional photographers, so I asked several of my friends how much they paid for such services.
    a. how fast the average person can do something
    b. the lowest price or salary for something
    c. the typical price or salary for something

11. **The odds are** that you prefer playing sports to doing laundry.
    a. it is true   b. it is obvious   c. it is likely

12. People choose to do some types of work because of various **incentives**, such as extra money or some sort of special benefit.
    a. help to make work easier   b. types of motivation   c. offers

iQ ONLINE   **C.** Go online for more practice with the vocabulary.

D. Complete the summary of Reading 1 in your own words.

Some leisure activities that were popular in the past are less popular today because of ___developments in technology___. On the other hand,

some activities that used to be considered _____
₂

are now popular as _____. Economists divide
₃

our time into market work, _____, and pure
₄

leisure. In one study, economists Valerie Ramey and Neville Francis found

that we do less _____ than in 1900 but more
₅

_____. However, authors Stephen Dubner and Steven
₆

Levitt suggest a different definition of *work* and *leisure*: an activity is work if

_____ and leisure if _____.
₇   ₈

According to economists, people today do menial tasks when they don't need

to because _____.
₉

E. Skim the article to find the meaning of these numbers and statistics.

1. 76,966: _____the number of pianos sold in the US last year_____

2. 7.7: _____

3. 16 hours: _____

4. $20: _____

5. 1%: _____

6. 4.8: _____

F. Answer these questions. Use specific information from the article.

1. Was playing the piano considered work or leisure by many Americans in the late 19th and early 20th centuries? How do you know?

   _____

2. Is playing the piano considered work or leisure by many Americans now? How do you know?

   _____

3. How do the authors calculate that a homemade scarf costs $140?

   _____

4. Why do "gray areas" exist between home production and leisure?

   _____

5. How did Ramey and Francis distinguish between home production and leisure?

   _____

6. What problem do the authors note with Ramey and Francis's conclusions?

   _____

7. What non-financial incentives explain why the authors grow tomatoes and cook special meals?

   _____

G. Read the statements. Write *T* (true) or *F* (false). Then correct each false statement to make it true.

_____ 1. A homemade scarf costs more when you put a value on the time you take to make it.

_____ 2. An example of menial labor that is not popular today as a hobby is growing vegetables.

_____ 3. The difference between market work and household production is that market work happens outside the house.

_____ 4. Ramey and Francis classify knitting, gardening, and cooking as leisure activities.

_____ 5. According to Ramey and Francis, men do more chores today than in 1920.

_____ 6. If you mow your own lawn because you want to, you probably would not accept money to cut your neighbor's lawn.

_____ 7. Evolutionary biologists might say that we have a natural desire to do as little work as possible.

_____ 8. The author who likes growing tomatoes enjoyed visiting his grandparents' farm as a child.

_____ 9. The other author prefers cooking to growing vegetables because his parents owned a restaurant when he was a child.

 H. Go online to read *The Blurring of Work and Leisure* and check your comprehension.

 # WRITE WHAT YOU THINK

A. Discuss these questions in a group.

1. Think about the activities you do in your daily life. Which would you pay someone else to do for you if you could? Why?

2. The authors of this article both live in the United States, where it is possible for many people to buy food and clothes cheaply. Do you think their opinions would be different if they lived in another country? Why or why not?

3. The authors of "Laid Back Labor" claim that economists do not agree about the definition of *leisure*. After reading this article, how would you define *work* and *leisure*? Use your own examples to support your opinion.

B. Choose one question and write a paragraph in response. Look back at your Quick Write on page 37 as you think about what you learned.

Reading Skill | Identifying contrasting ideas

Authors often present several different opinions in order to provide a balanced argument. They may also add their own opinion, which might differ from those of other experts. To follow the authors' arguments and main ideas, it is important to recognize whose opinion you are reading and to be aware of different opinions in a text. Here are some words and phrases you can look for to identify a new opinion or a different opinion.

Words that introduce an opinion	Words that show a different opinion
According to economists, . . .	. . . but/yet this is not always true.
In a recent study, Dubner found . . .	Some say . . . while/whereas others argue . . .
A critic might say . . .	However/On the other hand, . . .
Some people regard/see this as . . .	I disagree with Dubner about . . .
Francis argues/claims/states that . . .	Gardening is not work, but rather/instead . . .
We believe/think that . . .	A different/alternative/contrasting idea is . . .

A. Read the paragraph. Circle words that introduce an opinion and underline words that show a different opinion. Then compare your answers with a partner.

Do Americans have more leisure time than in the past? Economists cannot reach a consensus on this question. For example, Ramey and Francis argue that Americans have about the same amount of leisure time as they did in 1900 and slightly less than they did about 40 years ago. However, according to another study by Aguiar and Hurst, American adults actually have more leisure time than they did about 40 years ago. The differences result from disagreement over what constitutes work. Ramey and Francis consider the whole population, whereas Aguiar and Hurst only look at working-age adults, and they do not regard engaging in schoolwork and homework as labor. Rather than focusing on this difference, we believe that both studies support an alternative conclusion: Americans certainly do not have less leisure time than in the past.

Source: Adapted from Kristie M. Engemann and Michael T. Owyang (2007, January), "Working Hard or Hardly Working? The Evolution of Leisure in the United States." *The Regional Economist*, 10–11.

B. Complete the chart with the different opinions on the question *Do Americans have more leisure time now than in the past?* Use your annotations from Activity A to help you.

Do Americans have more leisure time now than in the past?	
Ramey and Francis's opinion	
Aguiar and Hurst's opinion	
The authors' opinion	

C. Reread the article "Laid-Back Labor: The $140 Homemade Scarf." Circle the words and phrases in paragraphs 7–11 that introduce an opinion and a different opinion. Then compare your answers with a partner.

Critical Thinking Tip

In Activity D, you will paraphrase the definitions and opinions from the article. Paraphrasing helps you understand and remember information better. It is also very important in writing. You will practice this skill more thoroughly in Unit 6.

D. Complete the charts. Use your own words to describe the definitions and opinions.

What is the definition of *leisure*?	
Levitt and Dubner	Leisure is something you choose to do; no one tells you to do it.
Ramey and Francis	

Why do people choose to do menial labor when they don't have to?	
Evolutionary biologists	
Economists (including the authors)	

 E. Go online for more practice identifying contrasting ideas.

READING 2 | Tae Kwon Do for Health

You are going to read an article from *Black Belt Magazine* about tae kwon do. Tae kwon do is a martial art (a fighting activity like karate or judo) that originated in Korea and is now included in the summer Olympic Games. Use the article to gather information and ideas for your Unit Assignment.

PREVIEW THE READING

A. **PREVIEW** Do you think martial arts like tae kwon do are sports or leisure activities? Why? Write three reasons.

_____

_____

_____

B. **QUICK WRITE** What characteristics does a sport need to be included in the Olympic Games? Write for 5–10 minutes in response. Remember to use this section for your Unit Assignment.

C. **VOCABULARY** Check (✓) the words or phrases you know. Then work with a partner to locate each word or phrase in the reading. Use clues to help define the words and phrases you don't know. Check your definitions in the dictionary.

boost (v.)	it dawned on me (phr.)
devotion (n.)	pass your prime (phr.)
emerge (v.) 🔑	regard as (phr. v.) 🔑
estimate (v.) 🔑	rhythm (n.) 🔑
evolve (v.)	sophisticated (adj.)
execute (v.)	strategy (n.) 🔑

🔑 Oxford 3000™ words

D. Go online to listen and practice your pronunciation.

A. Read the article and gather information on the differences between work and fun.

Tae Kwon Do for Health

by Kim Soo
Kim Soo is a Houston-based martial arts pioneer and member of the Black Belt Hall of Fame.

Tae kwon do

1   The martial arts have **evolved** over the past century, and their purpose has changed. In an earlier era, they were used mainly for warfare. A person studying martial arts trained to become a superior soldier and better serve his country or his emperor. His highest honor was to die in combat. The emphasis in training was on physical ability, while the values centered on loyalty, **devotion**, and discipline. The health of the person was of low importance. No one trained for self-improvement; indeed, some of the traditional methods in martial arts were detrimental to physical well-being. For example, punches used to be performed with the mouth closed, exhaling on impact. Although this **boosts** speed and power, practicing it daily will take a toll on your health. But of course, soldiers back then didn't live long enough to develop long-term health problems.

2   Today, many martial arts enthusiasts **regard** what they do as sport, which means importance is placed on awards and tournament victories. Indeed, modern tae kwon do is an Olympic event, and as such, it emphasizes tournament fighting. During training, practitioners learn how to perform **sophisticated** moves in order to defeat their opponents and win medals.

During demonstrations, extreme acrobatics[1] and deadly-looking movements are the focus. However, this misses the true purpose of the martial arts.

3   In fact, sparring[2] should benefit both parties, which means that there should be no winners or losers. Additionally, tournament fighting sets the stage for martial arts enthusiasts to lose sight of the goals of training. They may be left thinking that after **passing their prime**, there's no more reason to train. Therefore, the question **emerges**: what is the true purpose of martial arts?

4   The purpose of martial arts today is to promote health and longevity,[3] and training must reflect those goals. Students today aren't preparing to die for their country, and fortunately most of us will never encounter a physical attacker. Modern-day enemies are internal rather than external: stress, depression, worry, and insecurity. Many of us must fight these enemies on a daily basis and defeat them through training that develops mental and physical balance.

[1] **acrobatics:** acts and movements
[2] **sparring:** to make the movements of a fight for practice
[3] **longevity:** long life

5   Some tae kwon do masters brag[4] about staying healthy by running on treadmills and lifting weights at the gym. In reality, though, traditional tae kwon do forms have everything a person needs to stay mentally and physically healthy. At the same time, if practice is conducted in the wrong way, it has the power to cause harm. Focusing on only speed and power is like taking small amounts of poison every day, while practicing the right way has the power to heal.

6   When I started the martial arts, we had to figure all this out by ourselves while training to exhaustion. Consequently, many of us suffered serious injuries such as broken bones. The instructors' attitude was that the toughest would survive. Most students didn't see the benefits of training and soon dropped out.

7   I suffered serious health problems while training, all because of poor training methods. Ironically, I became less healthy than people who didn't practice martial arts. After enduring pain for 10 years, I was advised to undergo back surgery with only an **estimated** 50–50 chance of improvement. Since the surgery would require me to stay in bed for a long time, I chose physical therapy, traditional Chinese medicine, and acupuncture[5] instead. However, nothing provided much relief.

8   One day during this dark period in my life, I exited the health studio on a gorgeous day with a bright blue sky, but to me, it looked as gray and gloomy as my future. The thought of martial arts making me sick had brought me to that low point. However, through meditation and training, I came to the understanding that the principles and teaching methods I was using were wrong, which was the real reason for my poor health. Instead of doctors and acupuncturists, the solution to my problem lay in my training. In essence, I was putting too much emphasis on the technical and physical aspects. **It dawned on me** that my focus should be on balance, breathing, and **rhythm**.

9   There is balance of movement and balance of mind. When techniques are practiced, they must be balanced to ensure the body isn't harmed by repeated unbalanced movements that may strain the anatomy. At the same time, without proper breathing, your health will be at risk. Not only is proper breathing fuel for the body, but it also establishes proper rhythm. The body can then follow this rhythm to **execute** a safe, powerful tae kwon do movement. Running provides a useful comparison: you may be able to run five miles without rhythm, but if you run like that every day, eventually your health will suffer.

10   So how did I cure my back problem? I practiced the aforementioned[6] principles while training. I practiced the basic forms with a new focus on breathing, balance, and rhythm every day, over and over. Incorrect training had harmed my body, and correct training was healing it. My way of teaching these principles came to be known as "natural way martial arts," or *Chayon-Ryu*. Its goal is to preserve and enhance the martial arts enthusiast's health.

11   I'd like to share another personal story. A friend sent me a shocking demo video. He was performing fancy moves in preparation for a competition. When I saw him a few months later, he said he couldn't sleep or eat and felt nervous and anxious all the time. I said I wasn't surprised. His training lacked proper breathing and rhythm. He could kick high and demonstrate impressive techniques, but there was no balance. I told him his problem was his own workouts.

12   The simple question of whether martial arts training is good for your health can be answered with a not-so-simple response: yes and no. Tae kwon do can save your life, but it can also destroy it. You have to practice correctly, using the right principles. The traditional Asian method of instruction is sometimes part of the problem. Few people have the patience to train long enough to understand the basic principles.

---

[4] **brag:** talk too proudly about something you've done
[5] **acupuncture:** a method of treating pain by pushing thin needles into particular parts of the body

[6] **aforementioned:** mentioned before, in an earlier sentence

13 Martial arts teachers in my home country, South Korea, are astonished to learn that I have students who have been with me for 20, 30, or 40 years. That fact strengthens my message that an incorrect understanding of the purpose of the martial arts results in poor teaching methods, which leads to students who have the wrong attitude, get injured, and ultimately give up. Today, people should study tae kwon do to increase personal happiness, not to die in battle. They're seeking health, longevity, and relaxation, in addition to self-defense.

14 A martial art is more than a sport, more than tournament **strategy**, more than self-defense. When taught right, tae kwon do is a way of life that combines philosophical insight with physical training to create mentally strong and independent individuals who can fight frailty and weakness as well as internal enemies like doubt, insecurity, and stress.

B. **VOCABULARY** Here are some words and phrases from Reading 2. Read the sentences. Then write each bold word or phrase next to the correct definition. You may need to change verbs to their base form and nouns to the singular form.

1. Fighting techniques have **evolved** from simple to very complex.

2. Professional athletes practice daily and show great **devotion** to their sport.

3. Studying hard should **boost** your performance in school.

4. Martial arts are **regarded as** a waste of time by those who do not understand their benefits.

5. Martial arts enthusiasts make very **sophisticated** moves in competitions.

6. In many sports, professional athletes over age 30 have **passed their prime**.

7. A question which **emerges** from this discussion is whether tae kwon do is a sport or a leisure activity.

8. It is **estimated** that tae kwon do is practiced in over 100 countries.

9. When I started running long distances, **it dawned on me** that I needed to do more training.

10. It is important to have good **rhythm** in your arms and legs when you run.

11. Good training in a sport allows athletes to **execute** techniques perfectly.

12. Checkers is a game of **strategy** that requires players to think ahead to their next several moves.

a. _____ (*v.*) to guess the approximate size of something

b. _____ (*n.*) a careful plan to reach a goal

c. _____ (*phr. v.*) to consider (as); to see in a certain way

d. _____ (*adj.*) complicated or highly developed

e. _____ (*v.*) to appear or start to exist

f. _____ (*v.*) to develop gradually

g. _____ (*v.*) to perform an action

h. _____ (*n.*) spending a lot of time or energy on something

i. _____ (*n.*) a regular, repeated pattern of movements

j. _____ (*phr.*) to be too old to do something at a high level

k. _____ (*v.*) to make something increase a lot

l. _____ (*phr.*) to become obvious or easy to understand

iQ ONLINE **C. Go online for more practice with the vocabulary.**

D. Cross out the incorrect answer to each question. Write the paragraph numbers where you found the correct answers.

1. What are the main ideas of the article?
   a. Tae kwon do is emerging as a popular sport.
   b. Tae kwon do should be practiced mainly for its health benefits.
   c. Tae kwon do has filled different purposes throughout its history.

Paragraph(s): _____

2. What does the article say about the early history of tae kwon do?
   a. It was a way of fighting.
   b. It was a competitive sport.
   c. It combined physical skill with devotion to country.

Paragraph(s): _____

3. What is the author's opinion about tae kwon do tournaments?
   a. They encourage bad training habits.
   b. They are exciting to watch.
   c. They make winning too important.

Paragraph(s): _____

4. What should be the purpose of tae kwon do today, according to the article?
   a. Mental balance
   b. Long-lasting physical health
   c. Speed and power

Paragraph(s): _____

5. How did the author injure himself?
   a. He did dangerous moves in a competition.
   b. His instructors believed that injuries were part of learning tae kwon do.
   c. He trained too hard because little was known about the effects of this type of training.

Paragraph(s): _____

6. What remedies did the author try to solve his health problems?
   a. Surgery
   b. Acupuncture
   c. Different training techniques

Paragraph(s): _____

7. What did the author contribute to the world of martial arts?
   a. An improved method of teaching tae kwon do
   b. A new strategy for winning tournaments
   c. An ideal purpose for martial arts

Paragraph(s): _____

8. In what ways can martial arts be good for you, according to the author?
   a. They make you emotionally stronger.
   b. They can help you to live longer.
   c. They give you techniques to fight your enemies.

Paragraph(s): _____

E. Summarize the main ideas of the article by completing the table in your own words.

Stage	Purpose(s) of tae kwon do	Training techniques	Advantages and disadvantages of training techniques
Early history			
Martial arts as a modern sport			
Chayon-Ryu ("natural way martial arts")			

F. With a partner, explain the meaning of these statements from the article.

1. "Soldiers back then didn't live long enough to develop long-term health problems" (Paragraph 1).

   _____

2. "There should be no winners or losers" (Paragraph 3).

   _____

3. "Modern-day enemies are internal rather than external" (Paragraph 4).

   _____

4. "Focusing on only speed and power is like taking small amounts of poison every day" (Paragraph 5).

   _____

5. "Proper breathing is fuel for the body" (Paragraph 9).

   _____

6. "Martial arts teachers in my home country, South Korea, are astonished to learn that I have students who have been with me for 20, 30, or 40 years" (Paragraph 13).

   _____

G. As you read in the article, tae kwon do is an event in the summer Olympic Games. Supporters of this status might make these arguments in favor of tae kwon do as a competitive sport. With a partner, use evidence from the reading to argue against these positions.

1. The purpose of tae kwon do has always been to defeat your enemies, so it is appropriate to use it for competition.

   _____

   _____

2. Sporting events encourage tae kwon do practitioners to develop new and more sophisticated moves and kicks.

   _____

   _____

3. Sports are supposed to be tough. Only the strongest athletes should be able to survive the training and compete at the highest levels.

_____

_____

4. Martial arts are methods of self-defense, so the focus of tae kwon do should be on speed, power, and technique. Competitions show which athletes have the best skills in these areas.

_____

_____

WRITE WHAT YOU THINK

A. Discuss these questions in a group. Look back at your Quick Write on page 46 as you think about what you have learned.

1. Do you think that physical activities such as martial arts can improve your mental health?

2. After reading the article, do you think tae kwon do should be considered a sport? Why or why not?

3. When an activity like a hobby or martial art becomes a competitive sport, do you think there is always a risk that it will lose its original purpose?

B. Think about the unit video, Reading 1, and Reading 2 as you discuss these questions. Then choose one question and write a paragraph in response.

1. In Reading 1, the authors suggested this definition of *work* and *leisure*: "Whether or not you're getting paid, it's work if someone else tells you to do it, and leisure if you choose to do it by yourself." Do the examples in the video and Reading 2 support or challenge this definition? Why?

2. The authors of Reading 1 described research that divided work and leisure according to how enjoyable people find an activity. Based on this definition, would amateur and professional sports be considered work or leisure? Why?

When writing academic papers (research reports, essays, etc.), you often need to report information, ideas, or research by other authors. The choice of verb in the main clause can show your attitude toward the source. The verb can imply a supporting, distancing, or neutral attitude about the author's ideas or opinions. Use a dictionary to help you understand the exact meaning and use of different verbs so that you can accurately express your opinion and recognize other authors' attitudes.

Example	Type of verb	Explanation
The authors **prove** that leisure time has increased.	Supporting	*Prove* means "to use facts or evidence to show that something is true;" the authors have convinced you that leisure time has increased.
The authors **say** that leisure has increased.	Neutral	*Say* means "to give information;" you are reporting the information the authors gave without expressing your own opinion.
The authors **claim** that leisure time has increased.	Distancing	*Claim* means "to say that something is true although it has not been proved and other people may not believe it;" you do not accept the authors' conclusion that leisure time has increased.

Adverbs can also have a supporting or distancing effect on a sentence. For example, "The authors argue **convincingly** . . . " means you are persuaded by the argument, whereas "The authors **supposedly** prove that . . . " shows doubt about their conclusions.

A. Read the sentences. Do the words in bold have a supporting, neutral, or distancing effect? Circle the correct answer.

1. Although most people would prefer to have more leisure time, a minority of experts **unconvincingly argue** that people don't need any leisure time at all.

   a. supporting   b. neutral   c. distancing

2. Research **unfailingly demonstrates** that people are more productive after they've had a vacation.

   a. supporting   b. neutral   c. distancing

3. The author's analysis and the scientific evidence **validate** the position that individuals do not need the same amount of leisure time to be satisfied.

    a. supporting   b. neutral   c. distancing

4. A United Nations report **states** that a certain amount of unemployment is inevitable in all economies.

    a. supporting   b. neutral   c. distancing

5. The authors **incorrectly contend** that people value their leisure time more than their time at work.

    a. supporting   b. neutral   c. distancing

6. Some economists **tell** politicians how to present employment data in different ways to support their position.

    a. supporting   b. neutral   c. distancing

B. Choose five ideas, opinions, facts, or statistics about sports, work, or leisure. Write sentences that show your attitude. Use a dictionary or thesaurus to find other reporting verbs or adverbs.

1. _____

_____

2. _____

_____

3. _____

_____

4. _____

_____

5. _____

_____

C. Exchange your sentences from Activity B with a partner. Read each sentence. Identify your partner's attitude.

D. Go online for more practice with reporting verbs.

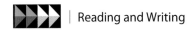

WRITING

UNIT OBJECTIVE ▶▶▶▶ At the end of this unit, you will write an argumentative essay on why a particular leisure activity should or should not be considered work. This essay will include specific information from the readings, the unit video, and your own ideas.

Writing Skill   Using evidence to support an argument

Most academic writing requires you to make an argument and try to persuade the reader that your opinion is correct. Writers use evidence (examples, quotations, statistics, explanations, etc.) to make their arguments more convincing. All evidence must be relevant (meaningful and connected to the topic), or it will confuse and not convince the reader.

The authors of Reading 1, for example, used several types of evidence to support their argument. They argued that activities that were once considered work are now considered hobbies. They used these types of evidence:

- **statistics** (Twenty-five percent of Americans grow vegetables.)
- **comparisons** (Only 1 percent of Americans live on farms now, compared with 30 percent in 1920.)
- **personal examples** (The sister of one of the writers runs a yarn store.)
- **analysis/mathematical calculations** (If we calculate labor at $10 an hour, the actual cost of a homemade scarf is $140.)

Tip for Success

Different academic subjects have different rules for good evidence, so always find out what kind of evidence your reader will accept. Ask your teacher or look closely at your readings for examples.

A. Read each section of this draft outline of an essay. The essay will argue that playing video games is a sport. Answer the question after each section.

> ### Video Games Are a Real Sport
>
> The gaming industry has seen a boom in recent years. Video games have developed from childhood hobbies into a massive, worldwide industry. As with other leisure activities, this has resulted in "professional amateurs" and finally full-time professional video gamers. As a result, video-game playing can now be called a real sport.

1. What evidence could the writer add to this section of the essay? Check (✓) all the appropriate answers.

☐ a. Dubner and Levitt define *sport* as "an activity that you do for pleasure and that needs physical effort or skill, usually done in a special area and according to fixed rules."

☐ b. Video games are similar to rugby, which began as a game at an English school and became an international professional sport.

☐ c. The video-game industry is worth roughly $5 billion in South Korea.

☐ d. My friend plays video games all the time, and she even won a prize at a regional competition last year.

> Video games are a sport because they are played by amateurs and professionals for both pleasure and profit.

2. What evidence could the writer add to this section of the essay? Check (✔) all the appropriate evidence.

☐ a. I conducted an informal survey of students in my class, and 85 percent said that they sometimes or often played video games.

☐ b. I think that about 85 percent of teenagers play video games.

☐ c. National and international professional gaming leagues exist. This makes video games similar to baseball, which is played in community parks and also in major leagues.

☐ d. Some video games are expensive, so some young people cannot afford them.

> Critics of professional video-game leagues suggest that gaming does not qualify as a sport because it is not a physical activity and it is a game of chance more than skill and strategy. However, these objections are not valid.

3. What evidence could the writer add to this section of the essay? Check (✔) all the appropriate evidence.

☐ a. Good video-game players need excellent motor control and reflexes in the arms, hands, and fingers.

☐ b. Not all sports involve movement; shooting is an Olympic sport, for example.

☐ c. Some people argue that card games should be a sport because they also take skill and practice to master.

☐ d. More sophisticated video games clearly require strategy; for example, players may have to control a character, solve puzzles, and shoot at monsters.

B. **WRITING MODEL** Read a student's essay arguing that playing video games should not be regarded as a sport.

Competitive Video Gaming

When most people think about sports, they imagine athletes engaged in intense physical and mental competition. They probably do not imagine young people sitting in front of flat-screen TVs or staring at their cell phones. Remarkably, professional video gamers claim that their hobby should be regarded as a sport alongside soccer, golf, and tennis. However, competitive video gaming does not meet any of the criteria for a sport, and its players are not athletes.

Professional sports demand a level of devotion and skill that exceeds the ability of amateurs. For example, I play golf in my leisure time, but I might only play once or twice a month, whereas a professional will play every day. Thanks to their physical strength and knowledge of the game, professional golfers achieve scores that most amateurs could not dream of reaching. In fact, professional and amateur golfers do not even play on the same courses, and when they do, they start from different places on the course. Video games, on the other hand, are commercial products that are the same for everyone. They demand little physical ability, and high scores can be reached by almost anyone with enough time. Therefore, there is simply nothing special about successful video gamers.

Furthermore, in real sports, the only limit is the skill level and physical fitness of the participants. In 1954, an amateur British athlete, Roger Bannister, became the first man in the world to run a mile in less than four minutes. His record stood for just over a month. Today, the world record for a mile is more than 15 seconds faster than Bannister's famous run. Video games, on the other hand, are limited by the capacity of the software and hardware. Top scores are determined as much by the game designers as by the players, who have few opportunities for truly game-changing innovations, strategies, and techniques.

In fact, the role of the computer is the most important reason why video games cannot be considered a sport. A sport is a contest between humans to see who is the strongest, fastest, most strategic, or most skillful. However, even when players compete against each other in a video game, a machine decides how the game will run. Today's game consoles, computers, and cell phones are highly sophisticated devices, and they can surely affect the outcome of the competition. There is no guarantee of fairness. Supporters of the video game industry could argue that nature influences the result of sporting events, for instance high winds during a golf tournament or rain at a soccer game. The comparison is not persuasive, though, because natural conditions affect all athletes equally. The computer could give an unfair advantage to one player. Hacking is even possible, so the outcome of a game could be fixed, and perhaps no one would ever know.

For all these reasons, video games should remain a popular and enjoyable leisure activity or even a profession for some. However, gaming is not a sport, and players are not professional athletes. Real sports are not decided by a combination of luck and computer technology.

C. Complete this outline of the model essay in Activity B.

Introduction: _____

Thesis: _____

First reason: _____

    Supporting explanation: _____

Second reason: _____

    Supporting example: _____

Third reason: _____

    Supporting explanation: _____

    Counter-argument: _____

    Reasons why the counter-argument is wrong: _____

Conclusion: _____

D. Evaluate the essay. Discuss these questions with a partner.

1. Do you find the argument persuasive? Why or why not?

2. Are there any claims or reasons that you find weak? Why?

3. One argument that could be added is that sports require physical fitness, whereas video games do not. Where could you add this point? How could you develop it into a paragraph?

4. What advice would you give this writer to revise the essay?

 E. Go online for more practice with using evidence to support an argument.

Grammar | Noun clauses

When writers include other people's speech, thoughts, questions, or results in their writing, they often use **noun clauses**. A noun clause is a dependent clause that can replace a noun or pronoun as a subject or object.

>   main clause   noun clause
> Some economists say that we have less free time now than in the past.

There are three types of noun clauses:

- Noun clauses formed from statements

>   noun clause
> Many Americans say (**that**) they cook for fun.

 Tip for Success

The word *that* may be deleted in a noun clause, but it is usually kept in academic writing.

- Noun clauses formed from *wh-* questions

  noun clause

  We asked the man **why** he plays video games.

- Noun clauses formed from *yes/no* questions

  noun clause

  TV networks wonder **if/whether** people will watch video-game competitions.

Noun clauses formed from questions always have sentence word order (subject-verb). They do not have the inverted word order typically used in questions, and they omit the form of *do* that is needed to form questions.

  ✗ We asked the man why does he play video games.

Remember that you can use different verbs in the main clause to show your attitude toward the information in the noun clause. (See page 54.)

A. Complete the paragraph with words from the box. Use each word once.

if	how	that	which	who	why

Although most people would say _____ gardening is
                                        1
a hobby, for a few enthusiastic gardeners, it is almost a sport. If you've

ever wondered _____ anyone would grow a one-meter-long
                      2
cucumber or a 770-kilogram pumpkin, here's your answer. Amateur

gardeners bring their produce to competitions where judges measure

them to determine _____ fruits and vegetables are the
                          3
largest. Every year, pumpkin growers gather near San Francisco to see

_____ has grown the heaviest orange gourd. After the results
        4
are announced, all the gardeners want to know _____ the
                                                        5
winners will share their secrets. But few champion growers will reveal

_____ they turned ordinary vegetables into giants.
        6

B. Complete each sentence using a noun clause with an appropriate reporting verb from the box. Use each verb once.

argue	discuss	~~feel~~	study	wonder

1. Cooking food is less enjoyable than eating it.

   Most Americans _feel that cooking food is less enjoyable than eating it._

2. How much time do we spend doing work?

   Ramey and Francis _____

3. What makes an activity work for one person and leisure for another?

   The authors _____

4. Something is leisure if you choose to do it yourself.

   Dubner and Levitt _____

5. Are video games as popular in rural places as in urban areas?

   Some readers _____

 C. Go online for more practice with noun clauses.

D. Go online for the grammar expansion.

 Unit Assignment **Write an argumentative essay**

UNIT OBJECTIVE In this assignment, you will write an argumentative essay arguing why a particular leisure activity should or should not be considered work. As you prepare your essay, think about the Unit Question, "What is the difference between work and fun?" Use information from Reading 1, Reading 2, the unit video, and your work in this unit to support your essay. Refer to the Self-Assessment checklist on page 62.

 Go to the Online Writing Tutor for a writing model and alternate Unit Assignments.

PLAN AND WRITE

A. **BRAINSTORM** Think of an activity that you enjoy and do not get paid to do. Choose one of the examples from the chapter or something else. Brainstorm ideas why it should or should not be considered work.

Activity:

_____

It should / shouldn't be regarded as work because:

_____

_____

B. **PLAN** Follow these steps to plan your argumentative essay.

1. List your three best ideas from Activity A that support your position.

 2. Go to the Online Resources to download and complete the graphic organizer and outline for your argumentative essay.

 C. **WRITE** Use your **PLAN** notes to write your essay. Go to *iQ Online* to use the Online Writing Tutor.

1. Write your essay, arguing whether the leisure activity you chose should be considered work or not. Support each main idea with evidence from your knowledge, experience, and reading.

2. Look at the Self-Assessment checklist to guide your writing.

REVISE AND EDIT

 A **PEER REVIEW** Read your partner's essay. Then go online and use the Peer Review worksheet. Discuss the review with your partner.

B. **REWRITE** Based on your partner's review, revise and rewrite your essay.

C. **EDIT** Complete the Self-Assessment checklist as you prepare to write the final draft of your argumentative essay. Be prepared to hand in your work or discuss it in class.

SELF-ASSESSMENT		
Yes	**No**	
☐	☐	Does the essay build a convincing argument using main ideas supported with good evidence?
☐	☐	Are contrasting ideas introduced clearly?
☐	☐	Did you use noun clauses effectively?
☐	☐	Are there a variety of reporting verbs?
☐	☐	Does the essay include vocabulary from the unit?
☐	☐	Did you check the essay for punctuation, spelling, and grammar?

D. **REFLECT** Go to the Online Discussion Board to discuss these questions.

1. What is something new you learned in this unit?

2. Look back at the Unit Question—What is the difference between work and fun? Is your answer different now than when you started the unit? If yes, how is it different? Why?

TRACK YOUR SUCCESS

Circle the words and phrases you have learned in this unit.

Nouns	**Verbs**	**Adjectives**
boom	boost	menial
consensus AWL	emerge 🔑 AWL	sophisticated
devotion AWL	estimate 🔑 AWL	thriving
incentive AWL	evolve AWL	**Adverb**
labor 🔑 AWL	execute	respectively
leisure	**Phrasal Verb**	**Phrases**
rhythm 🔑	engage in	it dawned on me
strategy 🔑 AWL	regard as 🔑	gray area
		pass your prime
		the going rate
		the odds are

🔑 Oxford 3000™ words

AWL Academic Word List

Check (✓) the skills you learned. If you need more work on a skill, refer to the page(s) in parentheses.

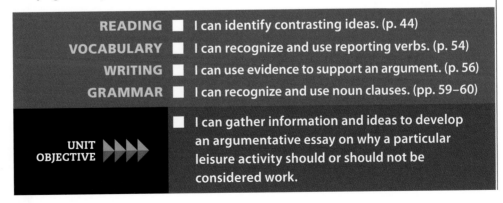

READING	☐ I can identify contrasting ideas. (p. 44)
VOCABULARY	☐ I can recognize and use reporting verbs. (p. 54)
WRITING	☐ I can use evidence to support an argument. (p. 56)
GRAMMAR	☐ I can recognize and use noun clauses. (pp. 59–60)
UNIT OBJECTIVE ▶▶▶	☐ I can gather information and ideas to develop an argumentative essay on why a particular leisure activity should or should not be considered work.

UNIT

3

Media Studies

READING ▶ previewing a text
VOCABULARY ▶ Latin and Greek roots
WRITING ▶ writing with unity
GRAMMAR ▶ quantifiers

UNIT QUESTION

How well does a picture illustrate the truth?

A Discuss these questions with your classmates.

1. How can a photograph change what we see?

2. How can advertisements alter your view of a product or service?

3. Look at the photo. Which parts of the photo are real? What visual tricks are being used? Why?

B Listen to *The Q Classroom* online. Then answer these questions.

1. How did the students answer the question?

2. Do you agree or disagree with their ideas? Why?

 C Go to the Online Discussion Board to discuss the Unit Question with your classmates.

UNIT
OBJECTIVE ▶▶▶▶ Read an article from *Fast Company* and an excerpt
from a textbook. Gather information and ideas to
create a proposal for a print or Web advertisement.

D Work with a partner. This chart lists several different types of images and graphics. In what kinds of texts can you find these images and graphics? Why would this type of image or graphic be used in this type of text? Complete the chart with your answers.

Image or graphic		What kind of text?	Why?
Photograph		newspaper	to show people and events in the article
Map			
Graph			
Cartoon			
Diagram			
Drawing			

E Number the types of images and graphics from 1 (most objective, or realistic) to 6 (most subjective, or influenced by personal feelings). Explain your decisions to your partner.

F Have you ever seen images or graphs that were deceptive? Where?

READING

READING 1 | Infographics Lie: Here's How

You are going to read an article about infographics (graphs, figures, maps, and other ways of displaying data) by Randy Olson from the business magazine *Fast Company*. Use the article to gather information and ideas for your Unit Assignment.

Reading Skill | Previewing a text

Before you read a text, it is helpful to make guesses about its content. **Preview a text** by following these steps:

- Look at the text without reading it: What type of text is it? Who wrote it? Who is it written for?
- Read the title and subtitles or headings: What is the topic of each section?
- Look at the pictures, illustrations, and graphs, and read the captions: What do you expect to read about in the text?

Previewing a text helps you:

- predict the content of the reading using your existing knowledge about the topic.
- read faster because you have already thought about the ideas.
- make connections between the text and the graphics.
- recognize main ideas and details or examples.

A. Preview Reading 1 on pages 69–71. Circle the answer that best completes each statement.

1. This reading is probably from ____.
   a. an online magazine
   b. an academic book
   c. a student essay

2. According to the title and first sentence, the article is probably about ____.
   a. the benefits of using infographics
   b. ways that infographics can trick readers
   c. techniques for creating infographics on computers

3. The three headings within the text are probably recommendations for ____.
   a. readers of infographics
   b. designers of infographics
   c. critics of infographics

4. Color and structural cues are ____.
   a. features of data presentation
   b. parts of the data source
   c. types of data alterations

5. Excluding data, transforming data, and the use of statistics are ____.
   a. features of data presentation
   b. aspects of the data source
   c. types of data alterations

B. Look at the infographics (the graphs and maps) in Reading 1. Discuss your predictions with a partner.

1. Which states in the map in Figure 1 stand out to you the most? Why?

   _____

2. Could the two graphs in Figure 2 represent the same data? Why or why not?

   _____

3. What do you think Figure 3 means?

   _____

iQ ONLINE **C.** Go online for more practice previewing a text.

PREVIEW THE READING

A. PREVIEW Based on the preview you have just done, predict three main ideas you will read in the article.

1. _____

2. _____

3. _____

B. QUICK WRITE How do you think graphs and other graphical representations of data might be unreliable? Write for 5–10 minutes in response. Remember to use this section for your Unit Assignment.

C. **VOCABULARY** Work with a partner to find these words and phrases in the reading. Circle clues in the text that help you understand the meaning of each word or phrase. Then use a dictionary to define any unknown words and phrases.

campaign *(n.)* 🔑	**scale** *(n.)* 🔑
distort *(v.)*	**skyrocket** *(v.)*
error-prone *(adj.)*	**take . . . with a grain of salt** *(phr.)*
manipulate *(v.)*	**transformation** *(n.)*
misleading *(adj.)*	**unprecedented** *(adj.)*
prominent *(adj.)*	**visualize** *(v.)*

🔑 Oxford 3000™ words

D. Go online to listen and practice your pronunciation.

WORK WITH THE READING

A. Read the article and gather information on how well a picture illustrates the truth.

Infographics Lie: Here's How
by Randy Olson

1 We live in an age of Big: Big Computers, Big Data, and Big Lies.

2 Faced with an **unprecedented** torrent[1] of information, data scientists have turned to the visual arts to make sense of big data. The results of this unlikely marriage—often called "data visualizations" or "infographics"—have repeatedly provided us with new and insightful perspectives on the world around us.

3 However, time and time again we have seen that data visualizations can easily be **manipulated** to lie. By misrepresenting, **distorting**, or faking the data they **visualize**, data scientists can twist public opinion to their benefit and even profit at our expense. We have a natural tendency to trust images more than text. As a result, we're easily fooled by data visualizations. Fortunately, there are three easy steps we can follow to save ourselves from getting duped[2] in the data deluge.

Check the data presentation

4 The subtlest way a data visualization can fool you is by using visual cues to make data stand out that normally wouldn't. Be on the lookout for these visual tricks.

5 1. Color cues: Color is one popular tool for making certain data more **prominent** than the rest. When considering the map below,

---

[1] **torrent:** a large amount of something that comes suddenly and violently

[2] **dupe:** to trick or cheat someone

Kentucky and Utah (the darkest and the lightest) will most likely stand out to us first.

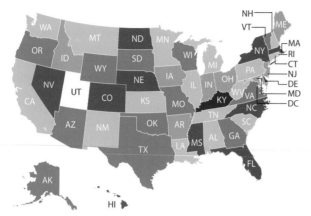

Figure 1: Percentage of smokers by US state

6   If the map in Figure 1 were showing percentage of the population that smokes (where dark colors indicate more smokers and light colors fewer smokers), we might quickly conclude that Kentucky has a serious smoking problem. But what if we looked at the raw numbers and saw that 27% of Kentuckians and 23% of Utahans smoke? Now, there's not so big of a difference after all. Make sure to look at what the colors actually represent before drawing a conclusion from the visualization.

7   2. Structural cues: Structure is another popular tool for making data immediately stand out. In the bar charts in Figure 2, we're looking at the same data, but with different **scales** on the y-axes[3]. Notice how such a simple structural change can make differences in the data look much more significant. Is an increase of 15 fraudulent visualizations from last year really "**skyrocketing**"? Don't let the structure of the visualization decide that for you. Always check the numbers that the visualization is representing.

Check the data source

8   Make sure the data source is reliable. Data collected by an amateur is more **error-prone** than data collected by a professional scientist. Do a quick Web search to see if the people who collected and organized the data have a good track record of collecting and distributing data.

9   You should also make sure the data source isn't biased. A drug company may be inclined to present fake data showing that their latest drug is more effective than it really is, or a political **campaign** may manipulate data to discredit their political opponents. Think twice when considering data provided by biased groups.

10   Generally, we can trust data provided by government organizations, university research centers, and non-partisan[4] organizations. However, we should look more closely at data provided by for-profit companies, political

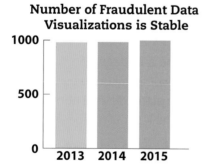

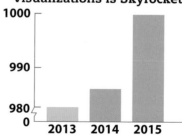

Figure 2: Changes in fraudulent visualizations, 2013–2015

[3] **y-axis:** the vertical axis (a fixed line against which the positions of points on a graph are measured)

[4] **non-partisan:** not supporting the ideas of one particular political party or group of people strongly

organizations, and advocacy groups. If the data source isn't listed, **take the data visualization with many grains of salt.**

Check the data alterations

11   Many data sets require a little bit of housecleaning before they can be visualized, but excessive editing can be a sign of misrepresented data. Every good data visualization will come with explanations describing how the data was manipulated from its raw form into the visualization you see. Read the explanations, and watch out for the following data alterations.

12   1. Excluded data: Ensure that the explanations for excluding that data are reasonable. Sometimes the "explanation" may be that the data inconveniently contrasted with the story the author wanted to tell.

13   2. Transformed data: Data **transformation**, the process of converting data from one format to another format, can complicate the relationships between data. It's difficult to interpret a finding such as "The log transform[5] of a city's productivity is related to the log transform of the city's population." See how that doesn't make any sense to us in practical terms? While a transformation can make complicated mathematics accessible, it can also potentially be **misleading**. Be wary if several transformations have been applied to the data.

14   3. Statistics: Statistics are an often-abused tool in data science. "Fatal shark attacks have risen 100% this year" sounds like an alarming statistic until you realize that only one person was fatally attacked by a shark last year. Check the raw numbers when data visualizations present only the statistics.

15   Comparing statistics is even trickier. If a survey shows that 50% of Latinos and only 30% of Caucasians[6] enjoy watching baseball, those results could easily have been purely due to chance if the survey interviewed only 20 people of each ethnicity (Figure 3). If the visualization doesn't indicate the researchers' confidence in the comparison (called statistical significance), then we shouldn't be confident in their comparisons.

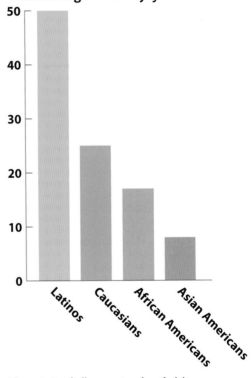

Percentage Who Enjoy Baseball

Figure 3: Baseball supporters by ethnicity

16   If the details on the data alterations aren't provided with the visualization, always keep in mind how easy it is to make data lie when it's visualized.

17   Remember: To save yourself from getting tricked by deceitful data, check the presentation, data source, and alterations.

---

[5] **log transform:** a statistical procedure that can be applied to raw data

[6] **Caucasian:** a member of any of the races of people who have pale skin

**Vocabulary
Skill Review**

In Unit 1, you
learned how to use
a thesaurus to check
the meaning of
synonyms. Look up
distort, manipulate,
and *misleading* in
your dictionary or
thesaurus to find
other similar words.

B. **VOCABULARY** Here are some words from Reading 1. Choose one to
complete each sentence. You may need to change the form of the word
or phrase to make the sentence grammatically correct.

campaign *(n.)*	manipulate *(v.)*	scale *(n.)*	transformation *(n.)*
distort *(v.)*	misleading *(adj.)*	skyrocket *(v.)*	unprecedented *(adj.)*
error-prone *(adj.)*	prominent *(adj.)*	take . . . with a grain of salt *(phr.)*	visualize *(v.)*

1. A graph must not _____ important data by
   making differences look greater than they actually are.

2. The photograph was in a(n) _____ position on
   the home page of the website.

3. The _____ of the map made the distance look
   short, but it took all day to drive between the two cities.

4. Our last advertising _____ was successful; a
   week's worth of ads increased sales by 20 percent.

5. A good graph helps readers to _____ the data
   described in the text.

6. The number of complaints _____ last year as
   readers became more aware of data misrepresentation.

7. _____ that email promising large cash rewards
   _____.

8. The picture has been _____ to hide cracks.

9. Analyzing data can often be a complex and _____
   process.

10. The chart is _____ because it does not state the
    number of people interviewed.

11. After so many _____, it was impossible to
    retrieve the raw data.

12. The newspaper took the _____ decision to
    publish an article explaining its policy for creating infographics.

D. Put the main ideas of the article in the correct order. Write the number(s) of the paragraph(s) where you found them. Two of the sentences are NOT main ideas. Write *X* next to them.

___ 1. Graphical choices in data representations can be deliberately deceptive.

Paragraph(s): _____

___ 2. More Latinos than Caucasians enjoy watching baseball.

Paragraph(s): _____

___ 3. Infographics help us visualize large amounts of information.

Paragraph(s): _____

___ 4. Some sources of data should not be trusted to present data accurately.

Paragraph(s): _____

___ 5. It is important to know how the information in an infographic has been

changed from the raw numbers. Paragraph(s): _____

___ 6. Pharmaceutical companies may produce infographics that exaggerate

the benefits of drugs they make. Paragraph(s): _____

___ 7. It is easy to be manipulated by infographics because most people believe

what they see more than what they read. Paragraph(s): _____

E. Look again at the infographics in the article. Complete the table using information from the text.

Figure	What does it appear to show?	What does it actually mean?
1		
2		
3		

F. Which pieces of advice are recommended in the article? Check the correct answers and write the paragraph number containing the advice.

☐ **1.** Make sure the scientists who collected the data are experienced professionals. Paragraph: ____

☐ **2.** Do not trust infographics that use color to show differences. Paragraph: ____

☐ **3.** Read the scale on the vertical axis (or y-axis) carefully. Paragraph: ____

☐ **4.** You should be highly suspicious of infographics that do not indicate the source of the data. Paragraph: ____

☐ **5.** It is important to check the actual numbers when reading a graph that displays percentages. Paragraph: ____

☐ **6.** You should look carefully for the date when the information was collected, as infographics sometimes present old information. Paragraph: ____

G. Why should readers be careful if they see the following infographics? Support your answer with ideas from the article.

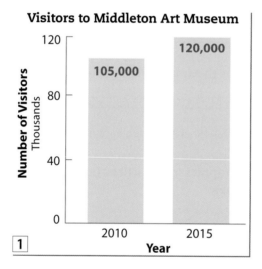

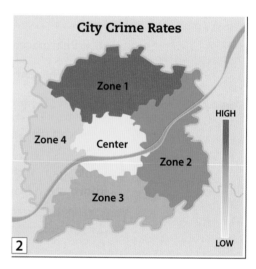

1. _____

_____

2. _____

_____

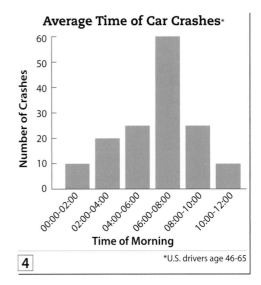

Customers Prefer Shop Smart Orange Juice

3 | Our brand   Other brands

Average Time of Car Crashes*

Number of Crashes / Time of Morning

4 | *U.S. drivers age 46-65

3. _____

_____

4. _____

_____

H. Go online to read *The Many Lives of Identity Thieves* and check your comprehension.

WRITE WHAT YOU THINK

A. Discuss these questions in a group.

1. Have you seen graphs, tables, or infographics that have been distorted using the tricks described in Reading 1? Why do you think this was done?

2. Do you agree with the author that people are more easily persuaded by images than by text? Why or why not?

3. In what other ways can graphs, infographics, maps, or diagrams be misleading?

B. Choose one question and write a paragraph in response. Look back at your Quick Write on page 68 as you think about what you learned.

READING 2 | Phototruth or Photofiction?

 **UNIT OBJECTIVE** ▶▶▶▶ You are going to read an excerpt from the college textbook *Phototruth or Photofiction? Ethics and Media Imagery in the Digital Age* by Thomas Wheeler. It asks how far journalists can go when manipulating photographs. Use the excerpt to gather information and ideas for your Unit Assignment.

PREVIEW THE READING

A. **PREVIEW** Think about the title and look at the picture on page 77. What do you predict the writer will say about manipulating photographs in journalism?

☐ It is always acceptable.   ☐ It is never acceptable.

☐ It is sometimes acceptable.

B. **QUICK WRITE** Why might someone want to change a photograph? Write for 5–10 minutes in response. Remember to use this section for your Unit Assignment.

C. **VOCABULARY** Read aloud these words from Reading 2. Check (✓) the ones you know. Use a dictionary to define any new or unknown words. Then discuss with a partner how the words relate to the unit.

alteration *(n.)*	document *(v.)* 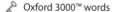	legitimate *(adj.)*
bias *(n.)*	ethical *(adj.)*	provoke *(v.)*
concoct *(v.)*	inherent *(adj.)*	scrutinize *(v.)*
credible *(adj.)*	left in the dark *(phr.)*	tempting *(adj.)*

🔑 Oxford 3000™ words

 D. Go online to listen and practice your pronunciation.

WORK WITH THE READING

🔊 **A.** Read the article and gather information on how well a picture illustrates the truth.

Phototruth or Photofiction?

1   Any discussion of "manipulated" photography must begin with the recognition that photography itself is an **inherent** manipulation—a manipulation of light, a process with many steps and stages, all subject to the **biases** and interpretations of the photographer, printer, editor, or viewer. Photography is not absolute "reality." It is not unqualified "truth." It is not purely "objective." It was never any of those things, and it has always been subject to distortion. Indeed, many of its earliest practitioners were more concerned with **concocting** fantasy than **documenting** reality. They were artists, not journalists.

2   Still, one branch of photography—called "photojournalism"—has acquired a special standing in the public mind. Newspaper and magazine readers generally believe that a photo can *reflect* reality in a **credible** way.

3   But why? Why has photography seemed so inherently realistic for so long? Much of the trust in photojournalism comes from average citizens' everyday experiences with personal photography. We point our cameras and cell phones at ourselves, our families, friends, and vacation sights and view the files and prints as **legitimate** documents that "capture" the events and scenes in meaningful ways. Countless millions of us take "selfies"[1] and snapshots or collect our photos in albums , on social media, and on hard drives for future generations, not only for entertainment or curiosity value but as evidence of the way we once looked and the way the world once worked. As Dartmouth College professor Marianne Hirsch has said, "People say if there was a fire, the first thing they would save is their photo albums. We almost fear we'll lose our memories if we lose our albums." The same is probably true now of digital photo collections.

4   This credibility has survived despite photography's history of occasional duplicity[2]. However, digital manipulation may challenge this trust more than a century and a half of other methods of fakery. Commentators have observed, "There's nothing new about faking photos," but that is not quite right. There is something new. Computer technology has made photo doctoring much easier to do and accessible to many more people with nothing more sophisticated than the phone in their pockets.

5   It seems that with each new graphics software program or photo app, the opportunities for fictionalizing images become ever more numerous and **tempting**. One result is that "the objective 'truth' of photographs has become something of a quaint[3] concept" (*American Photo*). Michael Morse of the National Press Photographers Association agrees: "People have no idea how much **alteration** is going on." This raises thorny **ethical** challenges for professionals, educators, and students alike.

6   For decades, photojournalists and editors have opposed misleading alterations, particularly in "hard news" photos (images of war, crime scenes, political events, natural disasters, etc.). As computer manipulations have become more common, however, adherence to photojournalistic norms has given way to the temptations of commerce, even in respected newspapers and news magazines.

7   For example, during the processing of *National Geographic's* February 1982 photo of the Great Pyramids of Giza, a pyramid was digitally shifted to make the image fit the cover. The alteration **provoked** much controversy, not so much because it was drastic (it was relatively insignificant)

National Geographic's **February 1982 photo of the Great Pyramids of Giza**

---

[1] **selfie:** a photograph you take of yourself with a smartphone or camera

[2] **duplicity:** dishonest behavior that is intended to make people believe something that is not true

[3] **quaint:** attractive in an unusual or old-fashioned way

but because it appeared in a magazine long respected for its authenticity.

8   In 1998, *National Geographic* editor Bill Allen said, "Nearly two decades ago we moved one pyramid to get the same effect as if the photographer had walked perhaps fifty yards to the left before taking the photograph. And yet after all that time, one of the most common questions I'm asked is, 'Do you guys still move pyramids?' This reminds all of us of just how fragile our credibility is. If you lose it, it's almost impossible to ever get it back. It's why we're such fanatics about disclosure[4] now at *National Geographic*."

9   Kenneth Brower's article in the May 1998 *Atlantic Monthly* listed a number of faked nature photos and sequences, including a polar bear in Antarctica that appeared in a full-page ad for *National Geographic Online* (there are no polar bears in Antarctica; there are polar bears in the Arctic—and also in the Ohio zoo where this particular animal was photographed!).

10   The following are just some of the many other examples of "photomanipulation" that have appeared in print:

- The winner of a spelling bee[5] sponsored by the *New York Daily News* was photographed for a story in the *New York Post*, which removed the name of its rival newspaper from the image of the winner's identification card.

- In all of their outdoor photos of the 1984 Summer Olympic Games, editors at the *Orange County Register* changed the color of the Los Angeles sky (notorious for its smog) to clear blue.

11   There are many more recent examples of digital deception, such as these:

- In March, 2012, after a number of tornadoes in the American Midwest, a graphic design student in Michigan posted a photo of a tornado on a popular social media site. The photo quickly spread until it was posted on the Web page of a local TV station and was even broadcast on the evening news. The student then admitted it was a fake. WNEM news director Ian Rubin said, "We've used this experience as a reminder to the whole news team to review viewer-submitted photos with the meteorologists before they go on the air."

- In Sydney, Australia, in 2013, a man called Dimitri di Angelis tricked investors into giving him $8 million, in part by showing them photographs of himself with world leaders and movie stars. The photos were, of course, created using computer software, and di Angelis was sent to prison for 12 years.

12   Some professionals might consider a few of this chapter's examples to be relatively innocuous[6], but in most cases readers and viewers were **left in the dark** until the truth was revealed. In these images, photography's presumed relationship to reality was disrupted. Readers might have a simpler description: they might call the photos lies.

13   The inherent trustworthiness once attributed to photography is withering[7], even as amateur photos flood the Internet. From now on, assumptions about the ability of photos to tell the truth will increasingly be **scrutinized**—for good reason. Visual journalists will have to accommodate these shifts and re-examine their own practices and ethics if they are to successfully separate their work from cartoons, fantasy, and fiction.

[4] **disclosure:** the act of making information public
[5] **spelling bee:** a competition in which participants have to spell difficult words correctly

[6] **innocuous:** not harmful or dangerous
[7] **withering:** growing weaker before disappearing completely

B. **VOCABULARY** Here are some words and a phrase from Reading 2. Read the paragraphs. Then write each bold word or phrase next to the correct definition. You may need to change verbs to their base form and nouns to the singular form.

Newspaper articles can never tell the entire truth: some element of lying is **inherent** in all journalism because it is impossible for one article to include all the details of the story. Journalists may also manipulate the order in which they present information to achieve more drama or other effects in their writing. Choosing details and the order to describe them is considered proper and **ethical** behavior for journalists. Editors can even reflect their paper's political **bias** when writing opinion pieces about elections and politics.

In book publishing, many companies do not always **scrutinize** the information authors write. A best-selling book can make a lot of money, so some authors find it **tempting** to make up lies. In one famous case, a writer **concocted** a completely fictitious history about himself. The writing seemed **credible**, so most readers believed his story. However, the writer later was unable to **document** the facts in the book, and he was revealed as a fake, which **provoked** controversy for him and his publisher. Although the writer's tale was not **legitimate**, many people still found it meaningful. Even these readers agree that they would rather not be **left in the dark**, wondering whether or not a story is true. They would rather be aware of any major **alteration** of facts that could turn a good true story into just a good story.

1. _____ (*v.*) to cause a particular reaction or have a particular effect

2. _____ (*phr.*) prevented from learning something

3. _____ (*v.*) to invent a story, an excuse, etc.

4. _____ (*n.*) a strong feeling in favor of or against one group of people or one side in an argument, often not based on fair judgment

5. _____ (*n.*) a change to something

6. _____ (*v.*) to look at or examine somebody or something carefully

7. _____ (*adj.*) can be believed or trusted

8. _____ (*adj.*) morally correct or acceptable

9. _____ (*adj.*) valid; fair

10. _____ (adj.) existing as a basic or permanent part of somebody or something

11. _____ (v.) to prove or support something with evidence

12. _____ (adj.) attractive, making people want to have it or do it

iQ ONLINE **C.** Go online for more practice with the vocabulary.

D. Answer these questions. Write the number of the paragraph where you found each answer. Then compare your answers with a partner.

1. Why are photographs always manipulated in some way? Paragraph ____

   _____

   _____

2. Why do most people trust the photographs they see in the news media? Paragraph ____

   _____

   _____

3. How is digital fakery different from earlier forms of photographic manipulation? Paragraph ____

   _____

   _____

4. What does the example of the pyramid in *National Geographic* say about the credibility of photojournalism? Paragraph ____

   _____

   _____

5. Why are the examples in this reading important even though many of them are relatively minor changes? Paragraph ____

   _____

   _____

E. Match each sentence with the correct person or publication.

____ 1.   Photographs have such great value for many people that we are almost afraid of losing our memories if our photo albums are lost.

____ 2.   It is old-fashioned to believe that photographs are inherently objective.

____ 3.   Most magazine readers do not realize how much photographs have been manipulated.

____ 4.   When people stop believing in your honesty, it is very hard to convince them otherwise.

____ 5.   Many nature photographs in magazines have been faked (for example, showing a polar bear in Antarctica).

a.   Bill Allen of *National Geographic*

b.   *Atlantic Monthly* article by Kenneth Brower

c.   *American Photo* magazine

d.   Professor Marianne Hirsch of Dartmouth College

e.   Michael Morse of the National Press Photographers Association

F.   What is your opinion? Rank the examples of manipulated photographs in the article in order from 1 (least serious) to 6 (most serious). Compare your answers with a partner or group and justify your rankings with specific evidence from the reading.

____ a.   *National Geographic's* pyramids

____ b.   *National Geographic Online's* polar bears

____ c.   The *New York Daily News's* report on a spelling bee

____ d.   The *Orange County Register's* photograph of Los Angeles

____ e.   The social media photo of a tornado

____ f.   Dimitri di Angelis's fake photographs

G. Find and write the phrase from the text that the pronouns in bold refer to.

1. **It** is not purely "objective." (Paragraph 1) _____ *photography* _____

2. **They** were artists, not journalists. (Paragraph 1) _____

3. However, digital manipulation may challenge **this** trust more than a century and a half of other methods of fakery. (Paragraph 4)

_____

4. **This** raises thorny ethical challenges for professionals, educators, and students alike. (Paragraph 5) _____

5. **It** was relatively insignificant. (Paragraph 7) _____

6. If you lose **it**, it's almost impossible to ever get **it** back. (Paragraph 8)

_____

WRITE WHAT YOU THINK

A. Discuss these questions in a group. Look back at your Quick Write on page 76 as you think about what you have learned.

1. Are photographs important to you? Why or why not?

2. Do you think of photography more as an art form or a type of journalism? Please explain.

3. Do you care if a photograph in a magazine or newspaper has been manipulated? Why or why not?

B. Before you watch the video, discuss these questions in a group.

1. What can images of space tell us about our universe?

2. Do you know the names of any patterns of stars? Why do you think many cultures have looked for familiar shapes in the stars?

3. How reliable do you think pictures created by telescopes are?

C. Go online to watch the video about the world's largest telescope. Then check your comprehension.

VIDEO VOCABULARY

constellation *(n.)* a group of stars that forms a shape in the sky and has a name

cosmos *(n.)* the universe

faint *(adj.)* cannot be clearly seen

inhospitable *(adj.)* difficult to stay or live in, especially because there is no shelter from the weather

orbit *(v.)* to move in a curved path around a much larger object, especially a planet or star

D. Think about the video, Reading 1, and Reading 2 as you discuss these questions. Then choose one question and write a paragraph in response.

1. Both readings suggest that images are persuasive but often untruthful. Should this affect the way we view images from the Very Large Telescope, or do different rules apply to astronomical pictures?

2. How could marketers use the manipulation techniques described in the readings to advertise products and services?

Vocabulary Skill Latin and Greek roots

Identifying **Greek and Latin roots** (or **stems**) will help you recognize and understand new words. Words with these roots are especially common in formal written English, so using these words will aid in reading comprehension and add sophistication to your writing.

Common roots

Root	Meaning	Examples
mot-/mov-/mob-	move	promote, immobile
just-/jur-	right, legal	justify, jury
her-/hes-	stick	coherent, cohesive
vid-/vis-	see, notice	evidence, visible

You should also watch for other roots when you recognize groups of words with similar meanings.

A. Read each sentence. Using your knowledge of roots, circle the word or phrase that best matches the meaning of each bold word.

1. The patient reported reduced **mobility**.
   a. ability to speak   b. ability to read   c. ability to move

2. You need to choose an **adhesive** that works on wood.

    a. paint   b. pencil   c. glue

3. I don't **envisage** any problem with this plan.

    a. remember   b. create   c. expect

4. She was angry at the **injustice** of the professor's decision.

    a. humor   b. unfairness   c. danger

5. The student was **motivated** to study hard by her teacher.

    a. moved   b. told   c. warned

6. There is an **inherent** problem with this type of car.

    a. unusual   b. unavoidable   c. annoying

7. She was unable to provide a **justification** for her behavior.

    a. plan   b. wish   c. good explanation

8. Successful companies are often led by great **visionaries**.

    a. people with a lot of money

    b. people with a lot of power

    c. people with a lot of imagination

Tip for Success

Learning Latin and Greek roots can improve your English spelling. For example, if you know *millimeter* comes from *milli-*, you will remember to write it with a double *l*.

B. Look at the sets of words below the box. The common root is bold. Choose the answer in the box that best defines each bold root. Then explain your choices to a partner.

| break | follow | life | thousand |
| circle/round | law | other/different | write |

1. hemi**sphere**, **spher**ical, atmo**sphere**   sphere   = _____

2. **alter**native, **alter**ation, **alter**   alter-   = _____

3. **sequ**ence, **sec**ond, **sequ**el   sequ-/sec-   = _____

4. sur**viv**e, **viv**id, re**viv**e   viv-   = _____

5. de**scrip**tion, post**script**, **scrib**ble   scrip-/scrib- = _____

6. **leg**itimate, **leg**al, **leg**islation   leg-   = _____

7. **mill**ennium, **milli**meter, **milli**pede   milli-   = _____

8. **frag**ile, **frag**ment, **fract**ion   frag-/fract- = _____

C. Go online for more practice with Latin and Greek roots.

WRITING

At the end of this unit, you will write an advertisement proposal. This proposal will include information from the readings, the unit video, and your own ideas.

Writing Skill | Writing with unity

In good writing, each paragraph has **unity**: it explores one idea. This helps readers understand all the main ideas in a text. If you mix different ideas in a paragraph, your readers may become confused, and your writing will not be effective. Sometimes, one idea needs several paragraphs, in which case each paragraph should describe one part of the idea. This keeps the reader focused on one point at a time.

The complete piece of writing (essay, article, report, etc.) also needs unity. All the points and ideas in the paragraphs should support one topic, argument, thesis, or purpose. This will keep your writing clear, interesting, and persuasive.

Writing Tip

In Unit 2, you learned to give evidence to support an argument. A proposal is another kind of persuasive writing, so you should give details and reasons to support your recommendations.

A. Read these paragraphs from an advertisement proposal for a café. Cross out one sentence to improve the unity of each paragraph. Explain your reason to a partner.

1. At the top of the Web page advertising Roy's Silver Spoon Café, three images will rotate. The first image is a digitally enhanced photograph of a cup of coffee that appears to show steam rising perfectly from the smooth surface of the drink. In the second picture, two friends are shown sitting at a table in the café. The Web page also shows the menu and weekly special coffees. The final photograph is of Roy himself, but we will manipulate the photo to make it look as if he is standing on top of the building to welcome customers.

2. The most important part of our proposed website design is your new logo. A shiny silver spoon stands proudly in the center of the café's name. A new, more modern font has been chosen to bring your business up to date. Roy's name appears in silver to make it more prominent and to match the color of the spoon. The next change we recommend is to include customer comments on the Web page.

3. The first page of your current website is dominated by a map of the town, showing the location of the café. We recommend moving this to another page, with directions and hours of operation. The home page is the first impression a new customer gets of your business, and while it is important to be able to find your café, thanks to navigation software and smartphones, an address is probably enough. There will also be a page to promote upcoming events at the café. In place of the map, we would like to write a paragraph explaining the history of the café and the atmosphere you create there.

B. A graphic designer working for an advertising agency is writing a proposal for a magazine advertisement for a local business, Rudy's Plumbing Supply. Look at the designer's notes in the cluster diagram. Then follow the instructions below.

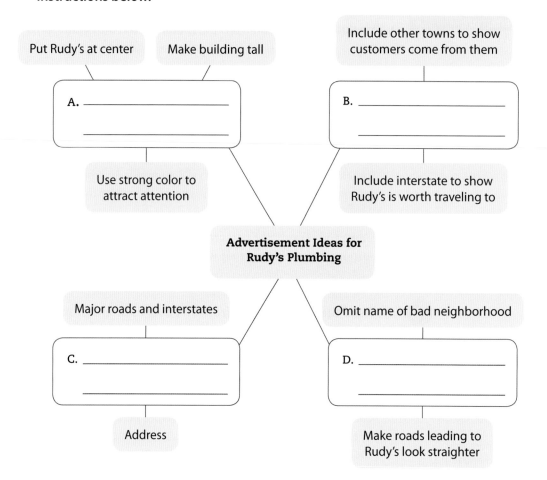

1. Label each cluster with an idea from the box. You will not use one idea.

Basic features of the map	Make Rudy's look more accessible
Information about other businesses	Stimulate demand
Make Rudy's look impressive	

2. Check (✓) each idea that the designer could include without affecting the unity of the proposal. Write *X* if an idea does not fit anywhere.

_____ a. Add this line of copy (text): "Just around the corner!"

_____ b. Include Rudy's website.

_____ c. Print a customer's review of Rudy's service.

_____ d. Suggest that people don't mind traveling a long way to go to Rudy's.

_____ e. Put a photograph of Rudy at the top to add personal appeal.

C. WRITING MODEL Read the model proposal and answer the questions.

Tildon Advertising
290 West Main, Tildon, PA

From: Liz Madison, Account Executive
To: Mr. Rudy Swenson, Manager, Rudy's Plumbing Supply
Date: March 14
Re: Ad Proposal
Dear Mr. Swenson,

1   Thank you for asking us to design a magazine advertisement for your store. Please find below a description of the ad we are proposing.

2   The centerpiece of the ad is a map. Maps are excellent attention-getters. The map will contain all the practical information customers need to find your business: the address, the major roads, and the nearby interstates. Obviously, most of your customers are local, and few of them need the interstate to get to your store. However, we want to show them that your store is so good that a number of customers might also come from far away. In this way, we can stimulate a great deal of demand for your business.

3   In addition to including the interstate, we will mention the names of several neighboring towns. You might attract a few customers from other towns, but mainly we will show that your business is popular and known throughout the region.

4   In our meeting, you asked us to stress the accessibility of your business, and our ad will make customers feel comfortable about visiting you. You told us you were concerned that your business is not located in the best part of town. Therefore, we recommend omitting the name of your neighborhood and some road names. The ad will encourage new customers to visit you and judge the quality of your service, not the neighborhood.

5   A good impression is also achieved by using strong colors in the ad and drawing your building from an angle that increases the scale of the building. The building will be at the center of the ad, and its prominent position and size will bring in plenty of new business.

6   We hope you approve of this proposal. We feel that it tells a truthful and persuasive story about Rudy's Plumbing Supply. Please do not hesitate to contact me if you have any questions.

---

1. Write the purpose or main idea of each paragraph. Use the cluster diagram in Activity B to help you.

Paragraph 1: _____

Paragraph 2: _____

Paragraph 3: _____

Paragraph 4: _____

Paragraph 5: _____

Paragraph 6: _____

2. What idea does the writer use to give unity through the entire proposal?

_____

D. Work with a partner. Add a new paragraph between paragraphs 5 and 6 of the writing model. Your paragraph should be about a slogan for Rudy's Plumbing Supply.

1. Choose a slogan from the suggestions below or write your own.

    ☐ "For service you can trust, call Rudy today!"

    ☐ "Your local plumbing expert"

    ☐ "Rudy's goes the extra mile!"

    ☐ Your idea: _____

2. Brainstorm ideas for your paragraph by answering these questions.
    a. Why does Rudy's need a good slogan?

    _____

    _____

    b. Why have you chosen this slogan?

    _____

    _____

    c. How will you use the slogan in the ad?

    _____

    _____

3. Organize your ideas and add a clear first and final sentence, plus any other ideas you have to write a paragraph that has unity.

4. Swap your paragraph with another pair. Discuss these questions.
    a. Does the paragraph have unity? Is every sentence related to the slogan?
    b. Are the ideas in the paragraph in a clear and logical order?
    c. What advice would you give the writers to improve their paragraph?

 E. Go online for more practice with writing with unity.

Quantifiers are words that modify nouns and noun phrases and talk about amounts. They give information about *how much* (for a noncount noun) and *how many* (for a plural count noun). Quantifiers generally come before the noun.

Noncount nouns

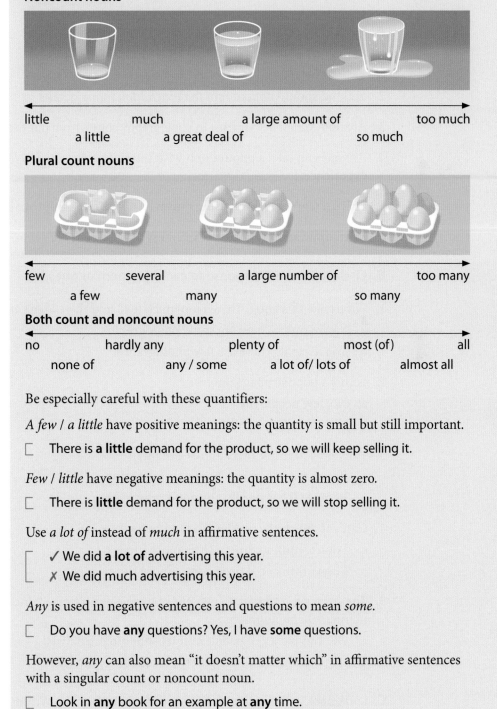

little	much	a large amount of	too much
a little	a great deal of	so much	

Plural count nouns

few	several	a large number of	too many
a few	many	so many	

Both count and noncount nouns

no	hardly any	plenty of	most (of)	all
none of	any / some	a lot of/ lots of	almost all	

Be especially careful with these quantifiers:

A few / a little have positive meanings: the quantity is small but still important.

☐ There is **a little** demand for the product, so we will keep selling it.

Few / little have negative meanings: the quantity is almost zero.

☐ There is **little** demand for the product, so we will stop selling it.

Use *a lot of* instead of *much* in affirmative sentences.

☐ ✓ We did **a lot of** advertising this year.
☐ ✗ We did much advertising this year.

Any is used in negative sentences and questions to mean *some*.

☐ Do you have **any** questions? Yes, I have **some** questions.

However, *any* can also mean "it doesn't matter which" in affirmative sentences with a singular count or noncount noun.

☐ Look in **any** book for an example at **any** time.

Almost all means nearly 100 percent.

Note: Do not use *almost* by itself; it is an adverb, not a quantifier.

> ✓ **Almost all** people take photographs.
> ✗ Almost people take photographs.

A. Circle the correct quantifier to complete each sentence.

1. *Some / Any* magazine photographs are manipulated.

2. Your ad should not contain *too much / too many* details.

3. *Almost / Almost all* our trust in photography comes from our experience with it.

4. Anyone can fake a photograph with the right software and *little / a little* experience.

5. *Few / A few* readers are using our map, so we must improve it.

6. I will draw attention to your business by using *a lot of / much* color.

B. Circle the correct response to each comment or question.

1. I don't like this book. There's too much text, and there aren't enough pictures.
   a. You're right. There are some photographs.
   b. You're right. There are few photographs.

2. Is this a popular magazine?
   a. No, few people read it.
   b. No, a few people read it.

3. Why do you think this ad uses a map?
   a. Because it has so much good information.
   b. Because it has hardly any good information.

4. Can you finish the proposal by tomorrow?
   a. I don't think so. I need little more time.
   b. I don't think so. I need a little more time.

5. The survey found that 45 percent of people expect magazines to manipulate photographs.
   a. OK, but plenty of people still trust photojournalists!
   b. OK, but almost all people still trust photojournalists!

C. Look back at the model proposal in Activity C of the Writing Skill on page 87. Circle the quantifiers in the proposal.

D. Go online for more practice with quantifiers.

E. Go online for the grammar expansion.

 In this assignment, you will pretend that you work for an advertising agency that designs print or Web advertisements. You will write a proposal for a client, describing your ideas for an ad. As you prepare your proposal, think about the Unit Question, "How well does a picture illustrate the truth?" Use information from Reading 1, Reading 2, the unit video, and your work in this unit to support your ideas. Refer to the Self-Assessment checklist on page 92.

 Go to the Online Writing Tutor for a writing model and alternate Unit Assignments.

PLAN AND WRITE

A. BRAINSTORM Complete the following tasks.

1. Work with a partner. Choose a product or service for another pair of students to advertise: for example, your school, a business you know, a product you use, or something that does not exist yet. Imagine you represent that product or service. Write a paragraph describing it and the type of advertisement you want to create, such as a poster, a website, or a newspaper ad.

2. Exchange paragraphs with another pair. Read and discuss the paragraphs. Ask for clarification as necessary. You are going to write a proposal to convince the other pair to hire you to design an ad for their product or service.

3. With your partner, answer these questions.
   a. What type of graphic will you use in the ad? Draw or describe in words the photograph, drawing, infographic, map, or other graphic you will use.

   _____

   _____

   _____

   b. How will the graphic make the ad persuasive?

   _____

   _____

   _____

c. How will the graphic help promote the product or service?

_____

_____

_____

 B. **PLAN** Go to the Online Resources to download and complete a cluster diagram and an outline for your proposal. In your cluster diagram, write your main ideas for the ad in the circles. Then connect supporting details, explanations, and examples outside each circle. Refer to the cluster diagram on page 86 if you need a guide.

 C. **WRITE** Use your **PLAN** notes to write your proposal. Go to *iQ Online* to use the Online Writing Tutor.

1. Write your proposal using your cluster diagram and any other ideas from your discussions in Activity A on page 91. Think about the unity of each paragraph and of the entire proposal.

2. Look at the Self-Assessment checklist to guide your writing.

REVISE AND EDIT

 A. **PEER REVIEW** Read your partner's proposal. Then go online and use the Peer Review worksheet. Discuss the review with your partner.

B. **REWRITE** Based on your partner's review, revise and rewrite your proposal.

C. **EDIT** Complete the Self-Assessment checklist as you prepare to write the final draft of your proposal. Be prepared to hand in your work or discuss it in class.

SELF-ASSESSMENT		
Yes	No	
☐	☐	Is each paragraph written with unity?
☐	☐	Does the entire proposal have unity?
☐	☐	Are quantifiers varied and used correctly?
☐	☐	Does the proposal include vocabulary from the unit?
☐	☐	Did you check the proposal for punctuation, spelling, and grammar?

ONLINE **D.** **REFLECT** Go to the Online Discussion Board to discuss these questions.

1. What is something new you learned in this unit?

2. Look back at the Unit Question—How well does a picture illustrate the truth? Is your answer different now than when you started the unit? If yes, how is it different? Why?

TRACK YOUR SUCCESS

Circle the words and phrases you have learned in this unit.

Nouns	**Verbs**	**Adjectives**
alteration AWL	concoct	credible
bias AWL	distort AWL	error-prone
campaign 🔑	document 🔑 AWL	ethical AWL
scale 🔑	manipulate AWL	inherent AWL
transformation AWL	provoke	legitimate
	scrutinize	misleading
	skyrocket	prominent
	visualize AWL	tempting
		unprecedented AWL

Phrase
left in the dark
take . . . with a grain of salt

🔑 Oxford 3000™ words

AWL Academic Word List

Check (✓) the skills you learned. If you need more work on a skill, refer to the page(s) in parentheses.

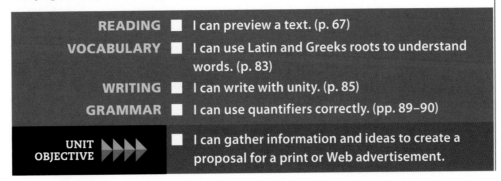

READING	☐ I can preview a text. (p. 67)
VOCABULARY	☐ I can use Latin and Greeks roots to understand words. (p. 83)
WRITING	☐ I can write with unity. (p. 85)
GRAMMAR	☐ I can use quantifiers correctly. (pp. 89–90)
UNIT OBJECTIVE ▶▶▶▶	☐ I can gather information and ideas to create a proposal for a print or Web advertisement.

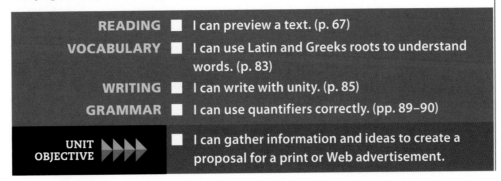

READING ▶ making inferences
VOCABULARY ▶ prefixes
WRITING ▶ organizing supporting ideas
GRAMMAR ▶ parallel structure and ellipsis

UNIT QUESTION

Why is global cooperation important?

A Discuss these questions with your classmates.

1. Have you ever worked with someone from another country? What were the benefits of cooperating with this person?

2. What issues or problems in your country do other countries also have? How do they affect you personally? Would cooperating with other countries help solve these problems?

3. Look at the photos. How do you think these people are working together? Why does global cooperation benefit different countries?

◉ **B** Listen to *The Q Classroom* online. Then answer these questions.

1. What ideas do Marcus, Felix, Yuna, and Sophy have about why global cooperation is important?

2. What ideas do you have to add to their discussion?

 C Go online to watch the video about saving endangered plant seeds. Then check your comprehension.

bank *(v.)* to collect and save for future use

fluctuating *(adj.)* changing frequently in size, amount, quantity, etc.

fortress *(n.)* a strong building or place that is protected against attack

leukemia *(n.)* a serious disease in which too many white blood cells are produced, causing weakness and sometimes death

properties *(n.)* qualities or characteristics something has

VIDEO VOCABULARY

 D Go to the Online Discussion Board to discuss the Unit Question with your classmates.

E Complete the survey. Compare your rankings with a partner.

Global Cooperation Survey

Rank the success of global cooperation in the following fields from 1 (highest) to 8 (lowest).

____ Stopping the spread of disease

____ Preventing hunger

____ Maintaining peace

____ Developing new technology

____ Advancing science and medicine

____ Protecting the environment

____ Exploring space

____ Improving education

F Choose a successful example of global cooperation from a field in the survey. Write three reasons why you think it was successful.

_____

_____

_____

G Discuss these questions with your partner.

1. Would the different countries in your example have achieved the same results working alone? Why was it important that the different countries in your example worked together?

2. Choose one of the fields in the survey for which you gave a low ranking. How might countries better cooperate in this field?

3. In your opinion, are there any fields in which it is impossible for countries to work together successfully? Why?

READING 1 | In Norway, Global Seed Vault Guards Genetic Resources

 **UNIT OBJECTIVE** ▶▶▶▶ You are going to read an article from *The New York Times* that reports on the international response to the dangers threatening the genetic diversity of the world's food supply. Use the article to gather information and ideas for your Unit Assignment.

PREVIEW THE READING

A. **PREVIEW** What do you think might cause plants to become extinct? Write three possible reasons.

1. _____

2. _____

3. _____

Writing **Tip**

Brainstorming ideas before you write can help you to write more fluently.

B. **QUICK WRITE** How could countries work together to protect the world's plant life? Take a couple of minutes to brainstorm ideas. Then write for 5–10 minutes in response. Remember to use this section for your Unit Assignment.

C. **VOCABULARY** Work with a partner to find these words in the reading. Circle clues in the text that help you understand the meaning of each word. Then use a dictionary to define any unknown words.

confront *(v.)* 🔑	extinct *(adj.)*
conserve *(v.)*	genetic *(adj.)*
consolidate *(v.)*	inevitable *(adj.)* 🔑
crucial *(adj.)* 🔑	Plan B *(n.)*
devastating *(adj.)*	urgency *(n.)*
erosion *(n.)*	vulnerability *(n.)*

🔑 Oxford 3000™ words

 D. Go online to listen and practice your pronunciation.

WORK WITH THE READING

🔊 **A.** Read the article and gather information about why global cooperation is important.

In Norway, Global Seed Vault Guards Genetic Resources

By Elisabeth Rosenthal

1   LONGYEARBYEN, Norway: With plant species disappearing at an alarming rate, scientists and governments are creating a global network of plant banks to store seeds and sprouts[1]—precious **genetic** resources that may be needed for man to adapt the world's food supply to climate change.

Global Seed Vault

2   This week, the flagship of that effort, the Global Seed Vault, received its first seeds here—millions of them. Bored[2] into the middle of a snow-topped Arctic mountain, the seed vault has as its goal the storing of every kind of seed from every collection on the planet. While the original seeds will remain in ordinary seed banks, the seed vault's stacked gray boxes will form a backup in case natural disaster or human error erases the seeds from the outside world.

3   The seed vault is part of a far broader effort to gather and classify information about plants and their genes. In Leuven, Belgium, scientists are scouring[3] the world for banana samples and cryo-preserving their shoots[4] in liquid nitrogen before they become **extinct**. A similar effort is under way in France on coffee plants. A number of plants, most from the tropics, do not produce seeds that can be stored.

interior of the Global Seed Vault

4   For years, a hodgepodge network of seed banks has been amassing[5] seed and shoot collections. Labs in Mexico banked corn species. Those in Nigeria banked cassava. These scattershot efforts are being **consolidated** and systematized, in part because of better technology to preserve plant genes and in part because of rising alarm about the trajectory[6] of climate change and its impact on world food production.

---

[1] **sprout:** a new part growing on a plant
[2] **bore:** to make a long, deep hole with a tool or by digging
[3] **scour:** to search very carefully because you are looking for something

[4] **shoot:** the part that grows up from the ground when a plant starts to grow
[5] **amass:** to collect something, especially in large quantities
[6] **trajectory:** the direction that something is taking

5 "We started thinking about this post-9/11 and on the heels of Hurricane Katrina," said Cary Fowler, president of the Global Crop Diversity Trust, the nonprofit group that runs the vault. "Everyone was saying, 'Why didn't anyone prepare for a hurricane before?'

6 "Well, we are losing biodiversity every day—it's a kind of drip, drip, drip. It's also **inevitable**. We need to do something about it."

7 This week, the **urgency** of the problem was underscored as wheat prices reached record highs and wheat stores dropped to the lowest level in 35 years. Droughts[7] and new diseases cut wheat production in many parts of the world.

8 "The **erosion** of plants' genetic resources is really going fast," said Rony Swennen, head of crop biotechnics at the Catholic University of Leuven, who has cryo-preserved half of the world's 1,200 banana varieties. "We're at a critical moment, and if we don't act fast, we're going to lose a lot of plants that we may need."

banana varieties

9 The United Nations International Treaty on Plant Genetic Resources, ratified[8] in 2004, created a formal global network for banking and sharing seeds, as well as studying their genetic traits. Last year, its database received thousands of new seed varieties.

10 A well-organized system of plant banks could be **crucial** in responding to climate crises because it could identify genetic material and plant strains that are better able to cope with a changed environment. At the Global Seed Vault, hundreds of grey boxes containing seeds from Syria to Mexico were being moved this week into a freezing vault to be placed in suspended animation. Collectively they harbor[9] a vast range of characteristics, including the ability to withstand a drier, warmer climate.

11 Climate change is expected to bring new weather stresses as well as new plant pests into agricultural regions. Heat-trapping carbon dioxide emissions will produce not only global warming but also an increase in extreme weather events, like floods and droughts, the Intergovernmental Panel on Climate Change concluded.

12 Already, three-quarters of biodiversity in crops has been lost in the last century, according to the UN Food and Agriculture Organization. Eighty percent of corn varieties that existed in the 1930s no longer exist today, for example. In the United States, 94 percent of peas are no longer grown.

13 Seed banks have operated for decades, but many are based in agricultural areas, and few are as technologically advanced or secure as the Global Seed Vault. Earlier efforts had been regarded as resources for gardeners, scientists, farmers, and food aficionados rather than a tool for human survival.

14 The importance and **vulnerability** of seed banks have become apparent in recent years. Centers in Afghanistan and Iraq were destroyed during conflicts by looters who were after the plastic containers that held the seeds. In the Philippines, a typhoon demolished the wall of a seed bank, destroying many samples.

15 In reviewing seed bank policies a few years ago, experts looked at the banks in a new light, said Fowler of the Global Crop Diversity Trust. "We said, 'We may have some of the best seed banks in the world, but look at where they are: Peru, Colombia,

---

[7] **drought:** a long period of time when there is little or no rain
[8] **ratify:** to make an agreement officially valid by voting for or signing it

[9] **harbor:** to contain something and allow it to develop

Syria, India, Ethiopia, and the Philippines.' So a lot of us were asking, 'What's **Plan B**?'"

16 The goal of the new global plant bank system is to protect the precious stored plant genes from the vagaries[10] of climate, politics, and human error. Many banks are now "in countries where the political situation is not stable and it is difficult to rely on refrigeration," said Swennen, the biotechnics expert. Seeds must be stored at minus 20 degrees Celsius (minus 4 Fahrenheit), and plant sprouts that rely on cryo-preservation must be far colder.

17 "We are inside a mountain in the Arctic because we wanted a really, really safe place that operates by itself," Fowler said.

18 Underground in Longyearbyen, just 1,000 kilometers, or 600 miles, from the North Pole, the seeds will stay frozen regardless of power failures. The Global Crop Diversity Trust is also funding research into methods for storing genetic material from plants like bananas and coconuts that cannot be stored as seed.

19 The vault was built by Norway, and its operations are financed by government and private donations, including $20 million from the United Kingdom, $12 million from Australia, $11 million from Germany, and $6.5 million from the United States.

20 The effort to preserve a wide variety of plant genes in banks is particularly urgent because many farms now grow just one or two crops. They are particularly vulnerable to pests, disease, and climate change.

21 Just as efforts to preserve biodiversity increase, economics encourages farmers to focus on fewer crops. But those seeds may contain traits that will prove advantageous in another place or another time. Scientists at Cornell University recently borrowed a gene from a South American potato to make potatoes that resist late blight, a **devastating** disease that caused the Irish potato famine[11] in the 19th century.

22 "You need a system to **conserve** the variety so it doesn't go extinct," Fowler said. "A farmer may make a bowl of porridge with the last seeds of a strain that is of no use to him, and then it's gone. And potentially those are exactly the genes we will need a decade later."

23 Scientists are also working to learn more about the genetic characteristics of each banked seed—crucial knowledge that is often not recorded. Ultimately, plant breeders will be able to consult a global database to find seeds with genes suitable for the particular challenge **confronting** a region, like corn with a stalk that is strong enough to resist high winds or wheat that needs less water.

24 "The seed vault is adding a new dimension to an evolving global system," Swennen said. "We should have done it sooner. But the technology and the global interest weren't available."

---

[10] **vagaries:** changes that are difficult to predict or control   [11] **famine:** a lack of food during a long period of time in a region

---

Vocabulary Skill Review

In Unit 3, you learned to identify Latin and Greek roots (or stems) in new words. As you work through this unit, look for Latin and Greek roots and use them to help you understand new vocabulary.

B. **VOCABULARY** Here are some words and a phrase from Reading 1. Read the sentences. Circle the answer that best matches the meaning of each bold word or phrase.

1. The seeds of each plant carry all of the **genetic** information necessary to transfer characteristics from a parent plant to a new plant.
   a. related to nutrition or ingredients   b. related to development or origin

2. There are so few members of some plant species left that they are in danger of becoming **extinct**.
   a. gone forever   b. overgrown

3. The Global Seed Vault in Norway is trying to **consolidate** many smaller collections of rare plant seeds and shoots from all over the world.

   a. bring together in a single place

   b. sell for a large amount of money

4. Some scientists worry that the loss of plants and animals all around the world is **inevitable** because of global warming and human activity.

   a. faster   b. unavoidable

5. Fears of rapid climate change give many scientists a sense of **urgency** about gathering rare seeds and shoots while there is still time.

   a. immediate importance   b. value

6. Natural disasters, as well as the effects of **erosion** over time, can lead to the loss of a plant's natural habitat.

   a. human activities   b. destruction and wearing away

7. The Global Seed Vault will play a **crucial** role in protecting the world's food crops from weather disasters and climate change.

   a. small   b. very important

8. Plants have even more **vulnerability** to climate change and natural disasters than animals do because plants cannot move to other areas.

   a. ability to protect oneself

   b. openness to attack or damage

9. Seeds are stored in many different locations, but the Global Seed Vault is a **Plan B** in case of disasters at other storage sites.

   a. an alternative solution in case the first idea or arrangement does not succeed

   b. a single, obvious best solution to a problem

10. Food crops are always in danger from **devastating** diseases and natural disasters.

   a. extremely destructive and damaging

   b. minor and easy to stop

11. It is important to **conserve** seeds and shoots so that future generations can enjoy and use the same plants we have today.

   a. plant   b. look after and save

12. Many of the challenges **confronting** the world can be solved only through global cooperation.

   a. facing or threatening   b. hiding from or tricking

 C. Go online for more practice with the vocabulary.

D. Based on the information in Reading 1, each of the following statements is false. Correct the statements to make them true.

1. Plant species are disappearing quickly, but scientists and governments are not doing much to save them.

2. The Global Seed Vault has the goal of storing seeds from North America and Europe in case an emergency destroys any of them.

3. The United Nations International Treaty on Plant Genetic Resources created a global network for banking and sharing seeds, but it ignored the need to study their genetic traits.

4. The Intergovernmental Panel on Climate Change decided that plants will be affected by global warming, but not by extreme weather events.

5. The Global Seed Vault is located in a dangerous place that is too cold to protect seeds and plant sprouts.

6. Preserving plant genes in the Global Seed Vault won't protect the world's food supply from changing climate conditions or new plant diseases.

E. Match each detail with the country it is associated with.

_____ 1. Norway

_____ 2. Belgium

_____ 3. France

_____ 4. Mexico

_____ 5. Nigeria

_____ 6. the United States

_____ 7. Afghanistan

_____ 8. the Philippines

_____ 9. the United Kingdom

_____ 10. Ireland

a. This country is the location of the Global Seed Vault.

b. This country was the location of a potato famine in the 19th century.

c. This nation donated $20 million to the Global Seed Vault.

d. Ninety-four percent of peas are no longer grown here.

e. Scientists in this country are searching the world for banana samples and preserving their shoots.

f. A typhoon hit a seed bank here, destroying many samples.

g. Scientists in this country are searching for and preserving coffee plant samples.

h. Labs here banked cassava.

i. Seed banks in this country were destroyed in conflicts.

j. Labs here banked corn species.

F. Look back at Reading 1 and match each title to the most appropriate paragraph.

Paragraphs:

2   4   10   12   13   14   15   19   20   23

1. Seventy-five Percent of Plant Varieties Already Lost   Paragraph ____

2. Organizing Previously Uncoordinated Efforts   Paragraph ____

3. Finding Out More about Plant Genes   Paragraph ____

4. Funding from Around the World   Paragraph ____

5. Global Seed Vault Begins Operations   Paragraph ____

6. Geographical Motivation for an Alternative Plan   Paragraph ____

7. Many Seed Banks Exposed to Conflicts and Disasters   Paragraph ____

8. Safeguarding Against Negative Climate Changes   Paragraph ____

9. Previous Seed Banks Not Focused on Survival   Paragraph ____

10. Farmers Growing Fewer, More Vulnerable Crops   Paragraph ____

G. Based on the information in Reading 1, write five reasons for the creation of the Global Seed Vault. Then put a check (✓) beside the reason you think is the most important. Explain to a partner why you think that reason is the most important.

 H. Go online to read the magazine interview *Safeguarding the World's Network* and check your comprehension.

 # WRITE WHAT YOU THINK

A. Discuss these questions in a group.

1. Will the global partnerships formed while working on the Global Seed Vault help the world in other ways? Why or why not?

Writing **Tip**

In Unit 3, you learned about writing with unity. As you write your response to Activity B, be sure to maintain unity by checking that each of your sentences supports your main idea.

2. Do you think the scientists and governments in the article will be successful in preserving seeds and shoots from around the world? What are the consequences for humanity if the Global Seed Vault project is not successful?

3. Does your home country have any unique plants or crops that aren't found anywhere else? Should they be preserved in the Global Seed Vault? Why or why not?

B. Choose one question and write a paragraph in response. Look back at your Quick Write on page 97 as you think about what you have learned.

Reading Skill | Making inferences

Writers often use facts and opinions to suggest ideas rather than giving the ideas to the reader directly. The reader has to determine, or **infer**, what the writer is saying. Making an inference is making a logical conclusion about something based on the information that is given. Making inferences while reading a text can improve your overall comprehension and help you become a more critical reader.

This excerpt is taken from Reading 1:

◻ Bored into the middle of a snow-topped Arctic mountain, the seed vault . . .

The text doesn't need to say exactly what kind of place is best for preserving the world's seeds and shoots. From the information in the excerpt, you can infer that it is a place that needs to be safe and secure, as well as cold and far away. You come to this conclusion because of clues such as *bored, snow-topped, Arctic,* and *middle of a . . . mountain.*

Critical Thinking Tip

When you infer ideas from a text, you are using separate pieces of information as clues or evidence to support a conclusion. This analytical process shows a deeper understanding of the material.

A. Match each excerpt from Reading 1 with the correct inference.

Excerpts

_____ 1. With plant species disappearing at an alarming rate, scientists and governments are creating a global network of plant banks to store seeds and sprouts—precious genetic resources that may be needed for man to adapt the world's food supply to climate change. (Paragraph 1)

_____ 2. In Leuven, Belgium, scientists are scouring the world for banana samples and cryo-preserving their shoots in liquid nitrogen before they become extinct. (Paragraph 3)

_____ 3. Those [seed banks] in Nigeria banked cassava. (Paragraph 4)

_____ 4. Collectively they [seeds from many different countries] harbor a vast range of characteristics, including the ability to withstand a drier, warmer climate. (Paragraph 10)

_____ 5. Eighty percent of corn varieties that existed in the 1930s no longer exist today, for example. In the United States, 94 percent of peas are no longer grown. (Paragraph 12)

_____ 6. Seeds must be stored at minus 20 degrees Celsius (minus 4 Fahrenheit), and plant sprouts that rely on cryo-preservation must be far colder. (Paragraph 16)

Inferences

a. These seeds are important because the genetic information they contain will help grow food despite climate change and global warming.

b. Some food crops are more important in certain countries than others.

c. The world's food supply is in danger.

d. Some rare varieties of important food crops are hard to find, and they are in danger of disappearing soon.

e. Cold areas of the globe, such as the Arctic, are excellent locations for seed banks.

f. Farmers are growing fewer varieties of crops compared to the past.

B. Read each statement. What can you infer from the information in the statement? Write your inferences. Then compare your inferences with a partner.

1. **Statement:** Bored into the middle of a snow-topped Arctic mountain, the seed vault has as its goal the storing of every kind of seed from every collection on the planet.

   Inference: _As many of the world's seeds as possible need to be stored in a safe place that is cold and far away._

2. **Statement:** Mexico is the perfect place for corn seeds to be banked.

   Inference: _____

   _____

   _____

3. **Statement:** Scientists cheered when the United Nations International Treaty on Plant Genetic Resources finally created a formal global network for banking seeds and studying their genetic traits.

   Inference: _____

   _____

   _____

4. **Statement:** In the Philippines, a typhoon demolished the wall of a seed bank, destroying many valuable samples.

   Inference: _____

   _____

   _____

 C. Go online for more practice making inferences.

READING 2 | Building the Perfect Spaceman

 UNIT OBJECTIVE You are going to read an article from the weekly news magazine *Maclean's* about preparing to become an astronaut aboard the International Space Station. Use the article to gather information and ideas for your Unit Assignment.

PREVIEW THE READING

A. **PREVIEW** Look ahead to quickly read only the first sentences of paragraphs 2, 4, 6, 8, 10, and 12. Then discuss with a partner what examples of international cooperation you might find in this article. As you read, check to confirm if your ideas are included in the article.

 Writing Tip

Receiving feedback from a peer can be a valuable part of the writing process.

B. **QUICK WRITE** What kinds of international cooperation do you think are necessary for successful space exploration? Write for 5–10 minutes in response. When you are finished, exchange your Quick Write with a partner. Give your partner advice on how to improve his or her ideas. Remember to use this section for your Unit Assignment.

C. **VOCABULARY** Check (✓) the words you know. Then work with a partner to locate each word in the reading. Use clues to help define the words you don't know. Check your definitions in the dictionary.

daunting *(adj.)*	mission *(n.)*
devote *(v.)* 🔑	mundane *(adj.)*
dominate *(v.)* 🔑	navigate *(v.)*
inhabit *(v.)*	orbit *(n.)*
intensively *(adv.)*	quarantine *(v.)*
mediator *(n.)*	reassemble *(v.)*

🔑 Oxford 3000™ words

 D. Go online to listen and practice your pronunciation.

A. Read the article and gather information about why international cooperation is important.

Building the Perfect Spaceman

Inside NASA's training facility that turns mortals[1] into astronauts, and one into spaceship commander

by Kate Lunau

Canadian astronaut Chris Hadfield in training

1   FROM THE OUTSIDE, Building 9 at the NASA Johnson Space Center, a sprawling complex on the outskirts of Houston, is nondescript[2]. Inside, it's like Willy Wonka's factory, if Willy were a rocket scientist. The hangar-like facility is filled with robots, moon buggies, and spaceship mock-ups. Robonaut, a humanoid robot with a golden head, sits next to Spidernaut, a robot prototype with eight arched legs. There's an Orion capsule and a Russian Soyuz spacecraft. But what **dominates** the vast room is a full-size mock-up of the International Space Station (ISS), an Earth-orbiting spaceship built by 15 countries, including Canada.

2   One recent Monday morning, astronaut trainer Gwenn Sandoz waited there for Chris Hadfield, who will blast off from Kazakhstan aboard the Soyuz in December and soon after will become the first Canadian to take command of the ISS. Canada has invested heavily in the station, which has been **inhabited** by a rotating crew since 2000, but Canada only gets to send so many astronauts there. For 20 years, Hadfield has worked tirelessly to prove himself in an astronaut corps dominated by the US and Russia. Canada has paid its dues by contributing the robotics systems that built and maintain the ISS, finally earning a spot for one of its own at the controls of what Hadfield calls "the world's spaceship."

3   Sandoz knew her time with Hadfield was limited; this was his last week of training in Houston before the launch. At 10:15 a.m., right on time, he breezed in[3] wearing a neatly tucked-in polo shirt—the unofficial uniform at Johnson—with the crew patch of Expedition 35, which portrays a moonlit view of Earth from the ISS as the sun peeks from behind it. Assigned to Expedition 34/35 in September 2010, he's been training **intensively** in the US, Russia, and elsewhere for the **mission**. It isn't his first space flight, but it will be the longest he's spent off the ground. Hadfield will be on the ISS until May, making him only the second Canadian (after Robert Thirsk) to do a long-duration mission.

4   The list of skills to master is **daunting**. Hadfield has to be a scientist, a plumber, an electrician, trilingual, a spokesperson, a **mediator**, an engineer, and now, of course, a commander.

---

[1] **mortals:** ordinary people with little power or influence
[2] **nondescript:** having no unusual features

[3] **breezed in:** arrived in a cheerful and confident way

"The entire partnership is trusting the vehicle, and the crew, to his good judgment and command," says Edward Tabarah, deputy director of the astronaut office of the Canadian Space Agency (CSA).

5   On Dec. 19, Hadfield, US astronaut Tom Marshburn, and Russian cosmonaut Roman Romanenko will squeeze themselves into the Soyuz, their knees squished up to their chests. Good weather, bad weather, the Soyuz almost always leaves on schedule. Two days after they blast off, they'll arrive at the ISS, joining a crew of three other astronauts already there. Until March, Hadfield is the mission flight engineer. He then assumes command.

6   As he prepared to leave Houston for a last visit to Canada—then on to Germany for more training—Hadfield was his usual affable[4] self, but with an undercurrent[5] of intensity people around him noticed: he was wearing the weight of command. "I've **devoted** my whole life to being in a position where, at 53 years old, somebody would say, 'We want you to command our spaceship,'" Hadfield remarked one evening, sitting in the giant ISS mock-up after a busy day of training, "and I could say, 'Okay. I know what I need to do.'"

7   Hadfield, who was selected as one of four new Canadian astronauts in 1992—beating out about 5,330 hopefuls—has been into space twice. In 1995, he was the first Canadian mission specialist on a NASA space shuttle mission, visiting the Russian space station Mir, and the first Canadian to operate the Canadarm[6] in **orbit**. In 2001, on an 11-day space shuttle flight to the ISS to deliver and install the Canadarm2, Hadfield performed two spacewalks, another first for Canada. He spent more than 14 hours outside, traveling around Earth 10 times. (The ISS circles the world 16 times per day.)

8   He was also NASA's director of operations at the Yuri Gagarin Cosmonaut Training Centre in Star City, Russia, from 2001 to 2003, overseeing ISS crew activities. (Astronauts who travel to the ISS have to speak English and Russian; Hadfield is fluent in both. Canadians must speak French, too.) And he was chief of robotics at the NASA Astronaut Office at Johnson, then chief of ISS operations.

9   In 1992, the CSA assigned Hadfield to the Johnson Space Center, home to NASA's astronaut corps. Active Canadian and Japanese astronauts are based here permanently, and those from the European Space Agency (ESA) and Russia come frequently to train. Fresh recruits spend two years in basic astronaut training. Preparing for a mission to the ISS can take another 2 1/2 years.

10   In the years Hadfield has spent training for this mission, mainly split between Russia and Houston, even the most **mundane** aspects of life on the ISS have been endlessly rehearsed. In one five-hour drill, which consumed a recent Tuesday afternoon, Hadfield, Marshburn, and Romanenko convened[7] at Building 9 for a "daily ops" session, essentially a day in the life of the station. Hadfield took apart and **reassembled** the toilet. (Urine on the ISS is recycled into drinking water.) This training is important because life on the ISS is unpredictable. For example, on Sept. 5, American astronaut Sunita Williams and Akihiko Hoshide, from Japan, ventured out on a six-hour spacewalk to fix a failing component, one that carries power from the space station's solar arrays to its systems. The culprit[8], a faulty bolt, seemed to be jammed, so they used an improvised tool—a toothbrush—to clear the blockage.

11   Hadfield acknowledged the space program "goes in waves." We're currently in a dip. In 2011, NASA's 30-year space-shuttle program ended, leaving the Russians with the only viable way of getting astronauts to the ISS. (The U.S. has encouraged commercial companies to develop

---

[4] **affable:** pleasant, friendly, and easy to talk to
[5] **undercurrent:** a hidden feeling whose effects are felt
[6] **Canadarm:** a large robotic arm used to move, capture, and release objects in outer space

[7] **convene:** to come together for a formal meeting
[8] **culprit:** a thing responsible for causing a problem

new ways of bringing humans to low-Earth orbit.) The station is scheduled to be decommissioned in 2020, although many expect that to be extended. But while President Obama has talked about sending space explorers to asteroids or to Mars, in this age of cutbacks, such missions sound like science fiction. "Saying we'll go to Mars in 15 or 20 years, that's saying some other president, budget, and Congress," says astrophysicist Adam Frank, who blogs about the cosmos and culture for National Public Radio. "We need somebody to say 10 years. That's what Kennedy did with the moon."

12 Two weeks before the launch, Hadfield, Marshburn, and Romanenko will arrive in Kazakhstan and be **quarantined** with a small entourage of others, including Tabarah.

Four days before departure, the astronauts' families will arrive with Jeremy Hansen, the crew support astronaut, whose job is to escort them to the launch site and help them **navigate** the process. After a thorough health screening, Hadfield's immediate family will be allowed a short visit. Extended family can see him through a glass divider. Then he's gone, off to the International Space Station.

13 When asked what he'll miss most aboard the ISS, Hadfield cites the basics like being able to drive out for a slice of pizza on a whim. Then he becomes more somber. "The contact," he says. "This is a scientific monastery. It's not normal human life where you hug somebody, or can be with your family. I'll miss that." He shrugs. "But for me it's all part of the same life."

B. VOCABULARY Complete each sentence with one of the vocabulary words from Reading 2. You may need to change the form of the word or phrase to make the sentence grammatically correct.

daunting *(adj.)*	inhabit *(v.)*	mission *(n.)*	orbit *(n.)*
devote *(v.)*	intensively *(adv.)*	mundane *(adj.)*	quarantine *(v.)*
dominate *(v.)*	mediator *(n.)*	navigate *(v.)*	reassemble *(v.)*

1. Space station commanders must _____ themselves to the welfare of their crews. As a result, safety has to be their number one concern.

2. Astronauts have to know how to take apart and _____ equipment on the International Space Station in case it needs to be repaired.

3. The International Space Station is usually _____ by a crew of six people.

4. While many people are attracted to the idea of becoming an astronaut, there are many dangers involved, and the idea of spending so many days in space can be _____.

5. Crew members preparing to travel to the International Space Station are _____ so that they don't become sick before the big journey.

6. When people are working together in a small space like the International Space Station, it is important to have someone acting as a _____ who can help the crew avoid arguments.

7. One of the future _____ to the International Space Station is going to include the international recording artist Sarah Brightman.

8. Having an astronaut as part of the family can be very complicated, but NASA provides support to help families _____ the situation.

9. People who want to become astronauts have to study _____ in order to master the necessary science, math, and languages.

10. Although life on the International Space Station seems adventurous, there are still many _____ tasks that have to be performed, such as cooking and cleaning.

11. The training facility was _____ by a huge pool that took up all the space in the building.

12. The International Space Station is located in low-Earth _____, and it circles the planet about 16 times per day.

iQ ONLINE **C.** Go online for more practice with the vocabulary.

D. Number the main ideas in the order they are presented in Reading 2.

____ a. The space program has good times and bad times.

____ b. Boring duties on the International Space Station must be practiced many times.

____ c. Canada has contributed much to the International Space Station.

____ d. While the exterior of the NASA Johnson Space Center is quite plain, the interior resembles a fictional fantasy place made up of many strange-looking things.

____ e. There are many skills that have to be learned in order to become an International Space Station commander.

____ f. Hadfield's experience makes him ready to command and know what to do in almost any situation.

E. Match each detail with the main idea (a–f in Activity D) that it supports. There are two supporting details for each main idea.

_____ 1. The mission depends on Hadfield's sound decisions and ability to lead.

_____ 2. The plan is to stop using the International Space Station after the year 2020.

_____ 3. The Robonaut looks like a human with a golden head.

_____ 4. Canada contributed to the International Space Station mainly in the field of robotics.

_____ 5. Hadfield has many abilities, including being a scientist, plumber, electrician, and more.

_____ 6. Hadfield has operated the Canadarm in space.

_____ 7. Canada can send only a limited number of astronauts to the International Space Station.

_____ 8. Hadfield put a toilet back together after taking it apart.

_____ 9. The room is filled by a life-size model of the International Space Station.

_____ 10. Sunita Williams and Akihiko Hoshide fixed part of the International Space Station with a toothbrush.

_____ 11. Hadfield has been on spacewalks.

_____ 12. The space shuttle program has ended, and Russians have the only way to get to the International Space Station.

F. Based on the information in Reading 2, what has each of the following countries contributed to the International Space Station? You may have to infer a county's contribution. Include as many ideas as you can.

1. The United States: _____

2. Russia: _____

3. Canada: _____

4. Kazakhstan: _____

5. Germany: _____

6. Japan: _____

G. Match the following people in Reading 2 with the statements that best describe them.

a. Chris Hadfield	c. Roman Romanenko	e. Edward Tabarah
b. Akihiko Hoshide	d. Gwenn Sandoz	f. Robert Thirsk

_____ 1. An official in the Canadian Space Agency who comments on Hadfield's command and is together with Hadfield just before his mission.

_____ 2. The first Canadian to spend a long time in space on a mission.

_____ 3. An astronaut trainer who worked with Hadfield to help prepare him for his mission.

_____ 4. A Canadian astronaut with many years of experience preparing to become the commander of Expedition 35 to the International Space Station.

_____ 5. A Russian cosmonaut who is going to the International Space Station with Hadfield.

_____ 6. An astronaut who fixed a broken part of the International Space Station with a toothbrush during a six-hour spacewalk.

H. Answer the following questions based on the information in Reading 2. You will have to infer some of your answers.

1. Why does Hadfield call the International Space Station the world's spaceship? _____

_____

2. Why does Hadfield have to master so many skills? _____

_____

3. Why does Hadfield have to be trilingual, including English, Russian, and French? _____

_____

4. Why do the astronauts and cosmonauts come from different countries?

_____

_____

5. Why did Hadfield have to take apart and reassemble a toilet? _____

_____

6. Why did Sunita Williams and Akihiko Hoshide improvise with a
   toothbrush to fix the faulty bolt and clear out the blockage? _____

_____

7. What does Hadfield mean by saying the space program "goes in waves?"

_____

_____

8. Why is the US encouraging commercial companies to find ways of
   transporting people to low-Earth orbit? _____

_____

9. Why does a mission to Mars seem like science fiction? _____

_____

10. What does Hadfield mean by saying that the International Space Station
    is like a scientific monastery? _____

_____

11. What examples of global cooperation are found in Reading 2? _____

_____

 WRITE WHAT YOU THINK

**A. Discuss the questions in a group. Look back at your Quick Write on
page 106 as you think about what you have learned.**

1. What kinds of challenges do you think you would face if you were working
   on a collaborative global project like the International Space Station?
   Would you be successful working on a project like this?

2. Is global cooperation necessary for a project like the International Space
   Station to be successful? Why or why not?

3. Could the resources being used for the International Space Station be put
   to better use? In your opinion, what projects are more important than the
   International Space Station? Why?

B. Think about the unit video, Reading 1, and Reading 2 as you discuss these questions. Then choose one question and write a paragraph in response.

1. Which do you think is a better example of global cooperation—the Global Seed Vault or the International Space Station? Why?

2. Do you think there will be more of these sorts of global initiatives in the future? Why or why not?

Vocabulary Skill Prefixes

 for Success

Apply new ideas to information you have already learned. For example, while studying prefixes, remember what you learned about Latin and Greek roots in Unit 4.

Understanding the meanings of the different parts of a word is an important way to build vocabulary. A **prefix** can be added to the beginning of a word to change or add meaning, or to create an entirely new word. For instance, the *un-* in *unhappy* changes the root word, *happy*, to mean its opposite. Another example is *tele-* (over a long distance; far) and the word *vision* (the ability to see). They combine to create the word for a piece of electronic equipment with a screen to watch moving pictures (*television*). Use a dictionary to learn more about various prefixes. For example, in this dictionary entry for *co-*, you learn that it can be used with a variety of root words and in different parts of speech. It adds the meaning of "together with" to the root word.

> **co-** /koʊ/ *prefix* (used in adjectives, adverbs, nouns, and verbs) together with: *co-produced* ♦ *cooperatively* ♦ *co-author* ♦ *coexist*

In this dictionary entry for *mal-*, you learn that this prefix can also be used with a variety of root words and in different parts of speech.

> **mal-** /mæl/ *combining form* (in nouns, verbs, and adjectives) bad or badly; not correct or correctly: *malpractice* ♦ *malodorous* ♦ *malfunction*

All dictionary entries are from the *Oxford Advanced American Dictionary for learners of English* © Oxford University Press 2011.

A. Write the correct prefix from the box next to its definition below and on page 116. Then write as many words as you know that can use each prefix and their parts of speech. Check your answers in a dictionary and add to the chart if possible.

| bio- | dis- | im- | mal- | non- |
| cryo- | geo- | inter- | multi- | re- |

Prefix	Definition	Possible words	Possible parts of speech
1. multi-	more than one; many	multicolored, multimillionaire	nouns, adjectives
2.	not		
3.	involving the use of very low temperatures		
4.	(also *il-* / *in-* / *ir-*) not; the opposite of		
5.	of the earth		
6.	again		
7.	between; from one to another		
8.	bad or badly; not correct or correctly		

Prefix	Definition	Possible words	Possible parts of speech
9.	not; the opposite of		
10.	connected with living things or human life		

B. Complete each sentence with the correct prefix from the chart.

1. When parts of the Soyuz spacecraft break down, they need to be

   ___re___ placed before the Soyuz can travel to the International Space Station.

2. Some scientists use _____-preservation to store banana plant shoots.

3. The design of the Soyuz spacecraft is so strong that even if there are a couple

   of _____ functions, the crew will most likely land safely on Earth.

4. One of the main goals of the Global Seed Vault is to preserve the

   _____ diversity of the world's edible plant species.

5. The scientists working on the International Space Station don't worry

   about _____ politics because it's their job to solve engineering problems.

6. The Global Seed Vault is run by a(n) _____ profit group.

7. The space station was built by a(n) _____ national partnership.

8. The _____ governmental panel came to the conclusion that extreme

   weather events were going to increase in the future.

9. The age of the Soyuz spacecraft is _____ material because its design is robust.

10. Plant species are _____ appearing at a very fast rate all around the world.

 C. Go online for more practice with prefixes.

WRITING

UNIT OBJECTIVE
At the end of this unit, you will write an essay describing the importance of global cooperation. This essay will include information from the readings, the unit video, and your own ideas.

Writing Skill   Organizing supporting ideas

Tip for Success

Expository writing fully explains and describes an author's ideas on a subject. **Classification writing** puts people, things, or ideas into groups.

A piece of writing is **coherent** when the ideas are organized in a logical way. The order of ideas and supporting ideas depends on the writer's subject and purpose. Three of the most common methods of organization are explained below.

Specificity

Specificity works well with descriptive essays, expository writing, and classification essays.

- Organize your ideas from the more general to the more specific.
- Give one or more general ideas with increasingly specific supporting ideas, facts, and examples.

Emphasis

This form of organization works well with persuasive essays, comparison and contrast essays, and business letters.

- Organize your ideas from the least to the most important. Readers tend to remember best what they read last. This organization strengthens your argument by building up to the strongest ideas.

Time

Time organization works well with process essays, narrative essays, cause and effect essays, case studies, biographies, book reports, and short stories.

- Follow a chronological order.
- Organize your information from the past to the present or from the present to the past.
- Organize a process from the beginning to the end or from the end to the beginning.

A. Look at the brief outlines for short paragraphs answering the question "What is a good example of global cooperation?" Decide if the ideas have been organized according to specificity, emphasis, or time.

1. Type of organization: _____
   Global Polio Eradication Initiative
   a. In 1988, the World Health Assembly passed a resolution to eradicate polio.
   b. Nelson Mandela started the Kick Polio Out of Africa campaign in 1996.
   c. The service club *Rotary International* had raised $500 million in the fight against polio by 2003.
   d. In 2004, 23 countries in west and central Africa immunized more than 80 million children.

2. Type of organization: _____
   The World Health Organization (WHO)
   a. The WHO works towards the highest possible levels of health for people around the world.
   b. It supports the development and strengthening of health systems in every country.
   c. It sets health standards for health systems to follow.
   d. It carries out worldwide campaigns for people to eat healthier food.

3. Type of organization: _____
   International Migratory Bird Day
   a. International Migratory Bird Day is celebrated in Canada, the United States, Mexico, Central and South America, and the Caribbean.
   b. This day can involve bird walks and presentations.
   c. People learn about threats to migratory birds on this day.
   d. By raising public awareness of migratory birds, people can save them from danger and extinction.

B. **WRITING MODEL** Read this response to an essay question on a political science test. Then answer the questions with a partner.

What is a good example of global cooperation?

International peace parks are a good example of global cooperation. An increasing number of peace parks can be found all over the world. International peace parks are protected areas that are located on the borders of two or more countries. There are no fences between the countries in the parks, and animals are free to move wherever they want in the park. Three peace parks in particular illustrate how these sorts of global initiatives can bring different countries closer together.

The first peace park in the world, Waterton-Glacier International Peace Park, was established in 1932. It lies on the border between the United States and Canada, and it was created as a symbol of friendship and peace between these two countries. The United Nations Educational, Scientific and Cultural Organization (UNESCO) recognizes this park as a biosphere reserve and a World Heritage Site.

Another peace park that is also a UNESCO World Heritage Site is located in Central America. La Amistad International Park is shared by Costa Rica and Panama, and it was created in 1988. It is very remote, and Costa Rica and Panama work together to manage the park and maintain its fragile tropical environment.

Finally, the first peace park in Africa, Kgalagadi Transfrontier Park, was founded on May 12, 2000, between Botswana and South Africa. These two countries currently work together to manage the park as a single ecological unit. Kgalagadi is a large wildlife reserve in which people are also able to move freely across the international borders.

International peace parks such as Waterton-Glacer, La Amistad, and Kgalagadi show that global cooperation is possible. Because of these successful examples, the number of international peace parks is sure to increase in the future. It is hoped that people and organizations around the world will continue to promote the collaboration of different governments in the creation of more transfrontier parks like these.

1. What is the main idea of this essay?

2. What are the supporting ideas for the main idea?

3. How are the supporting ideas organized?

4. Is the organization of the supporting ideas effective? Why or why not?

5. Is there another way the supporting ideas could have been organized? If so, what is it?

 **Tip for Success**

When answering an essay question on a test, write out your thesis statement first, before you start writing your essay. This will help you organize your ideas and ensure you are happy with the most important sentence of your essay.

C. Complete these steps to write a brief outline for a paragraph on the topic *What is a good example of global cooperation?*

1. Decide on a good example of global cooperation that you are familiar with.

2. Brainstorm a list of five to six ideas that support your choice as a good example of global cooperation.

3. Check (✔) the three or four ideas that you are going to use in your outline.

4. Decide if you are going to organize your ideas according to specificity, emphasis, or time.

5. Number your ideas in the order that you want to include them in your outline.

D. WRITING MODEL During an essay exam, a student wrote the following response to the question, "Why is global cooperation important?" Read the essay. Then answer the questions that follow.

The Importance of Global Cooperation

Because of globalization, it is now easier than ever to share information and trade goods all around the world. Rapid advances in information and communications technology have resulted in what seems to be a much smaller world. One of the main benefits of a shrinking world is that global cooperation is now much easier. Global cooperation is very important because it can help countries solve problems that cannot be solved by one country alone, and it can promote peace and understanding between different nations.

Global cooperation is vital because many of the world's problems cannot be solved without help from other countries. Take, for example, the environment. There are, unfortunately, many environmental problems that affect the entire planet today. However, countries can work together to solve these environmental problems. At the world-wide level, the United Nations Environmental Programme (UNEP) coordinates international efforts that affect the land, sea, and air for the 192 member states of the United Nations. The UNEP promotes sustainability for the entire planet's environment. At a more regional level, the United States and Canada are working together to fight the air pollution that leads to acid rain. These two countries are members of an international joint commission that has agreed to work on air quality. They do this in a number of ways,

including exchanging information and conducting research. These countries have been very successful in reducing the harmful elements that cause acid rain. For example, according to Environment Canada, sulphur dioxide emissions that cause acid rain have been reduced by 57% in Canada and 67% in the United States since 1990. By working together, Canada and the US are protecting the environment on both sides of the border.

Global cooperation does not just help to preserve the environment. It can also promote peace among different countries. The European Union provides a good example of former enemies now working together. This cooperation started in the 1950s, when six European countries, including France and Germany, created the European Coal and Steel Community, which fostered economic cooperation in those industries. Soon, another agreement was signed, in 1957, to create a common market in Europe. Countries in the common market stopped charging customs duties when trading with other member countries. Agricultural cooperation also began around this time. The success of the European Common Market encouraged more countries to join, and in 1973 there were a total of nine members, including the United Kingdom. By 1979 there was a European Parliament, whose members were elected directly by the citizens of the member countries. More countries continued to join in the 1980s, and by 1993 there was a single market for all members. The cooperation continued with the introduction of the euro, with 12 countries using this currency in 2002. Now, people and money can move freely throughout the European Union, and former World War II enemies now live in peace.

Major world problems such as air pollution and acid rain are best solved through global cooperation. Peaceful coexistence is also promoted through countries working together. These two examples demonstrate the importance of global cooperation. The planet is sure to face more challenges in the future, but if countries can collaborate on the solutions, the problems are sure to be overcome.

1. What is the main idea introduced in the introductory paragraph? _____

_____

2. What is the main idea of the second paragraph? _____

_____

3. What supporting ideas are included in the second paragraph? _____

_____

4. Have the supporting ideas in the second paragraph been organized

according to specificity, emphasis, or time? _____

5. What is the main idea of the third paragraph? _____

_____

6. What supporting ideas are included in the third paragraph? _____

_____

7. Have the supporting ideas in the third paragraph been organized

according to specificity, emphasis, or time? _____

8. What is the conclusion in the last paragraph? _____

_____

 E. Go online for more practice with organizing supporting ideas.

When words, phrases, and clauses are used in a series in the same sentence, they should have **parallel structure**. That is, they should have the same grammatical form. Using parallel structure makes it easier for the reader to understand a text, especially when a sentence is more complex or contains several supporting points.

> **Noun**
> <u>Dedication</u> and <u>tolerance</u> are two things people need if they want to cooperate.
>
> **Adjective + noun**
> Those who work side by side with their Russian counterparts say that <u>strong relationships</u> and <u>mutual respect</u> have resulted from the many years of collaboration.

When you use parallel structure, you often omit words that are repeated in a phrase or sentence. This is called **ellipsis**. You can use ellipsis with modals or verb forms that have auxiliary verbs, such as the present continuous or present perfect. In parallel structure, the auxiliary verbs are usually omitted.

> **Modal *could***
> A collaborative space program <u>could build</u> greater understanding, <u>promote</u> world peace, and <u>improve</u> scientific knowledge.
>
> **Present perfect auxiliary verb *have***
> Scientists <u>have identified</u> and <u>solved</u> several problems related to the Global Seed Vault.

A. Read each sentence. Underline and correct each error in parallel structure.

1. The French scientists are taking part in an expedition to the Amazon rain forest, a conference in Rio de Janeiro, and <u>discussing</u> with Brazilian coffee farmers.   *a discussion*

2. Russian cosmonauts and American astronauts are working on experiments, build new space station modules, and learning together.

3. The scientists cataloged the seeds, cryo-preserved the shoots, and have sent them to the Global Seed Vault.

4. Global warming has many people worried, feeling concerned, and frustrated about the future.

5. The rusty launch site, abandoned buildings, and uneven sidewalks are surprising to Americans because of the dependability, famous, and prestige of the Russian space program.

B. Complete the sentences with your own ideas. Use parallel structure.

1. The Global Seed Vault is an important resource that could save many plants,

   _____.

2. Future global collaborations should focus on promoting peace, _____

   _____.

3. Peace parks encourage global cooperation, _____

   _____.

4. The World Health Organization has monitored health problems, _____

   _____.

5. Global cooperation is important in order to fight poverty, _____

   _____.

 **C.** Go online for more practice with parallel structure and ellipsis.

D. Go online for the grammar expansion.

Unit Assignment | Write an essay

 In this assignment, you will write an essay that answers the Unit Question, "Why is global cooperation important?" Use information from Reading 1, Reading 2, the unit video, and your work in this unit to support your ideas. Refer to the Self-Assessment checklist on page 124.

Go to the Online Writing Tutor for a writing model and alternate Unit Assignments.

PLAN AND WRITE

A. **BRAINSTORM** Based on the readings and your own personal knowledge, think about why global cooperation is important or why international cooperation is not important. Record your best two or three main ideas. Provide two or three supporting ideas or details for each main idea.

B. **PLAN** Review Activity A and decide which information you want to include in your answer. Then complete these tasks to organize your ideas.

1. Check (✓) the method of organizing your ideas that fits best with the information you plan to include in your essay.

   ☐ specificity   ☐ emphasis   ☐ time

2. Go to the Online Resources to download and complete your outline of your essay based on the method you have chosen. Plan a four- or five-paragraph essay, depending on the number of main ideas you have to support your thesis statement.

 C. WRITE Use your **PLAN** notes to write your essay. Go to *iQ Online* to use the Online Writing Tutor.

1. Write an essay answering the Unit Question, "Why is global cooperation important?"

2. Look at the Self-Assessment checklist to guide your writing.

REVISE AND EDIT

 A. PEER REVIEW Read your partner's essay. Then go online and use the Peer Review worksheet. Discuss the review with your partner.

B. REWRITE Based on your partner's review, revise and rewrite your essay.

C. EDIT Complete the Self-Assessment checklist as you prepare to write the final draft of your essay. Be prepared to hand in your work or discuss it in class.

SELF-ASSESSMENT		
Yes	**No**	
☐	☐	Is there a logical order to the main ideas?
☐	☐	Is there a logical order to the supporting ideas?
☐	☐	Are parallel structure and ellipsis used correctly?
☐	☐	Are there words with prefixes?
☐	☐	Does the essay include vocabulary from the unit?
☐	☐	Did you check the essay for punctuation, spelling, and grammar?

 D. REFLECT Go to the Online Discussion Board to discuss these questions.

1. What is something new you learned in this unit?

2. Look back at the Unit Question—Why is global cooperation important? Is your answer different now than when you started the unit? If yes, how is it different? Why?

TRACK YOUR SUCCESS

Circle the words you have learned in this unit.

Nouns	**Verbs**	**Adjectives**
erosion AWL	confront 🔑	crucial 🔑 AWL
mediator	conserve	daunting
mission	consolidate	devastating
orbit	devote 🔑 AWL	extinct
Plan B	dominate 🔑 AWL	genetic
urgency	inhabit	inevitable 🔑 AWL
vulnerability	navigate	mundane
	quarantine	**Adverb**
	reassemble	intensively AWL

🔑 Oxford 3000™ words

AWL Academic Word List

Check (✓) the skills you learned. If you need more work on a skill, refer to the page(s) in parentheses.

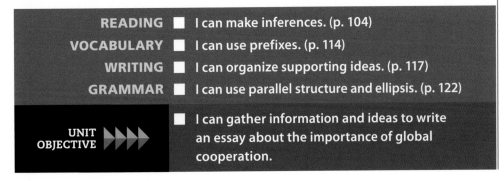

READING	☐	I can make inferences. (p. 104)
VOCABULARY	☐	I can use prefixes. (p. 114)
WRITING	☐	I can organize supporting ideas. (p. 117)
GRAMMAR	☐	I can use parallel structure and ellipsis. (p. 122)
UNIT OBJECTIVE ▶▶▶▶	☐	I can gather information and ideas to write an essay about the importance of global cooperation.

READING ▶ following ideas
VOCABULARY ▶ using the dictionary: verb complements
GRAMMAR ▶ passive voice to focus information
WRITING ▶ connecting information

UNIT QUESTION

What makes a public place appealing?

A Discuss these questions with your classmates.

1. What public places do you spend time in (for example, parks, libraries, banks, or malls)?

2. Does your hometown or the town where you are living now have many public places you can walk to? What are they?

3. Look at the photo. How can art affect a public place like a subway station? Why would a city plan a station like this?

B Listen to *The Q Classroom* online. Then answer these questions.

1. How did the students answer the question?

2. Do you agree with their ideas? Why or why not?

 C Go to the Online Discussion Board to discuss the Unit Question with your classmates.

127

D If you were designing a new library for your town or school, how important would each feature be? Complete the questionnaire. Circle the number that best corresponds to your opinion, from 1 (Not at all important) to 5 (Very important).

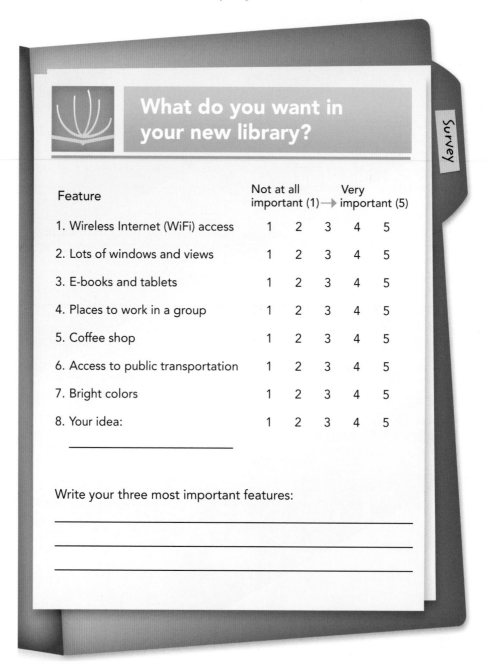

What do you want in your new library?

Survey

Feature	Not at all important (1) → Very important (5)				
1. Wireless Internet (WiFi) access	1	2	3	4	5
2. Lots of windows and views	1	2	3	4	5
3. E-books and tablets	1	2	3	4	5
4. Places to work in a group	1	2	3	4	5
5. Coffee shop	1	2	3	4	5
6. Access to public transportation	1	2	3	4	5
7. Bright colors	1	2	3	4	5
8. Your idea:	1	2	3	4	5

_____

Write your three most important features:

_____

_____

_____

E In a group, discuss your answers for Activity D and explain the reasons for your choices. As a group, agree on the three most important features. Present your group's top three features to the class.

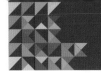

READING

READING 1 | The New Oases

You are going to read an article from the news magazine *The Economist* that describes a change in the design of public places caused by modern technology and lifestyles. Use the article to gather information and ideas for your Unit Assignment.

Reading Skill | Following ideas

When you read longer texts from newspapers, magazines, and books, you often have to follow complicated ideas and understand how the ideas develop. It is important not just to recognize these ideas, but also to understand how they connect to present a story or argument. Here are some tips that can help you follow ideas through a text:

When you see a pronoun (*it, they, them, her, who, which,* etc.), make sure you know the **referent** (the noun that the pronoun replaces). Find the referent by scanning back in the text.

The new library is a beautiful building. It is light, open, and welcoming.

Demonstrative pronouns such as *this* and *these* usually refer to the last idea, not just the last noun (for example, the last sentence or the entire last paragraph). Stop and ask yourself this question: What was the idea?

Many students rely on their laptops. This means that they can work anywhere.

A sentence or paragraph might begin with a word or phrase that acts as a summary of the previous idea. Often, the word is a different part of speech (for example, a noun instead of a verb).

When you see a summary word or phrase, check that you understood the last idea and expect examples, supporting details, or a new topic to come next. In this example, "This shift" refers to the change in the design of public buildings. Details regarding the change follow.

The design of public buildings **has changed.** This shift can be seen everywhere, from university libraries to public parks.

Critical Thinking **Tip**

Activity A asks
you to recognize
the referent for
each pronoun.
To understand
complicated texts,
you must understand
prior information
and apply your
knowledge of
grammar.

A. Read the paragraph about an urban designer named Ray Oldenburg.
Write the referent below each bold word or phrase.

> Ray Oldenburg is an urban sociologist from Florida **who** writes about the
> 1
> <u>Oldenburg</u>
>
> importance of informal public gathering places. In **his** book *The Great Good*
> 2
> _____
>
> *Place*, Oldenburg demonstrates why **these places** are essential to community
> 3
> _____
>
> and public life. **The book** argues that coffee shops, general stores, and other
> 4
> _____
>
> "third places" (in contrast to the first and second places of home and work)
>
> are central to improving communities. By exploring how **these places** work
> 5
> _____
>
> and what roles **they** serve, Oldenburg offers tools and insight for individuals
> 6
> _____
>
> and communities everywhere.
>
> Source: Adapted from Ray Oldenburg. *Project for Public Spaces*. Retrieved October 12, 2010, from http://www.pps.org/
> roldenburg.

B. Complete each second sentence with a noun from the box. Your choices should
reflect the meaning of the phrases in bold in the first sentence.

concept	spaces	problem	shift	term

1. In recent years, more effort has gone into the design of **public places**. These

   _____ function as an alternative to the home and the office.

2. Today, more people **are using smart phones and tablet computers for business**.

   This _____ makes the traditional office seem old-fashioned.

3. It has been nearly two decades since Oldenburg first used **the expression *third***

   places. Since then, many companies have used the _____ to

   describe their stores and restaurants.

4. Oldenburg believes that **third places could strengthen a community**.

   This _____ has been a powerful motivation for many urban

   planners.

5. Sometimes **people in third places interact with just their computers,
   not other people.** Some café owners are trying to solve this

   _____.

 C. Go online for more practice following ideas.

PREVIEW THE READING

A. PREVIEW Look at the photograph on page 133. It shows the Stata
Center at the Massachusetts Institute of Technology (MIT), a university
in the US. What do you think people do in this building? Write three
predictions. After you have read the article, check to see if your
predictions were correct.

1. _____

2. _____

3. _____

B. QUICK WRITE What makes public places like university buildings and
libraries attractive and functional for you? Write for 5–10 minutes in
response. Remember to use this section for your Unit Assignment.

C. VOCABULARY Check (✓) the words you know. Then work with a partner
to locate each word in the reading. Use clues to help define the words
you don't know. Check your definitions in the dictionary.

controversy *(n.)*	in decline *(phr.)*	neutral *(adj.)*
encounter *(v.)* 🔑	intentionally *(adv.)*	nomadic *(adj.)*
form bonds *(phr.)*	isolated *(adj.)*	pop up *(phr. v.)*
hybrid *(adj.)*	mingle *(v.)*	specialized *(adj.)*

 Oxford 3000™ words

 D. Go online to listen and practice your pronunciation.

WORK WITH THE READING

> **A.** Read the article and gather information on what makes a public place appealing.

The New Oases

1 Frank Gehry, a celebrity architect, likes to cause aesthetic **controversy**, and his Stata Center at the Massachusetts Institute of Technology (MIT) did the trick. Opened in 2004 and housing MIT's computer-science and philosophy departments behind its façade[1] of bizarre angles and windows, it has become a new landmark. But the building's most radical innovation is on the inside. The entire structure was conceived with the **nomadic** lifestyles of modern students and faculty in mind. Stata, says William Mitchell, a professor of architecture and computer science at MIT who worked with Mr. Gehry on the center's design, was conceived as a new kind of "**hybrid** space."

2 This is best seen in the building's "student street," an interior passage that twists and meanders through the complex and is open to the public 24 hours a day. It is dotted with nooks and crannies[2]. Cafés and lounges are interspersed with work desks and whiteboards, and there is free Wi-Fi everywhere. Students, teachers, and visitors are cramming for exams, napping, instant-messaging, researching, reading, and discussing. No part of the student street is physically **specialized** for any of these activities. Instead, every bit of it can instantaneously become the venue for a seminar, a snack, or relaxation.

> **❝** Flexibility is what separates successful spaces and cities from unsuccessful ones. **❞**

3 The fact that people are no longer tied to specific places for functions such as studying or learning, says Mr. Mitchell, means that there is "a huge drop in demand for traditional, private, enclosed spaces" such as offices or classrooms, and simultaneously "a huge rise in demand for semi-public spaces that can be informally appropriated to ad-hoc[3] workspaces." This shift, he thinks, amounts to the biggest change in architecture in this century. In the 20th century, architecture was about specialized structures—offices for working, cafeterias for eating, and so forth. This was necessary because workers needed to be near things such as landline phones, fax machines, and filing cabinets.

4 The new architecture, says Mr. Mitchell, will "make spaces **intentionally** multifunctional." Architects are thinking about light, air, trees, and gardens, all in the service of human connections. Buildings will have much more varied shapes than before. For instance, people working on laptops and tablets find it comforting to have their backs to a wall, so hybrid spaces may become curvier, with more nooks, in order to maximize the surface area of their inner walls.

5 This "flexibility is what separates successful spaces and cities from unsuccessful ones," says Anthony Townsend, an urban planner at

---

[1] **façade:** the front of a building
[2] **nooks and crannies:** small, quiet places that are sheltered or hidden from other people

[3] **ad hoc:** arranged or happening when necessary and not planned in advance

the Institute for the Future. Almost any public space can assume some of these features. For example, a not-for-profit organization in New York has turned Bryant Park, a once-derelict[4] but charming garden in front of the city's public library, into a hybrid space popular with office workers. The park's managers noticed that a lot of visitors were using mobile phones and laptops in the park, so they installed Wi-Fi and added some chairs with foldable lecture desks. The idea was not to distract people from the flowers but to let them customize their little bit of the park.

interior "student street" of the Stata Center of MIT

6   The academic name for such spaces is *third places*, a term originally coined by the sociologist Ray Oldenburg in his 1989 book *The Great Good Place*. At the time, long before mobile technologies became widespread, Mr. Oldenburg wanted to distinguish between the sociological functions of people's first places (their homes), their second places (offices), and the public spaces that serve as safe, **neutral**, and informal meeting points. As Mr. Oldenburg saw it, a good third place makes admission free or cheap—the price of a cup of coffee, say—offers creature comforts[5], is within walking distance for a particular neighborhood, and draws a group of regulars.

7   Mr. Oldenburg's thesis was that third places were **in** general **decline**. More and more people, especially in suburban societies such as America's, were moving only between their first and second places, making extra stops only at alienating[6] and anonymous locations such as malls, which in Mr. Oldenburg's opinion fail as third places. Society, Mr. Oldenburg feared, was at risk of coming unstuck without these venues for spreading ideas and **forming bonds**.

8   No sooner was the term coined than big business queued up to claim that it was building new third places. The most prominent was Starbucks, a chain of coffee houses that started in Seattle and is now hard to avoid anywhere. Starbucks admits that as it went global, it lost its ambiance[7] of a "home away from home." However, it has also spotted a new opportunity in catering to nomads. Its branches offer not only sofas but also desks with convenient electricity sockets. Bookshops are also offering "more coffee and crumbs," as Mr. Oldenburg puts it, as are YMCAs[8] and public libraries.

9   But do these oases for nomads actually play the social role of third places? James Katz at Rutgers University fears that cyber-nomads are "hollowing them out." It is becoming commonplace for a café to be full of people with headphones on, speaking on their mobile phones or laptops and hacking away at their keyboards, more engaged with their email inbox than with the people touching their elbows. These places are "physically inhabited but psychologically evacuated," says Mr. Katz, which leaves people feeling "more **isolated** than they would be if the café were merely empty."

---

[4] **derelict**: not used or cared for and in bad condition
[5] **creature comforts**: things that make life, or a particular place, comfortable, such as good food, comfortable furniture, or modern equipment

[6] **alienating**: making you feel as if you do not belong
[7] **ambiance**: the character and atmosphere of a place (also *ambience*)
[8] **YMCA (The Young Men's Christian Association)**: an association-run community and sports center

A Third Place . . .

- is not expensive, or is free;
- usually offers food or drink;
- is easily accessible to many people;
- has "regulars" (people who go there often);
- has a friendly atmosphere; and
- is a good place to meet old friends and new people.

10   Many café owners are trying to deal with this problem. Christopher Waters, the owner of the Nomad Café in Oakland, regularly hosts poetry readings, and he actually turns off the Wi-Fi at those times so that people **mingle** more. He is also planning to turn his café into an online social network so that patrons opening their browsers to connect **encounter** a welcome page that asks them to fill out a short profile and then see information about the people at the other tables.

11   As more third places **pop up** and spread, they also change entire cities. Just as buildings during the 20th century were specialized by function, towns were as well, says Mr. Mitchell. Suburbs were for living, downtowns for working, and other areas for playing. But urban nomads make districts, like buildings, multifunctional. Parts of town that were monocultures, he says, gradually become "fine-grained mixed-use neighborhoods" more akin[9] in human terms to pre-industrial villages than to modern suburbs.

[9] **akin:** similar to

B. **VOCABULARY** Here are some words and phrases from Reading 1. Read the sentences. Circle the answer that best matches the meaning of each bold word or phrase.

Vocabulary Skill Review

In Unit 4, you learned about prefixes that change the meaning of words. Which words in Activity B can you modify with a prefix to give them the opposite meaning?

1. Frank Gehry likes to create **controversy** to get people discussing his challenging, modern style of architecture.
    a. fun   b. disagreement   c. harmony

2. College students lead a **nomadic** lifestyle; every day they move among dormitories, classroom buildings, and libraries.
    a. traveling often   b. being busy   c. working hard

3. The new building is a **hybrid** space suitable for both work and play.
    a. different   b. mixed-use   c. beautiful

4. The building's design is not **specialized**, so it can easily be adapted to different purposes.
    a. made for a   b. unusual   c. finished
        particular use

5. To create a sense of community, city officials **intentionally** created a place where people could sit and work during their lunch hour.
    a. then   b. accidentally   c. deliberately

6. A good public space should be safe, **neutral**, and informal.
   a. brightly colored
   b. open only for some people
   c. open for all people

7. The city needs to spend more money downtown because many older buildings are **in decline**.
   a. being offered for sale
   b. getting worse
   c. being used

8. A community is stronger when people care about each other and **form bonds**.
   a. work together
   b. play sports
   c. develop relationships

9. Customers in many coffee shops never talk to other people there, so they feel **isolated**.
   a. alone
   b. intelligent
   c. private

10. In good public places, people can **mingle**, getting to know new people if they want.
    a. sit together
    b. make noise
    c. mix and chat

11. If possible, architects should design places so that visitors **encounter** a welcoming atmosphere in any public space.
    a. meet with
    b. hope for
    c. appreciate

12. New public places **pop up** all the time in growing cities.
    a. get larger
    b. appear suddenly
    c. fail

Barclay's Center, Brooklyn, NY

 C. Go online for more practice with the vocabulary.

D. Complete this outline of the main ideas in the article. Use the Reading Skill (Following ideas, page 129) to help you.

the Stata Center at MIT

Bryant Park in New York City

Example 1: Stata Center

A _____ space
1

Used for _____
2

Example 2: _____
3

A customizable space

Not only a park but also

_____
4

Academic term: _____
5

Definition: _____
6

Oldenburg thought they were _____.
7

New third places were built by _____.
8

Problem: _____.
9

Solution: _____
10

Conclusion: Third places change cities.

Districts become _____ (like the Stata Center).
11

E. Read the statements. Write *T* (true), *F* (false), or *I* (impossible to know from the article). Write the number of the paragraph that helped you. Correct the false statements.

_____ 1. Gehry's design is popular with everyone. (Paragraph: ____)

_____ 2. There is no need to make a formal appointment to use an area in the "student street" for a meeting. (Paragraph: ____)

_____ 3. Buildings in the 20th century followed a limited number of forms. (Paragraph: ____)

_____ 4. Curved walls will become more common because they increase the amount of possible meeting space. (Paragraph: ____)

_____ 5. Future construction will use more color inside buildings. (Paragraph: ____)

_____ 6. The term *third spaces* was first created by an architect. (Paragraph: ____)

_____ 7. Oldenburg blamed technology for the lack of third places. (Paragraph: ____)

_____ 8. At Christopher Waters's café, customers cannot use Wi-Fi at any time. (Paragraph: ____)

F. The article describes three reactions to three modern problems. Complete the chart with details from the article. Write the numbers of the paragraphs where you found the information.

	Problem	Solution	Paragraph(s)
1. Classrooms and office buildings	Spaces were specialized because workers needed access to landline phones and other equipment.		
2. Bryant Park			
3. Starbucks			

G. Circle the correct answers. Write a reason for your answer using information from the article.

1. Why does the "student street" in the Stata Center have twists and curves?
   a. to look inventive
   b. because there are no landline telephones
   c. to create controversy and something to discuss
   d. to create space that is comfortable for different uses

   Reason: _____

2. According to Oldenburg's definition, which is a third place?
   a. a bookstore that holds free weekly discussion groups for local residents
   b. a coffee shop with Internet access
   c. a suburban shopping mall
   d. a museum that charges people to attend public lectures

   Reason: _____

3. What can you infer from Reading 1 about people who live in the suburbs?
   a. They work longer hours than other people.
   b. They don't have much contact with other people outside work.
   c. They dislike shopping in urban centers.
   d. They do not have access to coffee shops.

   Reason: _____

4. What is causing the shift to multifunctional districts, according to the last paragraph of Reading 1?
   a. third places   c. modern architecture
   b. the Internet   d. changes in lifestyle

   Reason: _____

H. Use your understanding of Reading 1 to define these terms from the article.

1. "nomadic lifestyles" (paragraph 1): _____

2. "hybrid space" (paragraph 1): _____

3. "semi-public spaces" (paragraph 3): _____

4. "coffee and crumbs" (paragraph 8): _____

5. "cyber-nomads" (paragraph 9): _____

6. "monocultures" (paragraph 11): _____

I. Go online to read *The New Third Places* and check your comprehension.

WRITE WHAT YOU THINK

A. Discuss these questions in a group.

1. Do you know a building like the Stata Center or a place like Bryant Park that is multifunctional or has a hybrid purpose? Describe it and explain whether it is appealing to you.

2. Do you agree with the idea that technology such as smartphones and tablet computers can have an alienating effect? Do you like the ideas that Christopher Waters had to encourage customers to mingle more?

3. Do you think third places differ from country to country? Why might some third places in your country be less appealing elsewhere?

B. Choose one question and write a paragraph in response. Look back at your Quick Write on page 131 as you think about what you learned.

READING 2 | A Path to Road Safety with No Signposts

You are going to read a profile from *The New York Times* about Dutch traffic engineer Hans Monderman. Although he died in 2008, Monderman's ideas about cars, pedestrians, and bicyclists sharing roads are still popular today. Use the article to gather information and ideas for your Unit Assignment.

PREVIEW THE READING

A. **PREVIEW** Read the title, subheadings, and caption in the article. What do you think Monderman did to make roads safer? Make three predictions.

B. **QUICK WRITE** How do you think urban planners can make towns and cities friendly for motorists, cyclists, and pedestrians? Write for 5–10 minutes in response. Remember to use this section for your Unit Assignment.

C. **VOCABULARY** Work with a partner to find these words in the reading. Circle clues in the text that help you understand the meaning of each word. Then use a dictionary to define any unknown words.

accommodate *(v.)*	counterintuitive *(adj.)*	negotiate *(v.)*
anticipate *(v.)* 🔑	criteria *(n.)* 🔑	proponent *(n.)*
appealing *(adj.)* 🔑	division *(n.)* 🔑	regulated *(adj.)*
concede *(v.)*	fatal *(adj.)*	reinforce *(v.)*

🔑 Oxford 3000™ words

WORK WITH THE READING

A. Read the article and gather information on what makes a public place appealing.

A Path to Road Safety with No Signposts

By Sarah Lyall

1 DRACHTEN, The Netherlands. "I want to take you on a walk," said Hans Monderman, abruptly stopping his car and striding—hatless, and nearly hairless—into the freezing rain.

Pedestrians, bicycles, and cars all share this intersection in Drachten without the need for traffic lights or road signs.

2 Like a naturalist conducting a tour of the jungle, he led the way to a busy intersection in the center of town, where several odd things immediately became clear. Not only was it virtually naked, stripped of all lights, signs, and road markings, but there was no **division** between road and sidewalk. It was, basically, a bare brick square.

3 But in spite of the apparently anarchical[1] layout, the traffic, a steady stream of trucks, cars, buses, motorcycles, bicycles, and pedestrians, moved along fluidly and easily, as if directed by an invisible conductor. When Mr. Monderman, a traffic engineer and the intersection's proud designer, deliberately failed to check for oncoming traffic before crossing the street, the drivers slowed for him. No one honked or shouted rude words out of the window.

4 "Who has the right of way?" he asked rhetorically[2]. "I don't care. People here have to find their own way, **negotiate** for themselves, use their own brains."

5 Used by some 20,000 drivers a day, the intersection is part of a road-design revolution pioneered by the 59-year-old Mr. Monderman. His work in Friesland, the district in northern Holland that takes in Drachten, is increasingly seen as the way of the future in Europe.

6 His philosophy is simple, if **counterintuitive**.

7 To make communities safer and more **appealing**, Mr. Monderman argues, you should first remove the traditional paraphernalia[3] of their roads—the traffic lights and road signs; the center lines separating lanes from one another; even the speed bumps, speed-limit signs, bicycle lanes, and pedestrian crossings. In his view, it is only when the road is made more dangerous, when drivers stop looking at signs and start looking at other people, that driving becomes safer.

---

[1] **anarchical:** without order
[2] **rhetorically:** asked only to make a statement or to produce an effect rather than to get an answer
[3] **paraphernalia:** a large number of different objects, especially the equipment that you need for a particular activity

8   "All those signs are saying to cars, 'This is your space, and we have organized your behavior so that as long as you behave this way, nothing can happen to you,'" Mr. Monderman said. "That is the wrong story."

9   The Drachten intersection is an example of the concept of "shared space," a street where cars and pedestrians are equal, and the design tells the driver what to do.

10   "It's a moving away from **regulated** traffic toward space which, by the way it's designed and configured, makes it clear what sort of behavior is **anticipated**," said Ben Hamilton-Baillie, a British specialist in urban design and movement and a **proponent** of many of the same concepts.

11   Highways, where the car is naturally king, are part of the "traffic world" and another matter altogether. In Mr. Monderman's view, shared-space schemes thrive only in conjunction with well-organized, well-regulated highway systems.

Social Space

12   Mr. Monderman is a man on a mission. On a daylong automotive tour of Friesland, he pointed out places he had improved, including a town where he ripped out the sidewalks, signs, and crossings and put in brick paving on the central shopping street. An elderly woman crossed slowly in front of him.

13   "This is social space, so when Grandma is coming, you stop, because that's what normal, courteous human beings do," he said.

14   Planners and curious journalists are increasingly making pilgrimages[4] to meet Mr. Monderman, considered one of the field's great innovators, although until a few years ago he was virtually unknown outside Holland. Mr. Hamilton-Baillie, whose writings have helped bring Mr. Monderman's work to wider attention, remembers with fondness his own first visit.

15   Mr. Monderman drove him to a small country road with cows in every direction. Their presence was unnecessarily **reinforced** by a large traffic sign with a picture of a cow on it.

16   "He said: 'What do you expect to find here? Wallabies[5]?'" Mr. Hamilton-Baillie recalled. "'They're treating you like you're a complete idiot, and if people treat you like a complete idiot, you'll act like one.' Essentially, what it means is a transfer of responsibility to the individual and the community."

17   Dressed in a beige jacket and patterned shirt, with scruffy facial hair and a stocky build, Mr. Monderman has the appearance of a football hooligan[6] but the temperament of an engineer, which indeed he trained to be. He was working as a civil engineer building highways in the 1970s when the Dutch government, alarmed at a sharp increase in traffic accidents, set up a network of traffic safety offices. Mr. Monderman was appointed Friesland's traffic safety officer.

18   In residential communities, Mr. Monderman began narrowing the roads and putting in design features like trees and flowers, red brick paving stones, and even fountains to discourage people from speeding. This principle is now known as psychological traffic calming, where behavior follows design.

19   He made his first nervous foray into[7] shared space in a small village whose residents were upset at its being used as a daily thoroughfare for 6,000 speeding cars. When he took away the signs, lights, and sidewalks, people drove more carefully. Within two weeks, speeds on the road had dropped by more than half.

---

[4] **pilgrimage:** a journey to a place that is connected with someone or something that you admire
[5] **wallaby:** an Australian animal like a small kangaroo

[6] **hooligan:** someone who behaves in an extremely noisy way
[7] **make a foray into:** to attempt to become involved in (a new activity)

20   In fact, he said, there has never been a **fatal** accident on any of his roads.

Limits of Shared Space

21   Mr. Monderman **concedes** that road design can do only so much. It does not change the behavior, for instance, of the 15 percent of drivers who will behave badly no matter what the rules are. Nor are shared-space designs appropriate everywhere, like major urban centers, but only in neighborhoods that meet particular **criteria**.

22   Recently a group of well-to-do parents asked him to widen the two-lane road leading to their children's school, saying it was too small to **accommodate** what he derisively[8] calls "their huge cars."

23   He refused, saying the fault was not with the road, but with the cars. "They can't wait for each other to pass?" he asked.

[8] **derisively:** in a way that shows that he thinks something is ridiculous

---

B. **VOCABULARY** Here are some words from Reading 2. Read the sentences. Then write each bold word next to the correct list of synonyms.

1. In most countries, driving is a **regulated** activity.

2. Drivers learn traffic laws when they get their licenses, but signs **reinforce** the laws in case drivers forget them.

3. Urban planners try to **anticipate** conflict between cars and pedestrians when they design streets.

4. Most street planners try to create a strict **division** between the road and the sidewalk.

5. Whenever possible, roads are built to **accommodate** all the vehicles that are likely to use them.

6. Streets can be hard to **negotiate** if rules are complicated or there is a lot of traffic.

7. Despite many safety measures, sometimes there are **fatal** accidents on the roads.

8. Many home buyers think houses on large, busy streets are less **appealing** than those on small, quiet streets.

9. One street designer is a **proponent** of a planned shared-space movement and is trying to convince other people of the plan's value.

10. The shared-space approach is **counterintuitive** to traditional street design because it removes the traditional traffic signs and signals.

11. Shared-space designers **concede** that the idea does not work everywhere.

12. There are several **criteria** for a successful shared space; only streets that meet these guidelines are likely to succeed.

a. _____ (*v.*) admit • acknowledge • recognize

b. _____ (*v.*) expect • await • look for

c. _____ (*v.*) clear • get around • get past • pass

d. _____ (*v.*) adapt • fit • suit • receive • shelter • work with

e. _____ (*v.*) strengthen • cement • make stronger • repeat

f. _____ (*adj.*) surprising • unexpected • contrary to usual thinking

g. _____ (*adj.*) deadly • lethal

h. _____ (*adj.*) popular • attractive • desirable

i. _____ (*n.*) standards • measures • guides

j. _____ (*adj.*) overseen • policed • supervised • governed

k. _____ (*n.*) separation • split • partition

l. _____ (*n.*) advocate • champion • supporter • promoter

iQ ONLINE **C.** Go online for more practice with the vocabulary.

D. Check (✓) the techniques that Monderman used for improving intersections. Then discuss with a partner why he did or did not use each method.

____ 1. adding more road signs

____ 2. forcing cars, bikes, and pedestrians to share the same space

____ 3. removing lane divisions

____ 4. making roads wider

____ 5. adding more pedestrian crossings

____ 6. reducing the speed limit on highways

_____ 7. letting people negotiate their own behavior

_____ 8. changing roads in major cities

_____ 9. planting trees and flowers

_____ 10. making road surfaces look the same as sidewalks

E. **Answer these questions. Then circle and number information in the article that supports your answers.**

1. Why are intersections like the one in Drachten safe?

_____

_____

2. In Monderman's view, why are roads with road signs, speed limits, and lane markings more dangerous?

_____

_____

3. Why don't shared-space ideas apply to highways?

_____

_____

4. Why does Monderman find road signs and other traditional ways of regulating traffic to be insulting?

_____

_____

5. Why did Monderman refuse to widen a road leading to a school?

_____

_____

F. Read the statements. Write *T* (true), *F* (false), or *I* (impossible to know from the article). Write the number of the paragraph that helped you. Correct the false statements.

_____ 1. Monderman is compared to a naturalist in a jungle because people are out of place in his intersections. (Paragraph: _____)

_____ 2. Someone is directing traffic in the intersection in Drachten that the reporter visits. (Paragraph: _____)

_____ 3. There has been an increase in deadly car accidents since Monderman redesigned the roads in Drachten. (Paragraph: _____)

_____ 4. In the "traffic world," drivers do not respond to the design of the roads; they respond to road signs. (Paragraph: _____)

_____ 5. Hamilton-Baille met Monderman because the Dutchman's work was famous in Britain. (Paragraph: _____)

_____ 6. Monderman suggested that the Dutch government create traffic safety officers in response to increasing car accidents. (Paragraph: _____)

_____ 7. Monderman's experiment with psychological traffic calming was unsuccessful. (Paragraph: _____)

_____ 8. Monderman believed that even the worst drivers would respond positively to shared spaces. (Paragraph: _____)

WRITE WHAT YOU THINK

A. Discuss the questions in a group. Look back at your Quick Write on page 139 as you think about what you have learned.

1. Could Monderman's ideas work in your home country or in the place you live now? Why or why not?

2. In some cities, cars are not allowed or are heavily restricted in the downtown area. What do you think about this idea?

3. Who is responsible for making a town or city safe and friendly for all its citizens: urban planners, local authorities, or the citizens themselves?

B. **Before you watch the video, discuss these questions in a group.**

1. Many cities have areas that are not very attractive, such as unused factories or parking lots. What can be done to make them more appealing?

2. Think of a park you know well. How could you redesign it as a third place?

3. Do you think local governments should invest money in public parks, or should donors and businesses pay the costs?

C. **Go online to watch the video about Millennium Park in Chicago. Then check your comprehension.**

> **engage** *(v.)* to succeed in attracting and keeping someone's attention and interest
>
> **eyesore** *(n.)* a building or an object that is unpleasant to look at
>
> **raise the bar** *(phr.)* to set a new, higher standard of quality or performance
>
> **relic** *(n.)* an object, a tradition, or a system, etc. that has survived from the past
>
> **renowned** *(adj.)* famous and respected

VIDEO VOCABULARY

D. **Think about the unit video, Reading 1, and Reading 2 as you discuss these questions. Then choose one question and write a paragraph in response.**

1. Do you believe that the design of public spaces should change to better suit our behavior (as in Reading 1 and the video), or should we change our behavior to meet the expectations of the design (as in Reading 2)?

2. How do you think technology will affect the design of buildings, roads, parks, and cities in the future?

Vocabulary Skill | **Using the dictionary: verb complements**

The main verb controls the pattern of a clause or sentence. Knowing the **verb complements**, or the types of words and phrases allowed with the verb, is important in improving your writing and speaking. For example, some verbs can be followed by a direct object (transitive verbs), but others cannot (intransitive verbs). The dictionary can help you write better sentences by telling you which complements are possible or required with each verb: objects, prepositional phrases, noun clauses, infinitives, or gerunds.

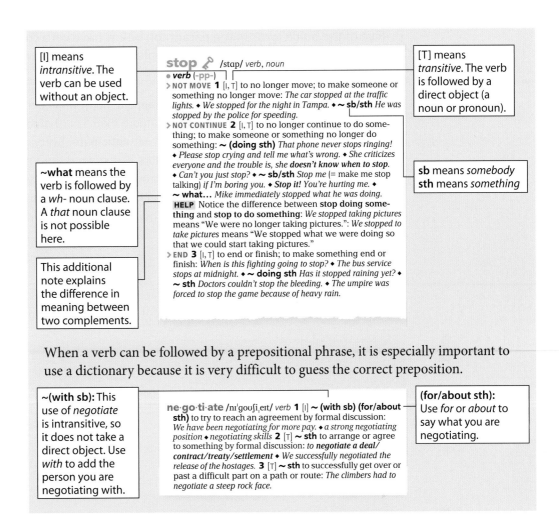

[I] means *intransitive*. The verb can be used without an object.

[T] means *transitive*. The verb is followed by a direct object (a noun or pronoun).

~what means the verb is followed by a *wh-* noun clause. A *that* noun clause is not possible here.

sb means *somebody*
sth means *something*

This additional note explains the difference in meaning between two complements.

stop /stɑp/ *verb, noun*
- **verb** (-pp-)
> **NOT MOVE 1** [I, T] to no longer move; to make someone or something no longer move: *The car stopped at the traffic lights.* ♦ *We stopped for the night in Tampa.* ♦ **~ sb/sth** *He was stopped by the police for speeding.*
> **NOT CONTINUE 2** [I, T] to no longer continue to do something; to make someone or something no longer do something: **~ (doing sth)** *That phone never stops ringing!* ♦ *Please stop crying and tell me what's wrong.* ♦ *She criticizes everyone and the trouble is, she **doesn't know when to stop**.* ♦ *Can't you just stop?* ♦ **~ sb/sth** *Stop me* (= make me stop talking) *if I'm boring you.* ♦ ***Stop it!** You're hurting me.* ♦ **~ what…** *Mike immediately stopped what he was doing.* **HELP** Notice the difference between **stop doing something** and **stop to do something**: *We stopped taking pictures* means "We were no longer taking pictures.": *We stopped to take pictures* means "We stopped what we were doing so that we could start taking pictures."
> **END 3** [I, T] to end or finish; to make something end or finish: *When is this fighting going to stop?* ♦ *The bus service stops at midnight.* ♦ **~ doing sth** *Has it stopped raining yet?* ♦ **~ sth** *Doctors couldn't stop the bleeding.* ♦ *The umpire was forced to stop the game because of heavy rain.*

When a verb can be followed by a prepositional phrase, it is especially important to use a dictionary because it is very difficult to guess the correct preposition.

~(with sb): This use of *negotiate* is intransitive, so it does not take a direct object. Use *with* to add the person you are negotiating with.

ne·go·ti·ate /nɪˈɡoʊʃiˌeɪt/ *verb* **1** [I] **~ (with sb) (for/about sth)** to try to reach an agreement by formal discussion: *We have been negotiating for more pay.* ♦ *a strong negotiating position* ♦ *negotiating skills* **2** [T] **~ sth** to arrange or agree to something by formal discussion: *to negotiate a deal/contract/treaty/settlement* ♦ *We successfully negotiated the release of the hostages.* **3** [T] **~ sth** to successfully get over or past a difficult part on a path or route: *The climbers had to negotiate a steep rock face.*

(for/about sth): Use *for* or *about* to say what you are negotiating.

A. Are the bold verbs transitive or intransitive? Write *T* (transitive) or *I* (intransitive). Check your answers in a learners' dictionary.

____ 1. This is best seen in the building's "student street," which twists and **meanders** through the complex.

____ 2. Architects **are thinking about** light, air, trees, and gardens.

____ 3. Bookshops **are** also **offering** "more coffee and crumbs."

____ 4. He **led** the way to a busy intersection.

____ 5. The drivers **slowed** for him.

____ 6. Mr. Hamilton-Baillie's writings **have helped** bring Mr. Monderman's work to wider attention.

____ 7. It does not change the behavior, for instance, of the 15 percent of drivers who **will behave** badly no matter what the rules are.

____ 8. Mr. Monderman **began** narrowing the roads.

B. Five of the bold words in the paragraph below have verb complement errors. Read the paragraph. Then complete the tasks below.

> The design of my high school did not **appeal** me. It was built to **accommodate** 1,000 students. However, more than 1,500 students **occupied** the building. The designers did not **anticipate**. Every day, we had to **negotiate** with the crowded corridors and staircases to **go** to class. The principal **told** that they could not **improve** the situation. However, he **conceded** that a better system was necessary. Consequently, some staircases were **called** as "up" stairs. When you wanted to go down a level, you **looked** for the "down" stairs.

1. Look up each bold verb from the paragraph in a learner's dictionary. Find the meaning that fits the context. Write the correct complement in the chart.

Verb	Complement	Correct in paragraph? Yes	No
a. appeal	verb + to somebody	☐	☐
b. accommodate		☐	☐
c. occupy		☐	☐
d. anticipate		☐	☐
e. negotiate		☐	☐
f. go		☐	☐
g. tell		☐	☐
h. improve		☐	☐
i. concede		☐	☐
j. call		☐	☐
k. look		☐	☐

2. Is the complement of each verb correct in the paragraph? Check (✓) *Yes* or *No* in the chart.

3. For each complement that is incorrect, write the correct sentence.

 C. Go online for more practice using the dictionary to identify verb complements.

WRITING

UNIT OBJECTIVE At the end of this unit, you will write an essay analyzing a place you know. This essay will include information from the readings, the unit video, and your own ideas.

Grammar | Passive voice to focus information *Part 1*

Forming the passive

In most **active** sentences, the subject of the verb is also the **agent**: that is, it does the action of the verb.

> active sentence
>
> The architect **designed** the new library in a modern style.
>
> subject/agent

In a **passive** sentence, the agent of the verb is not the subject. The passive voice is formed with *be* + the past participle of a transitive verb.

> passive sentence
>
> The new library **was designed** in a modern style (by some architect).
>
> subject   agent

The *by* phrase containing the agent is often omitted in academic writing.

Focusing information

The passive is used when you want to focus on the result or receiver of the action instead of the agent of the action.

> The entire structure **was conceived** with the nomadic lifestyles of modern students and faculty in mind.

The focus is on *The entire structure*, not the architect who conceived it.

The passive also allows writers to report opinions without saying whose they are.

> His work in Friesland . . . **is** increasingly **seen** as the way of the future in Europe.

The focus is on Monderman's work, and the sentence emphasizes his reputation; it is not important who specifically has this opinion.

Active voice is more common than passive voice. The passive should not be used in contexts where active sentences are more direct and easier to understand. However, the passive voice can be useful in academic and other formal writing.

A. Read each sentence. Circle the best sentence to follow it. Then explain your choice to a partner.

1. Monderman distinguished the "social world" of the town from the "traffic world" of the highway.
   a. Engineers design the traffic world for cars.
   b. The traffic world is designed for cars. *(circled)*

   The first sentence ends with "the traffic world," so the traffic world should be the focus of the next sentence. The engineers are not important.

2. Small towns and villages are examples of the social world.
   a. There, we decide how to behave based on politeness and human contact.
   b. There, behavior is determined by politeness and human contact.

3. Many drivers do not notice the schools, shops, and people that they pass.
   a. Road signs distract them from the social world.
   b. They are distracted from the social world by road signs.

4. Thanks to road signs, villages often appear to be part of the traffic world.
   a. Therefore, drivers often speed through them.
   b. Therefore, they are often driven through too fast.

5. Traditional traffic-calming techniques, such as stop signs, are ineffective.
   a. Drivers simply speed up between the stop signs.
   b. Cars are simply driven faster between the stop signs.

Source: Activity text adapted from Vanderbilt, Tom. *Traffic: Why We Drive the Way We Do (and What It Says About Us)* (2008). New York: Knopf, 189–190.

B. Read the paragraph. Complete each sentence with the correct passive or active form of the verb. Use your dictionary if you are not sure whether a verb is intransitive or transitive in this context.

Online social media sites _____ are considered _____ (consider) third
      1

places. According to some experts, these websites _____
                                                           2

(need) because they fit our nomadic lifestyle better than traditional third places.

For example, social media can _____ (access) from
                                        3

any computer or smartphone anywhere in the world. However, some users

_____ (encounter) unexpected problems. One study found
           4

that family time _____ (decrease) because of increased use
                        5

of the Internet. Ironically, we _____ (isolate) by technology
                                          6

that _____ (design) to connect us. Proponents of online
          7

social media _____ (concede) that these sites
8

should be used responsibly. Children's use of such sites, for example, should

_____ (regulate) by their parents.
9

| Grammar | Passive voice to focus information *Part 2* |

Focus information with passive infinitives and passive gerunds

Two other forms of the passive are the *passive infinitive* and the *passive gerund*. These structures, which both require complements, can help make sentences more logical and focused because they avoid introducing a new grammatical subject into the sentence. If you don't know whether a verb takes a gerund or an infinitive complement, look it up in a learner's dictionary. A few verbs allow both types of complement.

> **?** The road **needs** someone to widen it.
> ✓ The road **needs to be widened**.
>
> **?** Customers **like** coffee shop owners treating them as members of a community
> ✓ Customers **like being treated** as members of a community.

Remember that only transitive verbs can be used in the passive voice. Intransitive verbs do not have a passive form. However, many verbs have both transitive and intransitive meanings. (See the Vocabulary Skill on pages 146–147.)

C. Complete each sentence with a passive infinitive or a passive gerund. Use your dictionary if you are not sure which is the correct complement.

1. The architect agreed _____ *to be interviewed* _____ (interview) for this story.

2. The building seems _____ (design) for modern student life.

3. I appreciate _____ (tell) about the problem, and I will try to find a solution.

4. Cyclists keep _____ (hit) by drivers at this intersection.

5. The Internet has started _____ (see) as an obstacle to human interaction.

D. Go online for more practice with the passive voice.

E. Go online for the grammar expansion.

Good paragraphs have unity and are written in a logical order (see the Writing Skills in Units 3 and 4.). They contain clues to help readers follow the main ideas. To achieve this, most clauses and sentences follow a regular pattern of information: old information followed by new information. Often, the new information in one sentence becomes the old information—and, therefore, the beginning—of the next sentence.

The old-new pattern allows writers to connect sentences logically while developing ideas.

old (third place)   new
No sooner was **the term** coined than big business queued up to claim that it was building new third places.

old   new
The most prominent was Starbucks.

old   new
Starbucks admits that as it went global, it lost its ambiance.

This is called **linear information structure** because the logic flows in a straight line. The new information in one sentence becomes the old information in the next. You can use this pattern to create smooth, logical connections between the sentences in your paragraphs.

A. **WRITING MODEL** Read the first two paragraphs in a description of another third place. Then complete the tasks below.

"The Third Place" Coffeehouse

"The Third Place" is the name of a coffeehouse in Raleigh, North Carolina. Raleigh is the home of the state capitol and many businesses. However, many workers have not had options for spending their time in locations other than their first places (homes in the suburbs) and second places (downtown offices). The Third Place is a friendly café that fills this gap.

When you walk into The Third Place, you first see cozy, inviting chairs. Behind them, on the walls, are colorful rugs, suggesting an international theme. Between the rugs, you will see pictures taken by local photographers. The photos are changed monthly and really help to develop a sense of community. This feeling of community is enhanced by the customers, who represent the range of Raleigh's inhabitants. Businesspeople, students, and families can be found at The Third Place on any day of the week.

1. If a sentence contains old information, circle the old information.

2. Connect each circled phrase to the new information in the previous sentence.

3. Discuss with a partner how the last sentence in paragraph 1 is linked to the previous sentence.

4. Underline the three passive verbs in the second paragraph. Explain why the passive voice is used in each case.

Writing Skill | Connecting information *Part 2*

In Activity A, you saw an example of linear information structure, in which the new information in one sentence becomes the old information at the start of the next. An alternative organization is **constant information structure**. In this pattern, the same old information is used at the start of several sentences, and each sentence adds new information on the topic. Use constant information structure to define or explain a complex topic.

The new architecture . . . will make spaces intentionally multifunctional.
Architects are thinking about light, air, trees, and gardens, all in the service of human connections.
Buildings will have much more varied shapes than before.

Synonyms and pronouns help you to avoid repetition and make a smooth flow of information.

B. Read the next paragraph in the description of The Third Place coffeehouse. Then complete the tasks below.

> (1) The menu at The Third Place is varied. (2) It is available from 11 a.m. to 7 p.m. (3) Much of the food is homemade and includes creative sandwiches, delicious soups, and fresh salads. (4) All the meals are vegetarian and use local ingredients. (5) Weekly specials offer something new even to regular customers. (6) And, of course, good coffee is served all day and evening!
> (7) _____ will keep you coming back.

1. Discuss with a partner how the first words in sentences 2–6 are related to *The menu* in sentence 1.

2. With your partner, complete Sentence 7 with the appropriate information.

C. WRITING MODEL Read the model of a student's analysis essay about a third place.

A Third Way for Modern Libraries

1   Because of the recent rapid growth in e-books and e-readers, some have questioned the need for libraries, with their shelves of dusty books and outdated technology. Libraries have responded to the challenges and opportunities of digital reading in many different ways. One solution can be found at my local public library in Kirkwood, which is a good example of a relevant modern library that mostly succeeds in accommodating the needs of both traditional and digital users.

2   The overall design of the Kirkwood Library is fresh and appealing. Large picture windows look out over a children's playground and the woods beyond, giving the building an open and welcoming atmosphere. These windows also reduce the need for artificial lighting, which, in addition to the installation of solar panels and a rooftop garden, make this an environmentally friendly library. No barriers obstruct the entrance to the library from the lobby, and an information desk is positioned close by the entrance, but not so close that it might intimidate first-time visitors. Flat-screen TVs announce library events and community activities, which users can learn more about by scanning special codes on their smartphones or tablets. Most noticeably, visitors are greeted, not by stacks of books, but by a large reading room with comfortable chairs and tables that can be moved together for small-group discussions or separated for more isolated reading and studying.

3   In addition to these design features, the library's resources have also been updated. In fact, Kirkwood could be considered a hybrid library because of its commitment to both digital and print media. The library's e-book collection has been vastly expanded, and digital books can be borrowed in the library or by logging in at home. Databases of newspapers and academic articles are also available. E-readers and other technology can even be borrowed for a week at a time. Proponents of good old-fashioned books should also be satisfied at the library. To make room for the new seating, many of the books have been moved to the basement, but librarians promise to retrieve them in less than an hour. Furthermore, as a good example of Kirkwood's hybrid strategy, books can be requested online or by a smartphone app; the books will then be waiting at the information desk on the patron's arrival at the library.

4   Kirkwood Library meets most of the criteria for a successful modern-day library. It provides easy access to print and digital materials, and its flexible seating makes the space useful for multiple purposes. However, users may encounter two problems. One small difficulty is that the electric outlets in the reading area are all located along the walls, meaning that most users cannot charge their tablets and laptops from their seats. Patrons who are not yet familiar with digital resources may also encounter problems using the new technology, and there is currently little support available for them.

5   Both criticisms can easily be solved. Additional electric outlets can be provided around the building, with the possibility of new high-tech charging mats on the armrests of chairs in the future. Librarians could also do more to anticipate the needs of patrons who are new to digital libraries. They could offer workshops and provide written instructions for using the e-books and databases. With these improvements, Kirkwood is in a strong position to be a sustainable library of the future.

Writing Tip

In Units 3 and 4, you learned about unity and coherence. Notice how paragraphs that use these types of information structure have unity and form a coherent essay.

D. Highlight examples of these writing techniques in the essay.

1. linear information structure
2. constant information structure
3. passive voice to organize information
4. descriptive language
5. evaluative language

E. Answer these questions. Then decide whether the paragraphs below have linear (*L*) or constant (*C*) information structure.

__L__ 1. In paragraph 1, what old information does one solution (in the third sentence) refer to?

_____ 2. In paragraph 2, what do you notice about the subjects of the first five sentences?

_____ 3. In paragraph 3, what is the connection between the second and third sentences?

_____ 4. In paragraph 3, what is the old information in the last sentence?

_____ 5. In paragraph 4, what synonym is used for *problem*?

_____ 6. In paragraph 5, what does the phrase these *improvements* in the last sentence refer to?

 **F.** Go online for more practice connecting information.

Unit Assignment   Write an analysis essay

UNIT OBJECTIVE ▶▶▶▶   In this assignment, you will write an analysis essay about a particular public place and suggest ways to make it more appealing. As you prepare your essay, think about the Unit Question, "What makes a public place appealing?" Use information from Reading 1, Reading 2, the unit video, and your work in this unit to support your ideas. Refer to the Self-Assessment checklist on page 156.

 Go to the Online Writing Tutor for a writing model and alternate Unit Assignments.

PLAN AND WRITE

A. **BRAINSTORM** Choose a public place that you know well. Follow the steps below to brainstorm ideas about the place.

1. List descriptions of the place, its design, the people who use it, and the activities that happen there.

Tip for Success

When comparing and contrasting, it is important to develop strong criteria to support your conclusions.

2. Make a chart to evaluate the place. Write a list of criteria that make a public place appealing in the first column. Explain why your place does or does not meet those criteria in the second column.

Criteria	Evaluation + Reasons
easy to meet with others	yes: well-maintained tables with three or four comfortable chairs

3. Make a list of suggestions for improving the public place based on your negative evaluations. Use ideas from Readings 1 and 2 to help you.

 B. **PLAN** Go to the Online Resources to download and complete the graphic organizer and outline for your analysis essay.

 C. **WRITE** Use your **PLAN** notes to write your essay. Go to *iQ Online* to use the Online Writing Tutor.

1. Write your analysis essay to describe and evaluate a public place. Connect information using clear information structures.

2. Look at the Self-Assessment checklist to guide your writing.

REVISE AND EDIT

 A. **PEER REVIEW** Read your partner's essay. Then go online and use the Peer Review worksheet. Discuss the review with your partner.

B. **REWRITE** Based on your partner's review, revise and rewrite your essay.

C. **EDIT** Complete the Self-Assessment checklist as you prepare to write the final draft of your essay. Be prepared to hand in your work or discuss it in class.

SELF-ASSESSMENT		
Yes	**No**	
☐	☐	Did you use linear and/or constant information structure clearly?
☐	☐	Is your evaluation criteria clear?
☐	☐	Is the passive voice used appropriately?
☐	☐	Did you use the correct verb complements?
☐	☐	Does the essay include vocabulary from the unit?
☐	☐	Did you check the essay for punctuation, spelling, and grammar?

D. **REFLECT** Go to the Online Discussion Board to discuss these questions.

1. What is something new you learned in this unit?

2. Look back at the Unit Question—What makes a public place appealing? Is your answer different now than when you started the unit? If yes, how is it different? Why?

TRACK YOUR SUCCESS

Circle the words and phrases you have learned in this unit.

Nouns	**Adjectives**	**Adverb**
controversy AWL	appealing 🔑	intentionally
criteria 🔑 AWL	counterintuitive	**Phrasal Verb**
division 🔑	fatal	pop up
proponent	hybrid	**Phrases**
Verbs	isolated AWL	in decline
accommodate AWL	neutral AWL	form bonds
anticipate 🔑 AWL	nomadic	
concede	regulated AWL	
encounter 🔑 AWL	specialized	
mingle		
negotiate		
reinforce AWL		

🔑 Oxford 3000™ words

AWL Academic Word List

Check (✓) the skills you learned. If you need more work on a skill, refer to the page(s) in parentheses.

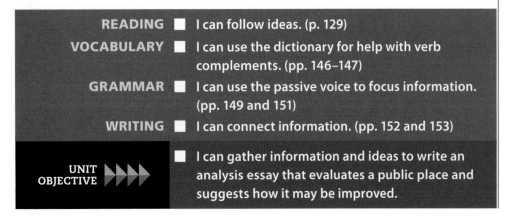

READING	☐ I can follow ideas. (p. 129)
VOCABULARY	☐ I can use the dictionary for help with verb complements. (pp. 146–147)
GRAMMAR	☐ I can use the passive voice to focus information. (pp. 149 and 151)
WRITING	☐ I can connect information. (pp. 152 and 153)
UNIT OBJECTIVE ▶▶▶▶	☐ I can gather information and ideas to write an analysis essay that evaluates a public place and suggests how it may be improved.

READING ▶ anticipating content through questions
VOCABULARY ▶ suffixes
WRITING ▶ paraphrasing
GRAMMAR ▶ modals of possibility

UNIT QUESTION

How can we turn trash into treasure?

A Discuss these questions with your classmates.

1. What do you do with things you no longer use? What do you throw away? What do you recycle?

2. Do you think society is wasteful? How could people decrease the amount of garbage they throw away?

3. Look at the photo. What materials were used to make this house? Would you live in this house? Is this a good way to use our trash?

B Listen to *The Q Classroom* online. Then answer these questions.

1. Why does Marcus think we should turn trash into treasure? Do you agree or disagree? Why?

2. How do Yuna, Felix, and Sophy answer the Unit Question? Whose ideas do you agree with the most? Why?

 C Go to the Online Discussion board to discuss the Unit Question with your classmates.

D Take the quiz on waste disposal. Write the letter of each definition next to the correct location. Then write two examples of things that can go in each location.

WHERE DO THINGS GO WHEN YOU DON'T WANT THEM ANYMORE?

a. a place for decaying organic waste that can eventually be mixed with soil to grow plants

b. a place where waste is sorted before it is used to make new products

c. a container or machine for burning garbage

d. a place where large amounts of garbage are put into the ground and covered with earth

LOCATION	DEFINITION	THINGS THAT CAN GO HERE
1. landfill		
2. incinerator		
3. composter		
4. recycling depot		

E What is the alternative to throwing away your garbage? Think about the five items in the chart below. What else could you do with them? Write your ideas.

Garbage	What else can you do with these items?
old cell phones	
plastic drink bottles	
old laptops	
old TVs	
bicycle wheels	

READING

READING 1 | Garbage of Eden

You are going to read an article from *New Scientist* magazine that examines the unique way that Singapore is dealing with its garbage. Use the article to gather information and ideas for your Unit Assignment.

Reading Skill | **Anticipating content through questions**

Being an active reader is the key to becoming a better reader. One way to be an active reader is to think about the topic of a text and form questions before you begin reading. Base your questions on the information or content you think will be in the reading. Use question words (*who, what, where, when, why,* and *how*). Then, while you read, keep your questions in mind and look for the answers.

For example, this title, subtitle, and photo are from a newspaper article.

Stop! I'm Full

No more room in local landfill; it will close at the end of this year.

These are possible questions to ask before reading the article:

⌐ **Who** is in charge of this landfill?
  What kinds of garbage are in this landfill?
⌊ **Where** is this landfill?

A. Read the title and subtitle of Reading 1 on page 163. Also look at the photos and landfill plan that accompany the article. Use the *wh*-word question chart to write six questions that you think the reading should answer.

Question	Answer
Who	
What	
Where	
When	
Why	
How	

B. As you read the article "Garbage of Eden," look for the answers to your questions. Annotate your text to remind you where you found the answers. Do not complete the chart yet.

 C. Go online for more practice anticipating content through questions.

PREVIEW THE READING

A. **PREVIEW** What are three possible ways Singapore could get rid of its waste in an environmentally friendly way? As you read, check to see if your ideas are similar to the ideas presented in the article.

1. _____

2. _____

3. _____

Writing

Using transitions between ideas can improve the smooth flow of information in your writing. Think of appropriate transitions to insert between your ideas.

B. **QUICK WRITE** How can a landfill site become a place of natural beauty? Write for 5–10 minutes in response. Remember to use this section for your Unit Assignment.

C. **VOCABULARY** Read aloud these words from Reading 1. Check (✓) the ones you know. Use a dictionary to define any new or unknown words. Then discuss with a partner how the words will relate to the unit.

abundant *(adj.)*	constraint *(n.)*	dubious *(adj.)*	obsolete *(adj.)*
anticipate *(v.)* 🔑	contaminated *(adj.)*	elimination *(n.)*	sustainable *(adj.)*
conservation *(n.)*	disposal *(n.)*	incinerate *(v.)*	thrive *(v.)*

🔑 Oxford 3000™ words

iQ ONLINE **D.** Go online to listen and practice your pronunciation.

WORK WITH THE READING

A. Read the article and gather information on how we can turn trash into treasure.

Garbage of Eden

Want to be at one with nature? Take a stroll around Singapore's island of trash.
By Eric Bland

ecotourists on Pulau Semakau

1   SINGAPORE'S only landfill is a 20-minute ferry ride south from the main island. On Pulau Semakau, coconut trees and banyan bushes line an asphalt road. Wide-bladed grass, short and soft, forms a threadbare[1] carpet. The only visible trash is a bit of driftwood on the rocky shore, marking high tide in an artificial bay. Water rushes out of the bay through a small opening, making waves in the Singapore Strait. The smell of rain is in the air.

---

[1] **threadbare:** thin layer

2   You would never know that all the trash from Singapore's 4.4 million residents is being dumped here 24 hours a day, seven days a week—as it will be for the next 40 years. This is no ordinary landfill: the island doubles as a biodiversity hotspot, of all things, attracting rare species of plants and animals. It even attracts ecotourists on specially arranged guided tours. Eight years in the making, the artificial island is setting an example for the future of **conservation** and urban planning.

3   Pulau Semakau, which is Malay for Mangrove[2] Island, is not the first isle of trash to rise from the sea. That **dubious** honor goes to a dump belonging to another island nation, the Maldives, off the southern coast of India. In 1992, the Maldives began dumping its trash wholesale into a lagoon on one of its small islands. As the island grew, it was named Thilafushi; its industries include a concrete manufacturing plant, a shipyard, and a methane bottler.

4   What distinguishes Semakau from Thilafushi—and most any other landfill—is that its trash has been **incinerated** and sealed off from its surroundings. Singapore burns more than 90 percent of its garbage, for reasons of space. Since its independence from Malaysia in 1965, Singapore has grown to become one of the world's 50 wealthiest nations. Not bad for a city-state little more than one-quarter the size of the smallest US state, Rhode Island. Its rapid rise, however, created a huge waste problem. In the early 1990s, the government began to heavily promote a national recycling program and to campaign for industry and residents to produce less waste.

From trash to ash

5   Since 1999, garbage **disposal** companies have been recycling what they can—glass, plastic, electronics, even concrete—and incinerating the rest. The Tuas South incineration plant[3], the largest and newest of four plants run by the Singapore government, is tucked away in the southwest part of the main island. A recent visit by *New Scientist* found it surprisingly clean and fresh. The incinerator creates a weak vacuum that sucks the foul air from the trash-receiving room into the combustion[4] chamber.

6   Not that incineration is problem-free. When Singapore began burning garbage, its carbon emissions into the atmosphere rose sharply while its solid carbon deposits dropped, according to data gathered by the Oak Ridge National Laboratory in Tennessee. During the last couple of years, however, its emissions have stabilized. "Our recycling program has been more effective than we **anticipated**," says Poh Soon Hoong, general manager of the Tuas South plant.

7   Once they started burning trash, the big question was where to put the ash. In 1998, the government built a seven-kilometer-long rock bund[5] to connect two offshore islands, Semakau and Sekang, and named the new island Pulau Semakau. The complex cost about 610 million Singapore dollars (US $400 million). The first trash was dumped there in April 1999, the day after the last landfill on the main island closed. "We weren't trying to design an island that would attract tourists," says Semakau's manager, Loo Eng Por. "Disposing of the waste was a matter of survival."

---

[2] **mangrove:** a tropical tree that grows in mud or at the edge of rivers

[3] **plant:** a factory
[4] **combustion:** the process of burning
[5] **bund:** embankment or wall

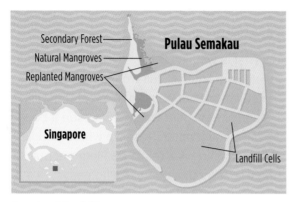

Semakau Island Plan

Labels: Secondary Forest, Natural Mangroves, Replanted Mangroves, Pulau Semakau, Singapore, Landfill Cells

8   How they do that is key to the island's success. At the receiving station, cranes[6] unload the ash from barges[7] into dumptrucks, which drive out to one of 11 interconnected bays, called cells, where they dump their debris (see Plan). The seawater is first pumped out of a cell, which is then lined with a layer of thick plastic to seal in the trash and prevent any leakage. Materials that can't be burned or recycled, such as asbestos, are wrapped in plastic and buried with dirt. Each month, samples are tested from the water surrounding a working cell, and so far there is no sign of any **contaminated** water seeping into the ocean. Four of the 11 cells have been filled to about two meters above sea level, then topped off with dirt and seeded with grass. A few trees dot the landscape. "Gifts from the birds," says Loo. "We plant the grass, but not the trees." Once all the cells are filled, which will be in 2030 or so, workers will start over again, dumping burnt trash onto the plots and covering it with earth, gradually forming taller hills. The government predicts that by 2045 its recycling and waste **elimination** programs will make its landfills **obsolete**.

9   One complaint about Pulau Semakau was that it called for the destruction of mangroves on part of the original island. Singapore's National Environmental Agency saw to it that the mangroves were replanted in areas adjoining the landfill. "We expected some of the new mangroves to die off," says Poh. "But they all survived. Now we have to trim them back." The island now has more than 13 hectares[8] of mangroves, which serve as a habitat for numerous species.

10   "Pulau Semakau is quite a success," says Wang Luan Keng of the Raffles Museum of Biodiversity Research at the National University of Singapore, and by all accounts the ecosystem is **thriving**—so much so that since July 2005, the island has been open for guided tours. "Visitors are stunned and amazed to see the rich biodiversity," says Ria Tan, an expert in ecology who runs wildsingapore.com, a website on nature-related activities in the area. At low tide, nature groups walk the intertidal zone, where they can see starfish, snails, and flatworms. Coral reefs are **abundant** off the western shore, and dolphins, otters, and green turtles have been spotted. Fishing groups come to catch and release grouper, barracuda, and queenfish. Birdwatchers look for the island's most famous resident, a great billed heron named Jimmy, as well as brahminy kites and mangrove whistlers[9]. In 2006, the island logged more than 6,000 visitors, and that number is expected to rise.

---

[6] **crane:** a tall machine with long arms, used to lift and move heavy objects

[7] **barge:** a large boat with a flat bottom, used to carry goods

[8] **hectare:** a measurement equal to 10,000 square meters; 2,471 acres

[9] **heron, kite, and whistler:** types of birds that live near water

11   The island is crucial to Singapore's future. "People may say the Semakau landfill is bad," Tan says. "What is the alternative? Toss it to some other country? Kill off some other habitat on the mainland? The garbage has to go somewhere. I see the Semakau landfill as an example of one aspect of successful, **sustainable** urbanization." Tan shares the concerns of city planners. "The resource **constraints** that Singapore faces today will be those the rest of the world will face eventually," she says.

12   That is why the rest of the world should be watching: time will tell whether Semakau is a useful model for conservation. Meanwhile, the island's managers would like to see it become a permanent nature reserve where people can come to hike, relax, and learn about nature, without a guide. As Loo says, "It's a great place to get away from the boss."

Vocabulary Skill Review

In Unit 5, you learned about verb complements and identifying whether or not verbs can be followed by a direct object. Consider the new verbs introduced in this unit and use a dictionary to confirm which complements are possible or required with each verb.

B. VOCABULARY **Here are some words from Reading 1. Read the sentences. Then match each bold word with its definition.**

_____ 1. Many people are interested in the **conservation** of Earth's resources so that future generations will benefit from them.

_____ 2. Some countries **incinerate** their garbage before it is put into a landfill. However, this often contributes to pollution in the atmosphere.

_____ 3. The safe **disposal** of garbage is very important in order to protect the environment.

_____ 4. The government **anticipates** that local landfills will become full in the next five years.

a. (*v.*) to expect and prepare for the fact

b. (*v.*) to burn

c. (*n.*) the protection of the natural world

d. (*n.*) the process of throwing away and removing

_____ 5. The local water supply became **contaminated** because someone dumped toxic waste into the river.

_____ 6. The **elimination** of recyclable materials from people's garbage reduces the amount of trash that goes to landfills.

_____ 7. Environmental activists hope that one day everything will be recycled and landfills will become **obsolete**.

_____ 8. The Maldives has the **dubious** honor of having the first island of trash to rise from the sea.

166   UNIT 6 │ How can we turn trash into treasure?

e. (*adj.*) dirty and unsafe

f. (*adj.*) no longer used because they are out of date

g. (*adj.*) that you cannot be sure about; that is probably not good

h. (*n.*) the process of taking away

___ 9. Although there are only a few trees on the island, they can **thrive** because they have enough sunshine and fresh water.

___ 10. Fish are **abundant** in this lake. They are everywhere you look!

___ 11. Many countries want long-term, **sustainable** economic growth that preserves their resources.

___ 12. Putting **constraints** on the amount of garbage we can throw away stops us from making more trash than the environment can handle.

i. (*adj.*) plentiful and existing in large numbers

j. (*n.*) a limit

k. (*adj.*) continued and environmentally friendly

l. (*v.*) to grow and develop well

iQ ONLINE **C.** Go online for more practice with the vocabulary.

D. Look at the questions you wrote in the Reading Skill activity on page 162. Complete the chart with the answers you were able to find in the reading.

E. Write short answers to these questions. Then tell a partner or group which of your questions from the chart on page 162 helped you.

1. What kind of landfill does Singapore have?

   _____

2. What does Singapore do with its trash?

   _____

3. How is trash disposed of in Singapore's landfill?

   _____

4. What is the state of the environment on and around the island?

   _____

5. What can the rest of the world learn from the Semakau landfill?

   _____

F. Read the statements. Write *T* (true) or *F* (false). Then correct each false statement to make it true.

_____ 1. The landfill is located 20 minutes by car from the main island.

_____ 2. The landfill took eight years to make.

_____ 3. Singapore incinerates less than 20 percent of its garbage.

_____ 4. Garbage disposal companies incinerate glass, plastic, electronics, and concrete.

_____ 5. Singapore has four incineration plants.

_____ 6. The rock wall that created the artificial island is 17 kilometers long.

_____ 7. The landfill is made up of 11 cells, which are being filled with waste.

_____ 8. Four of the eleven cells have been filled to about two meters above sea level.

_____ 9. The Government of Singapore plants trees on each filled cell.

_____ 10. Singapore's National Environmental Agency destroyed all of the mangroves on the original island.

G. Write the number of each true and corrected statement from Activity F next to the main idea it supports.

Main ideas of Reading 1	Supporting details
1. Singapore has an environmentally friendly and unique landfill.	
2. Singapore is able to reduce a large amount of the waste going into its landfill.	
3. Singapore has carefully planned the building of its island landfill.	
4. Singapore has done a lot to maintain the natural environment on and around its landfill.	

H. Based on the information in Reading 1, number the following events in the most logical order for creating an island out of trash. Compare your order with a partner and explain why you think your order is the most correct.

___ a.   Full landfill cells are covered with dirt and planted with grass seeds.

___ b.   Interconnected empty landfill cells are built.

___ c.   Landfill cells are full once they reach about two meters above sea level.

___ d.   Ash and debris arrive on barges and are loaded onto dump trucks by cranes.

___ e.   Once the cells are filled, workers start again by adding waste to make taller hills.

___ f.   A thick plastic liner is inserted in each empty landfill cell.

___ g.   Trucks drive to a working landfill cell to dump their loads of incinerated trash.

___ h.   Trash is burned in an incineration plant and taken to the island.

___ i.   Monthly seawater samples are taken near working cells to check for contamination.

___ j.   Seawater is pumped out of a landfill cell.

I. Go online to read the magazine article *From Fast Food to Fast Cars* and check your comprehension.

WRITE WHAT YOU THINK

A. Discuss these questions in a group.

1. How did Singapore turn its trash into treasure? Is this project worth 610 million Singapore dollars (about $400 million US dollars)? Why or why not?

2. Would Singapore's solution to its garbage problem work in other countries? Why or why not?

B. Choose one question and write a paragraph in response. Look back at your Quick Write on page 163 as you think about what you learned.

Pulau Semakau: no ordinary landfill

READING 2 | The Glorious Feeling of Fixing Something Yourself

You are going to read an article from the news magazine *The Atlantic* about repairing broken things so that they can be used again. Use the article to gather information and ideas for your Unit Assignment.

PREVIEW THE READING

A. PREVIEW Look ahead at the pictures accompanying Reading 2. Then write three or four questions that might be answered by this article.

B. QUICK WRITE Can old or broken items be repaired so that they can be used again? Write for 5–10 minutes in response. Remember to use this section for your Unit Assignment.

C. VOCABULARY Work with a partner to find these words in the reading. Circle clues in the text that help you understand the meaning of each word. Then use a dictionary to define any unknown words.

adjust (v.) 🔑	concept (n.) 🔑	craftsmanship (n.)	participant (n.)
appliance (n.)	consequence (n.) 🔑	device (n.) 🔑	permeate (v.)
aptitude (n.)	convene (v.)	founder (n.)	tinker (v.)

🔑 Oxford 3000™ words

 D. Go online to listen and practice your pronunciation.

WORK WITH THE READING

》 **A. Read the article and gather information on how we can turn trash into treasure.**

The Glorious Feeling of Fixing Something Yourself

When I mended my lamp at one of Portland's repair cafes, it was no longer "just" a lamp to me; I felt a fierce sense of attachment to it.

By Christina Cooke

Repair PDX volunteer Bryce Jacobson tries to twist the knob to my broken floor lamp.

1 Along with his broken toaster, Steve Vegdahl brought a slice of bread with him to Portland's repair cafe one day last month. By the time he left, his toaster was working again—and the sweet smell of toasted wheat **permeated** the room.

2 "This is the highlight of my day," Vegdahl said as he waited for the chrome Sunbeam, probably a 1950s model, to cool off so he could take it home. "I'm a software person; I don't have a lot of mechanical **aptitude**. I'm not good at taking things apart."

3 Since a woman named Martine Postma established the first repair cafe in Amsterdam in 2009, the **concept** of free events at which volunteers with repair skills assist **participants** with broken furniture, **appliances**, bicycles, clothing, and toys has spread far and wide.

4 More than 50 cafes operate throughout the Netherlands, France, Germany, and the United Kingdom, and, in the US, people have begun **convening** regularly at coffee shops and event spaces in New York, Chicago, Palo Alto, Los Angeles, Seattle, and—as of earlier this year—my hometown of Portland, Oregon, to fix busted items.

5 Repair PDX **founder** Lauren Gross, 33, says the Portland events attract people philosophically opposed to waste as well as those who simply want a favorite item to work again. Around 50 people attended the first gathering, held last May in a large, airy coffee shop, she said, and about 35 have shown up to the monthly gatherings since.

6 "We're going back to some of the old values our grandparents held and moving away from mainstream consumption," said Cindy Correll, one of the cafe's other organizers. "By reusing, we're keeping things out of the waste stream and eliminating the need to make another product." Plus, she said, reusing requires fewer resources than its more publicized counterpart recycling.

7 Correll attributes the success of fix-it ventures like Repair PDX in part to the recent economic downturn. When money was tight, she said, "people started looking at things differently."

8 When I carried my broken floor lamp into Portland's December gathering, held in a historic firehouse on the north side of town, numerous repairs were already underway.

9 At one table, Stan Jones shaved rotten foam from around a stereo speaker with a thin blade, preparing the surface for a new foam cover. At

another, Brett Stern tackled an electric stand mixer, eventually offering to take the contraption home for further inspection. Laurie Sugahbeare fixed a necklace a woman had snagged on her sweater earlier that day.

10 And Bryce Jacobson wrapped plumber tape around the center rod of a broken coffee grinder to compensate for the stripped threads. "We're just buying a little time from the landfill," he said, acknowledging the jankiness[1] of the solution.

11 Jacobson, who works as a regional solid waste planner by day, said he's always liked to **tinker**. Even as a kid, he would take home appliances he found in dumpsters, and he'd disassemble and rebuild them. As a Repair PDX volunteer, Jacobson wants to instill a repair ethic in participants—and teach them the practical skills to back up the ideal.

"I just have to admire the fixing of something—I love it!" says a woman looking on as Repair PDX volunteers Bryce Jacobson (left) and Randy Greb (right) tackle a broken coffee grinder.

12 "One of the most powerful things to realize is that you can actually fix your stuff when it's not working," he said. "I like seeing people make that connection."

13 Despite recent efforts by people like Repair PDX volunteers, repair culture stands counter to the dominant[2], disposable mentality. While products like disposable diapers and paper plates are unabashedly[3] designed for the dump, many other objects—radios, televisions, microwaves, etc.— are made to be tossed as well (though they're slightly less blatant[4] about it).

14 Last month when my washing machine began skipping the spin cycle, for example, my landlord's first response was to have a brand-new machine delivered to the house. Replacing the washer, he reasoned, would be cheaper and easier than diagnosing the problem, finding new parts, and paying a handyman to install them.

15 While I saw his point, I also regretted that the entire appliance would rust away in the landfill when probably just a small component had malfunctioned.

16 Though they're a determined bunch, Portland's fix-it volunteers say they often encounter objects that are not only impractical to repair, but impossible too.

17 "An old appliance makes it easy, because you can unscrew the bolts and take it apart," said volunteer Randy Greb, the man who revived[5] Vegdahl's toaster. "Newer stuff, you can sometimes get it apart, but it's often hard to get back together."

18 Across the board, tinkering is a challenge these days. Unlike the radios of generations past, it's hard to get inside an iPod, and once you do, you face a battery and computer chip rather than moveable components that can be tweaked and **adjusted**.

19 Even the businesses that supply the repair industry have become increasingly scarce: in an attempt to boost plunging profits, RadioShack switched in 2009 from selling cables, connectors, and widgets for garage and basement hobbyists to selling smartphones and other wireless **devices**.

20 The societal shift toward products that are untouchable, robotic, and useless when single parts break has given rise to a number of unfortunate **consequences**. First off, our landfills have swollen: The average American throws away 4.4 pounds of trash per day, compared

---

[1] **jankiness:** a slang word for a temporary solution that is not perfect
[2] **dominant:** more noticeable or common
[3] **unabashedly:** without being ashamed or worried about what people might think
[4] **blatant:** done in an obvious and open way
[5] **revive:** to make something start being used again

to 2.68 pounds in 1960, according to the US Environmental Protection Agency.

21   Additionally, we've been forced into shallow relationships with our material possessions and have become increasingly dependent on manufacturers. And finally, overall **craftsmanship** has declined, and we possess fewer objects worth taking pride in and passing to the next generation. (No one's going to inherit my $32 athletic watch.)

22   Back on the Repair PDX floor, I set my damaged lamp beside Jacobson's table and explained the problem: The on/off knob had become too stiff to turn, and though I'd been able to control the light by screwing and unscrewing the bulb, that strategy had stopped working as well.

23   Jacobson removed the shade, disconnected the socket, and tried cleaning the device with a solvent. When the knob still did not rotate easily, he advised me to install a new electrical connector and showed me how I'd fasten the lamp's wires to the new piece once I'd obtained it.

24   The next day, I visited the hardware store up the road: four dollars and a few at-home adjustments later, the bulb lit up. I felt a surge of pride—and a sudden, fierce attachment to the lamp.

25   While repairing rather than replacing may have become a rebellious action over the last few decades, Jacobson sees room for the concept to grow. From coffee grinders to speakers to lawnmowers to furniture, Repair PDX alone has endowed[6] a multitude of objects with new life.

26   "It might be a fringe activity, but so was stuff like Craigslist[7] at first," he said. "It's got to start with the curious ones, the people willing to take a risk."

---

[6] **endow:** to give something

[7] **Craigslist:** a popular classified advertisements Web site

B. VOCABULARY Here are some words from Reading 2. Complete each sentence with a vocabulary word from the box. You may need to change the form of the word to make the sentence grammatically correct.

adjust (v.) 🔑	concept (n.) 🔑	craftsmanship (n.)	participant (n.)
appliance (n.)	consequence (n.) 🔑	device (n.) 🔑	permeate (v.)
aptitude (n.)	convene (v.)	founder (n.)	tinker (v.)

1. After the coffeemaker was fixed, the smell of freshly brewed coffee

    _____ the room.

2. Although many people may think they don't have a(n) _____

    for fixing broken items, with a little help and patience, they can learn to repair

    many different kinds of things.

3. The repair cafe is a new _____ that is helping people learn

    how to fix old and broken items in a social atmosphere.

4. There were over 50 _____ at the repair cafe event last Saturday, and most of them were able to fix the items they brought along.

5. Instead of throwing them away when they are broken, _____ like toasters, coffeemakers, blenders, and electric kettles can easily be fixed and used again.

6. The university recycling club _____ every week in the student union building.

7. The _____ of the repair club started the organization about three years ago.

8. Many people enjoy _____ with broken appliances because fixing them results in a great sense of satisfaction.

9. The toast was popping out of the toaster too quickly. It was fixed by _____ the timer so that the bread stayed in the toaster for a longer period of time.

10. Many electronic _____, such as smartphones and tablets, are difficult for the average person to repair because they have so many complicated parts.

11. Fixing items instead of throwing them away can lead to a lot of positive _____, such as saving money and helping the environment.

12. Because of the high-quality _____, my father's wristwatch will last for many years.

iQ ONLINE   **C.** Go online for more practice with the vocabulary.

D. Match each subheading with the paragraphs it best describes.

Paragraphs	Subheadings
____ **1.** Paragraphs 1–2	**a.** Values of Repairing and Saving
____ **2.** Paragraphs 3–4	**b.** Serious Consequences of Modern Products
____ **3.** Paragraphs 5–7	**c.** Repair Cafes around the World
____ **4.** Paragraphs 8–9	**d.** Opposition to a Disposable Society
____ **5.** Paragraphs 10–12	**e.** Predict Future Growth
____ **6.** Paragraphs 13–15	**f.** Power of Tinkering
____ **7.** Paragraphs 16–19	**g.** Toaster Success
____ **8.** Paragraphs 20–21	**h.** Some Stuff Too Hard to Fix
____ **9.** Paragraphs 22–24	**i.** Old Lamp Fixed
____ **10.** Paragraphs 25–26	**j.** Variety of Items Being Repaired

E. Circle the answer that best completes each statement.

1. Steve Vegdahl brought a slice of bread with him to Portland's repair cafe because ____.
   a. he wanted to test his toaster after it was repaired to make sure it worked
   b. he wanted to make the entire room smell like toast
   c. he wanted to give the Repair PDX volunteer something to eat
   d. he wanted to highlight how delicious toast could be

2. More than ____ repair cafes can be found in the Netherlands, France, Germany, and the United Kingdom.
   a. 50   b. 33   c. 35   d. 20

3. Every month, about ____ people come to the repair events in Portland.
   a. 33   b. 35   c. 50   d. 20

4. Stan Jones, Brett Stern, and Laurie Sugahbeare were fixing a ____.
   a. toaster, coffee grinder, and a necklace
   b. stereo speaker, toaster, and a lamp
   c. stereo speaker, electric stand mixer, and a necklace
   d. coffee grinder, lamp, and an athletic watch

5. Bryce Jacobson is a ___.
   a. software person
   c. founder
   b. reporter
   d. volunteer

6. In 2009, RadioShack stopped selling ___.
   a. smartphones and other wireless devices
   b. lamps and stereo equipment
   c. cables, connectors, and widgets
   d. toasters and coffee grinders

7. People in the United States today throw away ___ trash per day than people in the 1960s.
   a. 1.72 pounds more
   c. 2.68 pounds more
   b. 6.4 pounds less
   d. 4.4 pounds less

8. Christina Cooke's athletic watch is an example of ___.
   a. an object worth taking pride in
   c. something inexpensive
   b. something she inherited
   d. high-quality craftsmanship

F. Match each of the following people with the statement that best describes them. There are two extra statements that are not needed.

People:

___ 1. Steve Vegdahl

___ 2. Martine Postma

___ 3. Lauren Gross

___ 4. Cindy Correll

___ 5. Stan Jones

___ 6. Bryce Jacobson

___ 7. Randy Greb

___ 8. Christina Cooke

Statements:

a. A person fixing a necklace

b. A person fixing an old coffee grinder with plumber tape

c. The owner of a toaster that was repaired at Repair PDX

d. A person who fixed a broken lamp by following the advice of a Repair PDX volunteer

e. A person who said that older items are easier to repair

f. The person who started the first repair cafe in Amsterdam

g. A person fixing a stereo speaker

h. The founder of the repair cafe in Portland

i. A repair cafe organizer who feels people are returning to the values of their grandparents

j. A person trying to fix an electric stand mixer

G. Based on Reading 2, what answers can you infer to the following questions?

1. Why was getting his broken toaster repaired the highlight of Steve Vegdahl's day?

2. Why have repair cafes become so popular around the world?

3. How would you describe the "old values our grandparents held" that Cindy Correll talks about?

4. Why would an economic downturn contribute to the success of repair cafes?

5. Why does Jacobson want to instill a repair ethic in people?

6. Why are products such as radios, televisions, and microwaves designed to be thrown away?

7. Why did the author's landlord want to replace the broken washer instead of fixing it?

8. Why did RadioShack switch from selling cables, connectors, and widgets to smartphones and other wireless devices?

9. Why isn't anyone going to inherit the author's athletic watch?

10. Why did the author feel such a sense of pride and fierce attachment to her lamp?

WRITE WHAT YOU THINK

A. Discuss these questions in a group. Look back at your Quick Write on page 170 as you think about what you have learned.

1. Which item fixed at the repair cafe do you think was the most valuable? Is this an item that you would fix if it ever became broken?

2. Why do you think Martine Postma started the first repair cafe?

3. Do you think that repair cafes will still be around in 10 years? Why or why not?

B. Before you watch the video, discuss these questions in a group.

1. Why could it be a good business idea to recycle garbage into organic fertilizer using worms?

2. How important is it to totally commit to a business idea and to put all of your time and energy into it?

C. Go online to watch the video about how the company TerraCycle creates its fertilizer. Then check your comprehension.

buzzword *(n.)* a popular technical term that is connected to a specific topic or subject

contraption *(n.)* a machine or piece of equipment that looks strange

gold mine *(n.)* a business or activity that makes a large profit

trade secret *(n.)* a secret piece of information that is known only by the people at a particular company

Writing **Tip**

In Unit 5, you learned about connecting information. Use linear information structure or constant information structure in your response to Activity D.

D. Think about the unit video, Reading 1, and Reading 2 as you discuss these questions. Then choose one question and write a paragraph in response.

1. Two different methods of turning trash into treasure were presented by the readings in this unit: (1) incinerating waste and creating an artificial island and (2) fixing broken items so they can be used again. What are some positive and negative aspects of each of these solutions?

2. Do you think governments or regular people are more effective at disposing of trash or finding ways to turn it into treasure? Why?

Vocabulary Skill | Suffixes

A **suffix** is an ending that is added to a root word. There are several **suffixes that form nouns**. Some of them indicate people or concrete objects or things, and others indicate more abstract nouns. The *Oxford Advanced American Dictionary for learners of English* has a list of suffixes with their meanings and uses. Understanding the meaning of suffixes will help you build your vocabulary by giving you clues to the meaning and function of new words.

Noun suffixes	Suffix meaning	Examples
-ation, -tion	an action or process, or the result of it	conservation, production
-er / -or	a person or thing that	manufacturer, editor
-ist	a person who does or believes in something	ecotourist
-ty, -ity	the quality or state of	biodiversity, clarity
-ment	the action or result of	agreement

A. Complete the chart with the correct form of each noun by using the most appropriate suffix from the skill box. Use your dictionary to help you.

Verb	Not a person / abstract idea	Person or thing
1. incinerate	incineration	incinerator
2. present		
3. fertilize		
4. invest		
5. invent		

B. Read the paragraph. Write the correct noun form of each word to complete the sentence.

Waste disposal is a big issue all around the world. Many countries have created new _____regulations_____ (regulate) about recycling that encourage
    1
_____ (retail) and _____ (manufacture)
        2   3
to recycle their waste. This recycling keeps waste materials from being burned in _____ (incinerate) or dumped into landfills. The
                    4
_____ (eliminate) of a large amount of garbage helps to
        5
protect the environment and the _____ (pure) of nearby lakes
                                    6
and rivers. Many of these retail and manufacturing companies have now started working with people such as _____ (environmental)
                                    7
to think of more ways to lower the amount of waste they produce. Also,
_____ (invest) are putting their money into recycling
        8
companies. With the increase in environmental awareness around the world,
their _____ (invest) are starting to make a profit. As greater
        9
numbers of _____ (corporate) become aware of the importance
            10
of recycling, recycling programs are sure to become more popular.

C. Go online for more practice with suffixes.

WRITING

UNIT OBJECTIVE ▶▶▶ At the end of this unit, you will write a business plan. This business plan will include information from the readings, the unit video, and your own ideas.

Writing Skill   Paraphrasing

Paraphrasing means putting someone else's words into your own words. A good paraphrase keeps the same meaning and is about the same length as the original text. Paraphrasing is a useful skill for both studying and integrating other people's ideas into your writing. However, it is important to cite the sources for other people's ideas that you use in your writing, even when you are paraphrasing.

Here are some tips for effective paraphrasing.

- Read over the text you want to paraphrase several times in order to completely understand it.
- Take notes in your own words.
- Find good synonyms for some of the key vocabulary in the text.

> **Around** 50 people **attended** the first **gathering**.
> **Approximately** 50 people **went to** the first **meeting**.

- Write the paraphrase using your own notes without looking at the original.
- Change the grammatical structure of your paraphrase by:

Changing the order of the clauses

> **Since its independence from Malaysia**, Singapore has become wealthy.
> Singapore has become wealthy **since its independence from Malaysia**.

Changing to active or passive voice

> Martine Postma **established** the first repair cafe in Amsterdam in 2009.
> The first repair cafe **was established** by Martine Postma in 2009.

Changing the word forms

> Pulau Semakau is quite a **success**.   Pulau Semakau is quite **successful**.

Check your paraphrases against the original texts to make sure that they are similar in content, but different in terms of vocabulary and grammar.

A. Rewrite each sentence according to the instructions. (Read each sentence carefully in order to fully understand the meaning.)

1. Find synonyms for the underlined words. Change the order of the clauses.

   Despite recent <u>efforts</u> by people like Repair PDX volunteers, repair culture stands counter to the <u>dominant</u>, <u>disposable mentality</u> (Cooke, 2014).

2. Find synonyms for the underlined words. Change from the active to the passive voice. Move the prepositional phrase "in the future" to the end of the paraphrased sentence.

   In the future, ecotourists will <u>visit</u> the island of Pulau Semakau on <u>specially arranged</u> guided <u>tours</u> (Bland, 2007).

3. Find a synonym for the underlined word. Change from active to passive voice. Move the final clause to the beginning of the sentence. Think of a different way of stating "according to the US Environmental Protection Agency."

   The <u>average</u> American throws away 4.4 pounds of <u>trash</u> per day, compared to 2.68 pounds in 1960, according to the US Environmental Protection Agency (Cooke, 2014).

Tip for Success

When paraphrasing someone else's words or ideas in your writing, you should always reference the source, or tell the reader where the ideas came from. This will help you avoid plagiarism.

B. Paraphrase each pair of sentences. Begin by reading the sentences carefully and taking notes. Then write the paraphrase without looking at the original. Use a variety of techniques as appropriate.

1. All the trash from Singapore's 4.4 million residents is dumped on an artificial island. This island could become one of Singapore's main tourist attractions in the near future (Bland, 2007).

   According to Bland, Singapore dumps the garbage from its 4.4 million citizens on an artificial island. In the near future, this island could become one of Singapore's main tourist spots.

2. Singapore burns more than 90 percent of its garbage for reasons of space. Singapore will need to recycle more of its garbage to lower carbon emissions in the atmosphere (Bland, 2007).

3. Along with his broken toaster, Steve Vegdahl brought a slice of bread with him to Portland's repair cafe one day last month. By the time he left, his toaster was working again—and the sweet smell of toasted wheat permeated the room (Cooke, 2014).

4. While repairing rather than replacing may have become a rebellious action over the last few decades, Jacobson sees room for the concept to grow. From coffee grinders to speakers to lawnmowers to furniture, Repair PDX alone has endowed a multitude of objects with new life (Cooke, 2014).

Bland, E. (2007). Garbage of Eden. *New Scientist Magazine.*

Cooke, C. (2014, Jan 10) The Glorious Feeling of Fixing Something Yourself. *The Atlantic.* Retrieved from http://www.theatlantic.com

C. WRITING MODEL Read the model business plan, making note of the underlined paraphrased ideas taken from Reading 1 and an article found on the Internet. Look back at Reading 1 on page 163 to find the original wording of phrases 1–3, and record the original quotes on the lines that follow the business plan. Then analyze with a partner how the quotes were turned into paraphrases.

The Clever Compost Company: Small Compost Bins for People Who Love the Environment

Introduction

The Clever Compost Company is an exciting new environmentally friendly company that manufactures small compost bins made of 100% recycled plastic. Compost bins are containers into which people can put their everyday kitchen scraps such as vegetable peels, coffee grounds, and many other things, rather than throwing them away. This food waste will soon turn into valuable compost that can be used as soil for growing plants.

The Clever Compost Company believes in the motto that garbage can be turned into gold. This approach has been inspired by what has been done in Singapore with its garbage. Singapore has created a nature filled island out of incinerated trash. (1) This island is an important place for many different kinds of natural life, and it is surprisingly appealing to infrequently seen types of animals and plants (Bland, 2007). Just like in Singapore, the Clever Compost Company wants to help people create a little natural oasis out of unwanted trash.

Business Description

With the goal of diverting garbage from local landfills and creating high-quality compost, the Clever Compost Company makes compost bins that are a conveniently small size for individuals living in apartments and townhouses with no gardens. The compost bins are made of 100% recycled plastic from old yogurt containers, margarine tubs, and other similar plastics. This product has been inspired by the success of TerraCycle. At TerraCycle, boxes of Capri Sun drink pouches, old computer components, and cookie packages have been recycled into pencil cases, picture frames, and kites, respectively (Feldman, 2009). However, TerraCycle does not make compost bins, and the Clever Compost Company fills this gap.

With landfills all around the world reaching their capacity, people everywhere need to start throwing away less. As a result, businesses that come up with a solution to prevent trash from being thrown away are going to be an excellent investment. A good example of what the future may look like can be found in Singapore, where (2) the limits on resources now are the same problems that other places around the globe will have to deal with soon (Bland, 2007). However, one of the drawbacks of Singapore's solution is that they burn their garbage. (3) When Singapore started to incinerate its trash, the amount of carbon it released into the air increased rapidly (Bland, 2007). In an age of global warming, it is not a good idea to release too many greenhouse gases into the atmosphere. The Clever Compost Company has one solution—the carbon in household kitchen waste is kept in solid form as compost that can be used to grow plants, which remove carbon dioxide from the atmosphere.

Finally, the creativity of this idea, coupled with its environmental goals, is sure to make money. Although TerraCycle has struggled from time to time, <u>since 2004, Tom Szaky has made money: inventive recycling has contributed to TerraCycle's income annually increasing twofold (Feldman, 2009)</u>. The industry as a whole appears ready to break into consistent profitability. More importantly, the Clever Compost Company will avoid mistakes such as when <u>the head of TerraCycle, instead of making a recycled tote bag in-house, choose to make them with a local producer that billed him $20 for each bag (Feldman, 2009)</u>.

Sales and Marketing

The potential customers for this product are environmentally conscious individuals living in apartments and townhouses with only a small amount of outdoor space, such as a balcony. In the first year of production, the compost bins will be available in hardware stores and garden centers across North America, but there are plans for global distribution.

Conclusion

The Clever Compost Company is set to create a highly successful product made of 100% recycled plastic that produces compost, instead of garbage headed toward a landfill. The small size of these compost bins makes them convenient for the majority of people living in city apartments today, and they help to fight global warming by keeping carbon in its solid form and avoiding incineration. All of these factors, plus the need for environmentally conscious companies, combine to create a financially solid investment in a product that will be a big seller in North America, and eventually around the world.

References

Bland, E. (2007). Garbage of Eden. *New Scientist Magazine*.

Feldman, L. (2009, March 25). Garbage mogul makes millions from trash. *CNN Money*. Retrieved from http://money.cnn.com

Quote 1: _____

_____

Quote 2: _____

_____

Quote 3: _____

_____

D. Choose three of the paraphrases in the model business plan, and rewrite them once more into your own words.

1. _____

   _____

2. _____

   _____

3. _____

   _____

 E. Go online for more practice with writing a business plan.

Grammar | Modals of possibility

We use modals to talk about possibilities in the future and to make predictions. The choice of modal depends on how certain you are about the possibility of something happening in the future.

Absolutely certain	The local landfill **will** be full in ten years.
	People **won't** be able to get free bags in grocery stores anymore.
	We **cannot** keep making more and more garbage without hurting the environment.
	With the building of the new nature reserve, the environmentalists **couldn't** be happier.
Very certain	With the new recycling laws, people **should** start recycling at least half of their garbage.
	The fertilizer company **should not** go bankrupt because new investors have been found.
	People are very concerned about the environment, so our new company **ought to** make a lot of money on our green products.
Somewhat certain	More people **may** start buying reusable tote bags if they become cheaper.
	Students **may not** buy our new recycled paper products because they are more expensive than regular paper products.
Less certain	The business **could** be making bracelets out of recycled toothbrushes by next year.
	Unrecyclable plastic **might** be banned in the next few years.
	Consumers **might not** buy nonrecyclable products in the future.

A. Check (✓) the most appropriate level of certainty for each prediction.

	Absolutely	Very	Somewhat	Less
1. The environment cannot be saved unless everyone starts recycling waste.	☐	☐	☐	☐
2. A lot of recyclable products might be banned from landfills soon.	☐	☐	☐	☐
3. Old-fashioned incandescent lightbulbs won't be sold in stores by 2050.	☐	☐	☐	☐
4. The city should start seeing the benefits of its new recycling program soon.	☐	☐	☐	☐
5. If something isn't done soon, the landfill ought to fill up quickly.	☐	☐	☐	☐
6. Consumers may be more interested in buying recycled products if they become less expensive.	☐	☐	☐	☐
7. The recycling program is a big success, and the mayor couldn't be happier.	☐	☐	☐	☐
8. A recycling depot could be built in the neighborhood if more people wanted one.	☐	☐	☐	☐

B. Read each green business idea and write a prediction about the success or failure of the business. Then write a reason for your prediction. Use modals of possibility in your predictions and reasons.

1. Recycle used toothbrushes into fashion bracelets for women.

   Prediction: _This idea might not be successful._

   Reason: _People may not want to wear somebody else's old toothbrush_

   around their wrists.

2. Make umbrellas out of recycled newspapers.

   Prediction: _____

   Reason: _____

3. Pay people to recycle their garbage (a garbage recycling company).

   Prediction: _____

   Reason: _____

4. Collect used coffee grounds from coffee shops and sell them to gardeners as fertilizer.

Prediction: _____

Reason: _____

5. Turn used cooking oil into gasoline for cars.

Prediction: _____

Reason: _____

C. You live in a large city, and the only landfill in the area is almost full. What is the future going to be like in this city? Write five sentences predicting the future. Each sentence should contain a different modal of possibility.

A new landfill might be built on a farm outside of the city.

 D. Go online for more practice with modals of possibility.

E. Go online for the grammar expansion.

Unit Assignment   Write a business plan

 In this assignment, you will pretend to start an innovative new company that reuses or recycles garbage. You must find investors for your company. As you prepare your business plan, think about the Unit Question, "How can we turn trash into treasure?" Use information from Reading 1, Reading 2, the unit video, and your work in this unit to support your ideas. Refer to the Self-Assessment checklist on page 188.

 Go to the Online Writing Tutor for a writing model and alternate Unit Assignments.

PLAN AND WRITE

Critical Thinking (Tip)

The Unit Assignment asks you to develop a business plan for an innovative new company. In developing this plan, you will synthesize the information from the unit with your own ideas and prior knowledge to create something new.

A. **BRAINSTORM** What kind of businesses turn trash into treasure? In a group or with a partner, discuss these questions. Then use a cluster diagram like the one on page 187 to map your ideas for one business.

1. What are three possible businesses that recycle or reuse trash?

2. What kind of services or products would each company provide?

3. Why would each business be attractive to potential investors?

4. Who would the customers be, and how would they buy the product or service?

Trash into treasure

B. PLAN Choose a business from Activity A. Follow these steps to prepare to write your business plan for the new company that you want to start.

1. These are questions commonly asked by investors before they invest in a new business. With a partner, answer each question.

   a. What is the name of your business? _____

   b. What kind of business is it? _____

   c. What product or service are you going to provide? _____

   d. Why is this business a great idea? _____

   _____

   e. What are the main goals for this business? _____

   _____

   f. Who are the customers going to be? _____

   g. Where will you sell the product or service? _____

   _____

 2. Go to the Online Resources to download and complete the outline for your business plan.

 C. WRITE Use your **PLAN** notes to write your business plan. Go to *iQ Online* to use the Online Writing Tutor.

1. Write a business plan for a company that reuses or recycles garbage. Use examples and paraphrase when necessary.

2. Look at the Self-Assessment checklist on page 188 to guide your writing.

REVISE AND EDIT

A. **PEER REVIEW** Read your partner's business plan. Then go online and use the Peer Review worksheet. Discuss the review with your partner.

B. **REWRITE** Based on your partner's review, revise and rewrite your business plan.

C. **EDIT** Complete the Self-Assessment checklist as you prepare to write the final draft of your business plan. Be prepared to hand in your work or discuss it in class.

SELF-ASSESSMENT		
Yes	No	
☐	☐	Does the business plan build a convincing argument using facts, reasons, and examples?
☐	☐	Has information from Reading 1 and Reading 2 been paraphrased correctly where appropriate?
☐	☐	Are modals of possibility used correctly to express predictions?
☐	☐	Do nouns have the correct suffixes where appropriate?
☐	☐	Does the business plan include vocabulary from the unit?
☐	☐	Did you check the essay for punctuation, spelling, and grammar?

D. **REFLECT** Go online to discuss these questions.

1. What is something new you learned in this unit?

2. Look back at the Unit Question—How can we turn trash into treasure? Is your answer different now than when you started the unit? If yes, how is it different? Why?

TRACK YOUR SUCCESS

Circle the words you have learned in this unit.

Nouns
appliance
aptitude
concept 🔑 AWL
consequence 🔑 AWL
conservation
constraint AWL
craftsmanship
device 🔑 AWL

disposal AWL
elimination AWL
founder AWL
participant AWL

Verbs
adjust 🔑 AWL
anticipate 🔑 AWL
convene AWL
incinerate

permeate
tinker
thrive

Adjectives
abundant
contaminated
dubious
obsolete
sustainable AWL

🔑 Oxford 3000™ words
AWL Academic Word List

Check (✓) the skills you learned. If you need more work on a skill, refer to the page(s) in parentheses.

READING ☐	I can anticipate content through questions. (pp. 161–162)
VOCABULARY ☐	I can recognize noun suffixes. (p. 178)
WRITING ☐	I can paraphrase. (p. 180)
GRAMMAR ☐	I can recognize and use modals of possibility. (p. 184)
UNIT OBJECTIVE ▶▶▶▶ ☐	I can gather information and ideas to prepare a business plan that describes a new recycling company to potential investors.

READING ▶ identifying the author's intent
VOCABULARY ▶ using the dictionary
WRITING ▶ summarizing
GRAMMAR ▶ subject-verb agreement

UNIT QUESTION

Why do people want to change who they are?

A Discuss these questions with your classmates.

1. If you could change any aspect of your personality, what would it be? How would this improve your life?

2. Have you ever changed or wanted to change your physical appearance? What did you change or want to change?

3. Look at the photo. What is this person changing? Why do you think this person wants to change?

▶ **B** Listen to *The Q Classroom* online. Then answer these questions.

1. How did the students answer the question?

2. Do you agree or disagree with their ideas? Why or why not?

 C Go to the Online Discussion Board to discuss the Unit Question with your classmates.

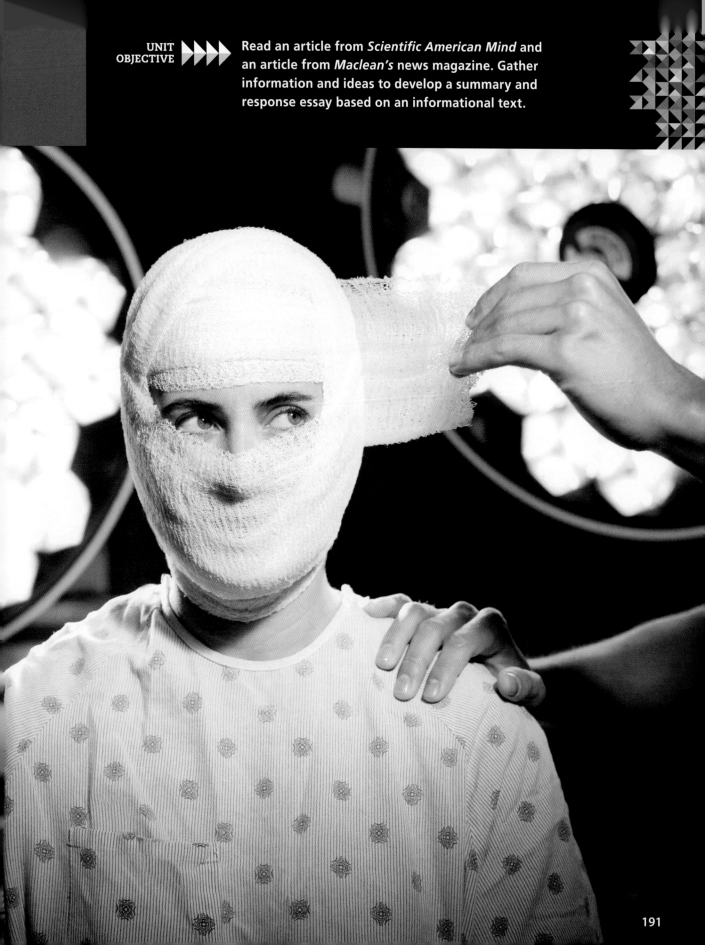

UNIT
OBJECTIVE ▶▶▶▶ Read an article from *Scientific American Mind* and
an article from *Maclean's* news magazine. Gather
information and ideas to develop a summary and
response essay based on an informational text.

D Read the list of changes. Check (✓) whether you think each change would affect a person's appearance, personality, or both. Discuss your answers in a group.

Change	Appearance	Personality
1. Dye one's hair brown, blond, or black.	☐	☐
2. Learn a new language.	☐	☐
3. Smile more.	☐	☐
4. Dye one's hair purple, blue, or green.	☐	☐
5. Go to a tanning salon.	☐	☐
6. Live abroad for a year.	☐	☐
7. Lose or gain weight.	☐	☐
8. Shave one's head.	☐	☐

E Work with a partner. Describe the personality and lifestyle of each person below. Give reasons for your descriptions. Be as detailed as possible.

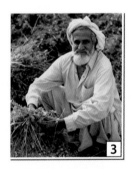

F The people above want to change. Read what each person wants and write some advice. Discuss your answers with a partner or a group. Would it be easy for them to change?

1. I think I'm too shy. I want to be more outgoing.

2. I want to look professional, but not too conservative.

3. I want to look the way I feel: young!

4. I want to live and work in another country.

READING 1 | Set in Our Ways: Why Change Is So Hard

You are going to read an article by Nikolas Westerhoff from the magazine *Scientific American Mind* that looks at why it is so difficult for people to change their lives and their personalities as they become older. Use the article to gather information and ideas for your Unit Assignment.

PREVIEW THE READING

A. **PREVIEW** Why is change so difficult for some people? List three reasons why people may not be able to change their lives or enjoy new experiences. As you read, check to see if your reasons are similar to the reasons presented in the article.

1. _____

2. _____

3. _____

B. **QUICK WRITE** Why do some people want to change their lives and personalities? Write for 5–10 minutes in response. Before you start, spend a couple of minutes planning what you are going to write about. Remember to use this section for your Unit Assignment.

C. **VOCABULARY** Check (✓) the words or phrases you know. Then work with a partner to locate each word or phrase in the reading. Use clues to help define the words or phrases you don't know. Check your definitions in the dictionary.

competence *(n.)*	intention *(n.)* 🔑
conceivable *(adj.)*	lose one's appetite *(phr.)*
conduct *(v.)* 🔑	novelty *(n.)*
conscientious *(adj.)*	the jury is still out *(phr.)*
consistency *(n.)*	undertake *(v.)*
impulsive *(adj.)*	

🔑 Oxford 3000™ words

 D. Go online to listen and practice your pronunciation.

WORK WITH THE READING

A. Read the article and gather information on why people want to change.

Set in Our Ways: Why Change Is So Hard

Millions of us dream of transforming our lives, but few of us are able to make major changes after our 20s. Here's why.

1   *"The shortest path to oneself leads around the world."* So wrote German philosopher Count Hermann Keyserling, who believed that travel was the best way to discover who you are.

2   That was how 22-year-old Christopher McCandless was thinking in the summer of 1990, when he decided to leave everything behind—including his family, friends, and career plans. He gave his bank balance of $24,000 to the charity Oxfam International and hitchhiked around the country, ending up in Alaska. There he survived for about four months in the wilderness before dying of starvation in August 1992. His life became the subject of writer Jon Krakauer's 1996 book *Into the Wild,* which inspired the 2007 film of the same name.

3   Not every newly minted college graduate is as **impulsive** and restless as McCandless was, but studies **conducted** since the 1970s by personality researchers Paul Costa and Robert R. McCrae of the National Institutes of Health confirm that people tend to be open to new experiences during their teens and early 20s. Young people fantasize about becoming an adventurer like McCandless rather than following in the footsteps of a grandparent who spent decades working for the same company. But after a person's early 20s, the fascination with **novelty** declines, and resistance to change increases.

People tend to be open to new experiences during their teens and early 20s.

As Costa and McCrae found, this pattern holds true regardless of cultural background.

4   Although people typically **lose their appetite** for novelty as they age, many continue to claim a passion for it. Voters cheer on politicians who pledge change. Dieters flock to nutritional programs advertising a dream figure in only five weeks. Consumers embrace self-help books promising personal transformation. And scientists tell us that novel stimuli[1] are good for our brains, promoting learning and memory.

5   Yet even as people older than 30 yearn for what is new, many find themselves unable or unwilling to make fundamental changes in their lives. Researchers say this paradox can be largely explained by the demands of adult responsibilities and that unrealistic expectations may also play a part in thwarting[2] our best **intentions**. Change is rarely as easy as we think it will be.

[1] **stimuli:** (pl. for *stimulus*) something that helps somebody or something to develop better or more quickly
[2] **thwart:** to prevent somebody from doing what they want to do

Nature or nurture?

6 Psychologists have long identified openness to new experiences as one of the "Big Five" personality traits, which also include extroversion[3], agreeableness, conscientiousness, and neuroticism[4]. Considerable disagreement exists about how much these personality traits change after age 30, but most research suggests that openness declines in adulthood.

7 The fact that an age-dependent pattern of decreasing openness appears around the globe and in all cultures suggests, according to biopsychologists, a genetic basis. But **the jury is still out**. As psychologist and personality researcher Rainer Riemann of Bielefeld University in Germany points out, it is **conceivable** that people all over the globe are simply confronted with similar life demands and societal expectations. Young men and women everywhere have to go out into the world and find a partner and a livelihood. Later, they have to care for their children and grandchildren. These life tasks require commitment and **consistency** and may serve as a catalyst for personality change.

8 Once a family and career are in place, novelty may no longer be as welcome. New experiences may bring innovation and awakening but also chaos and insecurity. And so most people dream of novelty but hold fast to the familiar. Over time we become creatures of habit: enjoying the same dishes when we eat out, vacationing in favorite spots, and falling into daily routines.

9 "The brain is always trying to automate things and to create habits, which it imbues[5] with feelings of pleasure. Holding to the tried and true gives us a feeling of security, safety, and **competence** while at the same time reducing our fear of the future and of failure," writes brain researcher Gerhard Roth of the University of Bremen in Germany in his 2007 book whose title translates as *Personality, Decision, and Behavior*.

10 But even negative events may have thoroughly positive results, according to sociologist Deborah Carr of Rutgers University. For example, many widows are able to start life over again and to develop talents they never knew they had. People who have been diagnosed with cancer learn to redefine themselves as a result of the disease—and may even conquer their cancer in the process. Survivors of natural catastrophes often discover new strengths. But we should not draw sweeping conclusions from these examples, says psychologist William R. Miller of the University of New Mexico. Many older people report that they have changed little in spite of major life experiences.

Over time we become creatures of habit.

11 The structure of one's personality becomes increasingly stable until about age 60. "That means that a person who is particularly **conscientious** at the age of 40 will be conscientious at 60 as well," says psychologist Peter Borkenau of Martin Luther University Halle-Wittenberg in Germany. Stability decreases again, however, after the age of 60. It seems that people are only able to become more open to new experiences once they have fulfilled their life obligations— that is, after they have retired from their careers and their children have flown the nest.

---

[3] **extroversion:** liveliness and confidence; enjoying being with other people
[4] **neuroticism:** the state of not behaving in a reasonable, calm way because you are worried about something
[5] **imbue:** to fill with strong feelings, opinions, or values

False hope springs eternal

12   Even after age 60, it is difficult to completely reframe your life. In fact, those who seek to make large changes often end up failing even to make the most minor corrections. The more an individual believes he can set his own rudder[6] as he pleases, the more likely he is to run aground[7]. That's one reason why so many smokers who tell you that they can quit whenever they want are still smoking 20 years later.

13   In 1999, psychologists Janet Polivy and C. Peter Herman of the University of Toronto Mississauga coined a term for this phenomenon: *false hope syndrome*. Over and over, they say, people **undertake** both small and large changes in their lives. Most of these attempts never get anywhere, thanks to overblown expectations.

14   Take the woman who believes that if she can lose 20 pounds, she will finally meet the man of her dreams and live happily ever after. This fantasy is based on the notion that one positive change—losing weight—automatically brings with it other desired changes. But the reality is that it is difficult to keep weight off over the long term, and finding an ideal life partner is often dependent on luck. Even if dieting proves successful, other goals may remain out of reach. But the false hope syndrome seduces people into trying to overhaul their entire lives all at once: the smoker and couch potato is suddenly inspired to become a nonsmoker and marathon runner, but because he attempts too much too fast, he is doomed to fail.

15   The cure for false hope is to set more reasonable goals and recognize that achieving even modest change will be difficult. And if you are older than 30, remember that your openness to new experiences is slowly declining, so you are better off making a new start today than postponing it until later. Perhaps most important of all, try to appreciate the person that you already are.

16   As the ancient Greek Epicurus put it: "Do not spoil what you have by desiring what you have not; but remember that what you now have was once among the things only hoped for."

---

[6] **rudder:** a piece of wood used to control the direction of a boat; figurative meaning: control your life

[7] **run aground:** when a ship touches the ground and cannot move; figurative meaning: to have trouble

---

Vocabulary
Skill Review

In Unit 1, you learned about using a thesaurus and how learning synonyms and antonyms is a good way to build your vocabulary. How many synonyms and antonyms can you find for the vocabulary words and phrases from Reading 1?

B. **VOCABULARY** Here are some words and phrases from Reading 1. Complete each sentence. You may need to change the form of the word or phrase to make the sentence grammatically correct.

competence *(n.)*	**consistency** *(n.)*	**novelty** *(n.)*
conceivable *(adj.)*	**impulsive** *(adj.)*	**the jury is still out** *(phr.)*
conduct *(v.)*	**intention** *(n.)*	**undertake** *(v.)*
conscientious *(adj.)*	**lose one's appetite** *(phr.)*	

1. The researchers are responsible for organizing the experiments, but their

    assistants actually _____ them.

2. People don't like too much change because familiar experiences give them a feeling of _____ and control over their lives.

3. Many people start a diet with the best _____ of losing weight, but they find it difficult to change their behavior.

4. Some scientists believe personality characteristics are genetic, but _____ on this issue because no research has proved this to be true.

5. As a person gets older, he may start to _____ for change and adventure, instead preferring to be comfortable and safe.

6. Some people are _____ workers and always try to do a good job.

7. Many young people are _____ and make quick decisions that are not based on a lot of thought.

8. Some people think that their hair needs to look different, so they style it in every _____ way.

9. When you _____ a diet or exercise program, you are also responsible for making a long-term change in behavior.

10. Lisa is learning English because she needs to have a high level of _____ in English in order to go to college in the United States.

11. The _____ of visiting a foreign country and experiencing a lot of new things can be very exciting.

iQ ONLINE **C. Go online for more practice with the vocabulary.**

D. Match each section of the article with its main ideas.
a. Introduction (Paragraphs 1–5)
b. Nature or nurture? (Paragraphs 6–11)
c. False hope springs eternal (Paragraphs 12–14)
d. Conclusion (Paragraphs 15–16)

_____ 1. People need to set reasonable goals, as even small changes are difficult. It is more important to be happy with who you are.

_____ 2. As people become older, they are less open to change. This is true around the world and in all cultures, suggesting that resistance to change has a genetic basis. However, it may also indicate that people all over the world simply have similar life demands and societal expectations.

_____ 3. While young people are usually open to new experiences, older people are less interested in new experiences and are more unwilling to change.

_____ 4. People who try to make big changes in their lives often end up failing to make even small changes. Their hopes are too high. Their desire for change is unrealistic.

E. **What is the overall main idea of Reading 1? Write down your ideas in one or two sentences and compare with a partner.**

_____

_____

F. **Refer back to the reading as you answer these questions. For each response, indicate the paragraph number(s) where you found your answers.**

1. What did Christopher McCandless do that is an extreme example of the impulsiveness and restlessness of youth? (Paragraph: _____)

_____

_____

2. How do the examples of voters, dieters, and consumers show that people continue to claim a passion for novelty as they get older? (Paragraph: _____)

_____

_____

3. What are the "Big Five" personality traits? (Paragraph: _____)

_____

_____

4. What evidence is there for a genetic basis to declining openness in adulthood? (Paragraph: _____)

_____

_____

5. What is the argument that there isn't a genetic basis to declining openness in adulthood? (Paragraph: _____)

_____

_____

6. According to the article, when are people able to become open to new experiences again? (Paragraph: _____)

_____

_____

7. What is meant by the subtitle "False hope springs eternal"? (Paragraph: _____)

_____

_____

8. What is false hope syndrome? (Paragraph: _____)

_____

_____

9. Why will the woman who believes that if she loses 20 pounds, she'll meet the man of her dreams and be happy probably not succeed? (Paragraph: _____)

_____

_____

10. What advice does the article give to people over the age of 30 who might want to change? (Paragraph: _____)

_____

_____

G. Who do you think is more likely to leave his or her friends and family behind and travel around the world for six months? Label the following five people in the order of most likely (1) to least likely (5). Write the reasons for your decisions and compare your answers with a partner.

_____ 19-year-old college student

Reason: _____

_____ 27-year-old plumber

Reason: _____

_____ 34-year-old writer

Reason: _____

_____ 42-year-old doctor

Reason: _____

_____ 68-year-old retired teacher

Reason: _____

H. Go online to read a book review of _The Tipping Point_ and check your comprehension.

WRITE WHAT YOU THINK

A. Discuss these questions in a group.

1. How open to new experiences are you? What are some examples of new experiences you have had?

2. Do you agree that the older people become, the harder it is for them to change? How does this idea compare with the experiences of people you know?

3. Based on what you have read and your own experiences, do you feel that the global pattern of being less open to change is genetic or a result of societal pressures?

B. Choose one question and write a paragraph in response. Look back at your Quick Write on page 193 as you think about what you have learned.

Authors can have many different reasons for writing. These reasons are the author's **intent**, or purpose. Everything you read has a purpose, and authors may have more than one purpose for writing something. They may want to inform, persuade, and/or entertain their readers. Authors do this through a combination of their writing style, the inclusion of certain facts and ideas, and their choice of particular words.

This chart gives three basic reasons authors have for writing something. Use the key indicators and examples to help guide you in judging an author's intent. Learning how to identify an author's intent will help you better analyze texts and become a more critical reader.

	Information	Persuasion	Entertainment
Intent	explains, describes, or informs the reader about something	tries to make the reader believe a particular idea, think in a certain way, or take action	entertains the reader
Style	expository writing	persuasive writing	narrative and descriptive writing
Key indicators	provides mostly factual information or gives instructions on how to do something	contains opinions, feelings, and beliefs	creates an image in the reader's mind that may make the reader feel a strong emotion; can be an interesting story or an anecdote
Examples	textbooks, lab reports, directions, cookbooks, some newspaper and magazine articles	some newspaper and magazine articles, editorials, advertisements, opinion essays, academic essays	fiction, short stories, novels, poetry, comics, graphic novels

A. Read these excerpts from Reading 1. Decide if the author is trying to inform (*I*), persuade (*P*), or entertain (*E*). More than one answer may be correct, so be prepared to defend your choices.

_____ 1. He gave his bank balance of $24,000 to the charity Oxfam International and hitchhiked around the country, ending up in Alaska. There he survived for about four months in the wilderness before dying of starvation in August 1992.

_____ 2. Studies conducted since the 1970s by personality researchers Paul Costa and Robert R. McCrae of the National Institutes of Health confirm that people tend to be open to new experiences during their teens and early 20s.

_____ 3. Psychologists have long identified openness to new experiences as one of the "Big Five" personality traits, which also include extroversion, agreeableness, conscientiousness, and neuroticism.

_____ 4. Over time we become creatures of habit: enjoying the same dishes when we eat out, vacationing in favorite spots, and falling into daily routines.

_____ 5. In 1999, psychologists Janet Polivy and C. Peter Herman of the University of Toronto Mississauga coined a term for this phenomenon: false hope syndrome.

_____ 6. The smoker and couch potato is suddenly inspired to become a nonsmoker and marathon runner, but because he attempts too much too fast, he is doomed to fail.

_____ 7. As the ancient Greek Epicurus put it: "Do not spoil what you have by desiring what you have not; but remember that what you now have was once among the things only hoped for."

Tip for Success

When you read a newspaper or a magazine, thinking about the author's intent will help you to decide on the trustworthiness and reliability of what you are reading.

B. Work in a group. Discuss these questions about the author's intent. Be sure to give reasons for your answers.

1. In your opinion, why did Nikolas Westerhoff write this article about the difficulty of change?

2. Find examples from the article to support your opinion of the author's purpose(s).

3. How does identifying the author's intent help you to become a better reader?

C. Go online for more practice identifying the author's intent.

READING 2 | Kids Want to Tan

You are going to read an article from the weekly news magazine *Maclean's* that considers why some people like to tan. It also discusses some of the drawbacks of getting too much sun. Use the article to gather information and ideas for your Unit Assignment.

PREVIEW THE READING

A. **PREVIEW** What do you think are some of the possible dangers of tanning? List three possible dangers of being exposed to too much sun. As you read, check to see if the dangers you have identified are mentioned in the article.

1. _____

2. _____

3. _____

B. **QUICK WRITE** Why do you think some people like to tan, despite the dangers? Write for 5–10 minutes in response. Use ideas and evidence that you already know about to support your argument. Remember to use this section for your Unit Assignment.

C. **VOCABULARY** Check (✓) the words or phrases you know. Then work with a partner to locate each word or phrase in the reading. Use clues to help define the words or phrases you don't know. Check your definitions in the dictionary.

dermatology *(n.)*	project *(v.)* 🔑
diagnosis *(n.)*	scorching *(adj.)*
doom *(v.)*	sun-kissed *(adj.)*
incidence *(n.)*	trigger *(v.)*
olive-toned *(adj.)*	urge *(v.)* 🔑
phenomenal *(adj.)*	with a vengeance *(phr.)*

🔑 Oxford 3000™ words

D. Go online to listen and practice your pronunciation.

WORK WITH THE READING

A. Read the article and gather information on why people want to change the way they look.

Kids Want to Tan

Sun is the new tobacco: Why the young, especially, just can't quit

1   In winter, if there's something special going on, Norah-Jean Howard, 19, heads to the tanning salon for a little color. In summer, though, Howard might join friends around the pool, or maybe at the trampoline in the backyard, to make sure she keeps that **sun-kissed** glow. The alternative—pallor[1]—is no alternative at all, and she doesn't spend a lot of time worrying about skin cancer.

2   Nevertheless, the Canadian **Dermatology** Association says, "No tan is a good tan," since all exposure to solar radiation[2]—whether from the sun or a tanning lamp—damages the skin to some extent. To the sun-obsessed, you might as well be saying, "No air is good air." Young people, especially, have embraced tanning **with a vengeance**, heading to tanning salons and, in warm weather, soaking up the sun. Recently, the American Academy of Dermatology released a survey indicating 79 percent of youths between 12 and 17 know sun tanning can be dangerous. Furthermore, 81 percent recognize that sunburns during childhood up the risk of skin cancer, yet 60 percent said they burned in the previous summer. It gets worse: while more than a third of those surveyed said they knew someone who had skin cancer, almost half said people with tans look healthier.

3   Teenage boys are the worst offenders, with only 32 percent of those 15 to 17 reporting they're either very or somewhat careful under the sun. "This lax[3] behavior could explain findings from a previous study published in the January 2003 issue of the *Journal of the American Academy of Dermatology* in which older white men had a higher **incidence** of skin cancer," the academy reported. The Centers for Disease Control and Prevention in the United States also confirms that white males have the highest rates of contracting skin cancer, with around 25 incidences of melanoma of the skin per 100,000 people in 2010.

4   North Americans are chasing ultraviolet (UV) radiation[4] more vigorously than ever. According to Statistics Canada, Canadians last year made almost 2.5 million trips to Bermuda and the Caribbean for stays of one night or more in 2010, a searing 190 percent increase over the 860,000 visits made in 2000. Similarly, the US 5-billion-dollar tanning-salon market in North America has shown **phenomenal** growth, going from fewer

---

[1] **pallor**: pale coloring of the face
[2] **solar radiation**: powerful and dangerous rays that are sent out from the sun

[3] **lax**: not strict, severe, or careful enough about work, rules, or standards of behavior
[4] **ultraviolet (UV) radiation**: radiation that causes the skin to darken

than 10,000 outlets in the early 1990s to about 50,000 today. "Gold equals healthy and white equals ill," says Daniel Maes, vice president of global research and development for Estée Lauder in Melville, NY. "Nobody wants to deal with people who look ill. This is what pushes people to go lie down on a beach and get burned. They look around and everybody looks better than them."

5   Skin cancer is the most common type of cancer in Canada, accounting for one-third of all **diagnoses** of the disease, with 82,600 cases forecast for 2014 by the Canadian Cancer Society. There are three kinds: basal, squamous, and melanoma. Basal and squamous are less serious and far more common than melanoma, and will account for roughly 76,100 cases in 2014. They're usually treated without hospitalization. However, the incidence of melanoma, with 6,500 diagnoses and 1,050 deaths **projected** for 2014, has risen alarmingly—an average of 2.4 percent a year in men and 1.8 percent in women since 1992. Various cancer agencies agree: since sun exposure is linked to most skin cancers, reduced exposure to ultraviolet radiation would cut the number of new cancer cases to the same extent that quitting smoking cuts cancer in tobacco addicts.

> " Gold equals healthy and white equals ill. . . . This is what pushes people to go lie down on a beach and get burned. "

6   Deborah Kellett grew up in Ontario and spent a lot of time sunning herself in cottage country north of Toronto. Kellett, 47, has **olive-toned** skin and generally didn't burn. Today, she lives in Bedford, Nova Scotia, and has had a year to think about her cancer. She had been keeping an eye[5] on a spot on her back, just below her armpit, for a few years when her family physician noticed it had grown. Kellett was in to see a specialist within a week, and a week after that, the dermatologist used a local anaesthetic and removed the growth, which was about the size of a baby fingernail. Her prognosis[6]—like any melanoma caught early—is very good. "I always thought I was safe—I was proud of the way I would tan—but I basically tell people that it's not worth it," says Kellett.

7   Sun suppresses the immune system. It works this way: dendritic cells with amoeba-like arms fight infections and are found in tissues throughout the body. They surround and swallow the infectious agent and deliver it to T cells[7], which **trigger** an all-out attack on the infection and also immunize the body against future assaults. The sun, however, "down regulates" dendritic cells, preventing their activation, says Bhagirath Singh, scientific director of the Institute of Infection and Immunity in London, Ontario. "Dendritic cells are really the central mechanism of the immune orchestra," says Singh. "They control how the immune system will mobilize."

8   Even when people put on sunscreen, they often don't put on enough to get the desired SPF[8] rating. That's why Canadian dermatologists have upped their recommendation of SPF 15 to SPF 30, says Dr. Jason Rivers, a professor of dermatology at the University of British Columbia and former national director of the sun awareness program for the Canadian Dermatology Association. "You can lead by example as a parent, so early education is important," suggests Rivers. In fact, it's not all bad news. The tanning-bed industry is under mounting pressure. In March 2005, the World

---

[5] **keep an eye on something:** to take care of something and make sure it is not harmful

[6] **prognosis:** an opinion, based on medical experience, of the likely development of a disease or an illness

[7] **T cell:** a kind of white blood cell that plays an important role in the human immune system

[8] **SPF:** sun protection factor

Health Organization—noting that more than two million cases of skin cancer, of which 132,000 are malignant[9] melanomas, occur worldwide each year—**urged** regulators to restrict artificial tanning with UV light to those 18 and older. Along those lines, Health Canada has taken steps that will require manufacturers to toughen warning labels on tanning equipment. As of 2013, six Canadian provinces have already banned young people under the ages 18 or 19 from using commercial indoor tanning services.

9   Under a **scorching** noonday sun in Toronto's Beaches neighborhood, Jason Remenda, 34, languidly[10] pushes his 21-month-old son Jaydn on a swing. Remenda, a parts manager for a Japanese car manufacturer, has a rare day off. He's wearing shorts, a baseball cap, and a thick gold chain around his neck. The only SPF lotion anywhere near him is on his son. It's his first time out this year, and he never uses sunscreen.

Thoughts of skin cancer cross his mind only when someone asks him about it. "I'm getting up there in age," shrugs Remenda. "I'm going to die of some kind of cancer, right?"

10   A few feet away, lying in the sand along the north shore of Lake Ontario, Gillian Parker feels guilty for being caught out in the sun. The 24-year-old TV production assistant—fair-skinned, strawberry blond and freckled—usually doesn't sunbathe. Nevertheless, here she is, although she says she's watching the time carefully. "I already know that I'll probably get skin cancer," says Parker, explaining how she's burned throughout her life. Four years ago, she fell asleep for 45 minutes in the sun and ended up with blisters all over her chin. Her mother has already had skin cancer—twice. "That's why I feel I'm pretty much **doomed**."

11   It's the cry of a tan addict. Many of us, especially young people, just can't say no to the kiss of the sun, even though it could be the kiss of death.

[9] **malignant:** that cannot be controlled and is likely to cause death
[10] **languidly:** moving slowly in an elegant manner, not needing energy or effort

B. **VOCABULARY** Here are some words and phrases from Reading 2. Read the sentences. Then match each bold word or phrase with its definition.

_____ 1. In the summer, Norah-Jean loves to stay outside in order to keep her **sun-kissed** glow.

_____ 2. The Canadian **Dermatology** Association says that sun tanning is bad for the skin.

_____ 3. Young people in North America have started tanning **with a vengeance**.

_____ 4. The American Academy of Dermatology reported that older white men have a higher **incidence** of skin cancer.

a. (*phr.*) to a greater degree than is expected or usual

b. (*adj.*) made warm or brown by the sun

c. (*n.*) the scientific study of skin diseases

d. (*n.*) the extent to which something happens or has an effect

_____ 5. In the last 20 years, the tanning-salon market has shown **phenomenal** growth.

_____ 6. Skin cancer is the most common form of cancer, accounting for one-third of all **diagnoses** of the disease.

_____ 7. Cases of skin cancer are **projected** to increase this year by five percent.

_____ 8. Some people with **olive-toned** skin don't think they need to worry about sunburns.

e. (*adj.*) yellowish-brown in color

f. (*n.*) the act of discovering or identifying the exact cause of an illness or a problem

g. (*adj.*) very great or impressive

h. (*v.*) to estimate what the size, cost, or amount of something will be in the future based on what is happening now

_____ 9. Toxic chemicals can harm our cells and **trigger** the growth of cancer in our bodies.

_____ 10. Last year, the World Health Organization **urged** governments to control artificial tanning.

_____ 11. The summer sun can be **scorching**, so it is important to protect your skin from burning.

_____ 12. Some people feel they are **doomed** to having skin cancer if their parents have had it.

i. (*v.*) to recommend something strongly

j. (*v.*) to make something happen suddenly

k. (*v.*) to be certain to fail, suffer, die, or experience a terrible and unavoidable event

l. (*adj.*) very hot

iQ ONLINE **C.** Go online for more practice with the vocabulary.

D. Answer these questions. Write the paragraph number(s) that contain information to support your answers.

_____ 1. What is the main issue in the article? _____

_____

_____ 2. Why do some people want to tan? _____

_____

_____ 3. What is the biggest danger associated with tanning? _____

_____

E. **Read the statements. Write _T_ (true) or _F_ (false). Then correct each false statement to make it true.**

_____ 1. Tanning under a solar lamp isn't as dangerous as tanning in the sun.

_____ 2. Few people between 12 and 17 realize that tanning can be dangerous.

_____ 3. The majority of youths between 12 and 17 got burned by the sun the summer before they answered a survey about tanning habits.

_____ 4. A research study from 2003 indicated that older white men had a lower rate of skin cancer than others.

_____ 5. Today there are fewer than 50,000 tanning salons in North America.

_____ 6. At the time the article was written, melanoma was less common than the other two types of skin cancers.

_____ 7. The incidence of melanoma is higher among women than men.

_____ 8. Although olive-skinned people may believe they are not at risk for skin cancer, they actually are.

_____ 9. A lot of sun exposure is good for the immune system.

_____ 10. The World Health Organization is in favor of limiting tanning with UV light to people over the age of 18.

F. **Each of the phrases below can be a subtitle for one of the paragraphs in the reading. Write the paragraph number beside the phrase that best represents that paragraph. Not all of the paragraphs in the reading are represented by the phrases in this activity.**

_____ Adolescent males take the least precautions

_____ An example of a woman who feels skin cancer is inevitable

_____ Skin cancer is widespread in Canada

_____ Young people tan despite knowing the dangers

_____ Having a darker complexion does not prevent skin cancer

_____ Stronger sunscreens and tanning bed warnings are suggested

_____ The sun hurts the body's ability to heal

_____ An example of a man who does not use sunscreen

G. Match the person with the ideas that are associated with them in the article. Note that there is one more person listed than the associated ideas.

a. Norah-Jean Howard	e. Jason Rivers
b. Daniel Maes	f. Jason Remenda
c. Deborah Kellett	g. Gillian Parker
d. Bhagirath Singh	

_____ 1. A darker skin color is not much protection from skin cancer. While she was happy with the way she could tan in her youth, she eventually found a skin cancer growth that had to be removed.

_____ 2. He never really thinks about skin cancer unless someone asks him about it. Because he is becoming older, he thinks he will get cancer anyway.

_____ 3. The sun negatively affects special cells that protect the body. This is dangerous because those cells are very important to the immune system, and they fight infections.

_____ 4. People look healthy if they have a tan, and they look unhealthy if they do not have a tan. People want to look as good as the other people around them.

_____ 5. Dermatologists have increased the suggested strength of sunscreen because people do not use enough. Parents should also teach their young children to use protection from the sun.

_____ 6. She has had very bad sunburns in the past. Her mother has had skin cancer two times. As a result, she thinks she will probably get skin cancer herself.

H. Read the questions. What answers can you infer based on the information in the reading?

1. Why does Norah-Jean Howard head to the tanning salon if there is something special going on?

_____

2. Why do older white men have a higher incidence of skin cancer?

_____

3. Why is skin cancer the most common type of cancer in Canada?

_____

4. Why did the World Health Organization urge regulators to restrict artificial tanning with UV light to people 18 and older?

_____

5. Why is the only SPF lotion anywhere near Jason Remenda on his son?

_____

6. Why does Gillian Parker feel guilty for being caught out in the sun?

_____

WRITE WHAT YOU THINK

A. Discuss the questions in a group. Look back at your Quick Write on page 203 as you think about what you have learned.

1. Why do people continue to tan despite the dangers of skin cancer?

2. Should governments control the amount of time people can use a tanning bed? Why or why not?

3. What determines whether or not someone is beautiful? Are attitudes toward physical beauty the same all around the world? Is the desire to change the way we look universal?

B. Before you watch the video, discuss these questions in a group.

1. How important are genetics in determining a person's personality?

2. How important are the environment and surroundings in determining a person's personality?

 C. Go online to watch the video about how a person can change his or her personality. Then check your comprehension.

> **aphorism** *(n.)* a short phrase that says something true or wise
>
> **missed the mark** *(phr.)* failed at something
>
> **mold** *(v.)* to strongly influence the way someone's character, opinions, and so on, develop
>
> **stumbling blocks** *(phr.)* things that cause problems and prevent you from achieving your aim
>
> **traits** *(n.)* particular qualities in your personality

VIDEO VOCABULARY

D. Think about the unit video, Reading 1, and Reading 2 as you discuss these questions. Then choose one question and write a paragraph in response.

1. Which is more difficult to change: your appearance or your life? Can changing your physical appearance change your personality or improve your life? Why or why not?

2. What positive actions can people take if they really want to change their personalities or improve their lives?

Vocabulary Skill   Using the dictionary

It is important to **make appropriate word choices** when you write. The first word that you think of when you are writing isn't always the best word to express your ideas. By looking critically at your vocabulary choices, you can choose words that are the best fit for your writing purpose.

Synonyms

Synonyms may be misleading as no two words are exactly the same. A synonym may be slightly different from the exact meaning you want, or it may be accurate, but inappropriate for the **audience, register,** or **genre** of your writing. If you are not sure of the exact definition or how to use the word, look it up in a dictionary.

Audience

The vocabulary choices you make need to match the audience for your writing. Who is the target audience? American English speakers? British? Academic scholars? The dictionary gives specific information about this sort of usage.

Register and genre

You should always be aware of the level of formality of a word or phrase. Formal and informal writing often require different vocabulary choices. Are you writing an article for a fashion magazine or for an academic journal? Are you posting a comment online? You can check your dictionary to see if the word you are using is appropriate or if a more suitable word exists.

> **ex·ac·er·bate** /ɪɡˈzæsərˌbeɪt/ verb ~ **sth** (formal) to make something worse, especially a disease or problem
> **SYN** AGGRAVATE: *The symptoms may be exacerbated by certain drugs.* ▶ **ex·ac·er·ba·tion** /ɪɡˌzæsərˈbeɪʃn/ noun [U, C]

From the example, you can see that *exacerbate* is a verb that means "to make something worse" and the noun form is *exacerbation.* You can also see that this word is used in formal language and that it is used when talking about diseases and problems, as in the example sentence. If you are writing or speaking in an informal way, it is more appropriate to say "made worse" than "exacerbated."

All dictionary entries are from the *Oxford Advanced American Dictionary for learners of English* © Oxford University Press 2011.

A. Circle the most appropriate word or phrase to complete each sentence in a formal piece of writing in a magazine. Use your dictionary to help you.

1. Many physicians (beg / urge) tanning-salon owners to set strict rules for the use of tanning beds by teenagers.

2. Some self-tanning lotions contain (bad things / toxic chemicals).

3. Consumers love self-help books that promise complete personal (transformation / change).

4. People who are able to make a big change in their lives at an older age are not afraid of (new stuff / innovation).

5. Because of false hope syndrome, people often (fail / mess up) when making big changes in their lives.

6. Couch potatoes who suddenly (are inspired / want) to become marathon runners may not have too much success.

B. Replace the words in bold with a more academic vocabulary word from Reading 1 or Reading 2.

scorching
1. The sun's rays are ~~really hot~~, so it is very important to protect your skin.

2. It is important to clearly define your goals before you **do** an experiment.

3. It's **possible** that skin cancer rates will increase significantly within the next year.

4. People lose their appetite for **new things** as they age.

5. Too much exposure to radiation can **set off** dangerous changes in skin cells.

6. My sister is thinking about becoming a doctor that specializes in **the study of the skin**.

C. Choose ten vocabulary words from this unit. Write a sentence using each word. Be sure to look up the words in the dictionary to see how they are used.

 D. Go online for more practice with using the dictionary.

WRITING

At the end of this unit, you will write a summary and response essay. This essay will include information from the readings, the unit video, and your own ideas.

Writing Skill | Summarizing

A **summary** is a shortened version of a text such as an article or textbook excerpt. It is an objective piece of writing that does not contain any of your opinions or ideas. To write a summary, determine the main ideas in the original text and write a paragraph about them. Summarizing is a useful study aid to help you remember and understand main ideas when you are taking an exam or doing research.

Here are some steps to help you write a summary.

Before you write: Read the text thoroughly. Use techniques you learned in Unit 1 ("Distinguishing main ideas from details," page 13) and Unit 4 ("Making inferences," page 104) to determine the main ideas the author is expressing.

As you write: Write a draft of the summary using your own words. Follow these guidelines:

- **Topic sentence:** Introduce the piece by giving the author's name, the title of the piece, the source, and the general topic of the text.
- **Body:** Write the main ideas in the order they appear. Do not include details.
- **Conclusion:** One way you can end a summary is to briefly restate the main ideas found in the reading.

After you write: Ensure that the summary is much shorter than the original text. Read over your summary to see if it makes sense and expresses the main ideas of the reading. Eliminate any unnecessary details. Then revise and edit your work.

- Always use your own words. Never copy the author's words. (See "Paraphrasing," page 180, in Unit 6.)
- Do not overuse quotes. Use mostly indirect speech. A short quotation of a key phrase may be included.
- Do not add your own ideas or opinions and do not change the writer's ideas and opinions.

A. Read this article from the British newspaper *The Guardian* about the dangers of sunbeds for children and teenagers. As you read, annotate the text and underline the main ideas.

Children as Young as 11 Use Sunbed Salons

By Sam Jones

a sunbed

1   Health campaigners have called for the rules governing tanning salons to be tightened after a study showed that up to 8 percent of 11- to 12-year-olds have used sunbeds in the past year, with some children visiting tanning shops daily after school. The survey, based in Merseyside, England, also found that some salons allowed mothers to take their babies into the booths while they used sunbeds, and one even offered children's events.

2   Philomena Zilinski of the campaign group Health in Knowsley said: "We surveyed young people because we wanted to find out why they were using sunbeds and how many times a week. Some were going in every day after school and many were using them four times a week. People don't seem to realize the health risks." Ms. Zilinski said many children were ignoring the damage they were doing to their skin because they thought tanning made them look better and slimmer or helped clear up complaints such as acne. "The problem is that schoolchildren can afford to use them. Parents don't have to give consent," she added.

3   The research has also prompted a crackdown on tanning salons by local authority officers in Knowsley's public health protection division. They have carried out an assessment of all 38 sunbed salons in the area and have sent written warnings to those that need to make changes. Any that fail to comply could be prosecuted.

4   Richard Fontana, Knowsley council's principal environmental health officer, said the survey had also revealed that some young people were refusing to wear goggles because they do not want white patches on their face, even though tanning without them can cause problems including eye cancer. "We were told one shop was holding tanning events inviting people to hire out the venue and turn it into a social event," he said.

5   Calls are growing for tighter restrictions on young people visiting tanning salons because the number of people with skin cancer has doubled in the past 10 years. Legally there is nothing to prevent children from using sunbeds, but the guidelines recommend they are only used by over-16s. Nina Goad of the British Skin Foundation said: "The advice of the World Health Organization is that people under 18 should not use sunbeds. It is widely reported that there are a number of short- and long-term health risks associated with using sunbeds. Some users have also reported dry, bumpy or itchy skin. However, of more consequence are the potential long-term risks of sunbed use, of which skin cancer is the most significant."

6   The popularity of tanning parlors among young people was highlighted this year when a 15-year-old girl was warned by doctors that she was likely to develop skin cancer by the age of 30 if she did not stop using sunbeds five times

a week. Hayley Barlow, from Liverpool, was dubbed a "tanorexic"[1] after experts found her skin was closer to that of a 25-year-old than a teenager. She has tried to give up visiting tanning salons but still goes at least three times a month. "All the girls you see in magazines are tanned and lots of my friends use sunbeds as well," she said. "But I'd like to warn other teenagers not to use them."

[1] **tanorexic:** someone who tans obsessively, to the point of making herself sick

Critical Thinking Tip

Activity B asks you to assess whether the summary is effective or not. When you assess, you use your own knowledge and opinions to judge another's ideas. People can form different, but equally valid assessments. Making judgments based on the information available and your own values and beliefs can help you understand a topic better.

B. **Read the summaries and answer the questions. Discuss your answers with a partner.**

The article "Children as Young as 11 Use Sunbed Salons" by Sam Jones tells us that 8 percent of 11- to 12-year-olds have used sunbeds in the past year. The article reports that children were ignoring the damage they were doing to their skin because they thought tanning made them look better and slimmer. There are 38 sunbed salons in the area, and some have been sent written warnings. Some young people were refusing to wear goggles because they do not want white patches on their face. The advice of the World Health Organization was that people under 18 should not use sunbeds. A 15-year-old girl was warned by doctors that she was likely to develop skin cancer by the age of 30 if she did not stop using sunbeds five times a week. She is a tanorexic, and she still goes at least three times a month to tanning salons.

1. Is this an effective summary? Why or why not?

_____

_____

The article from *The Guardian* newspaper "Children as Young as 11 Use Sunbed Salons" by Sam Jones looks at the use of tanning salons by children and teenagers. A survey has led health campaigners to ask for stronger government rules and has caused local authorities to crack down on salons. The survey showed that up to 8 percent of 11- to 12-year-olds have used sunbeds in the past year and that children are not protecting themselves properly in the salons because they want to look good. Another factor is that the number of people with skin cancer has doubled in the last ten years. Right now, children can use tanning salons, but government and World Health Organization guidelines state they should be restricted to people over ages 16 and 18, respectively. Children may be using tanning salons now, but health campaigners are working hard at changing the rules.

2. Is this an effective summary? Why or why not?

_____

_____

Sam Jones, in the article "Children as Young as 11 Use Sunbed Salons," informs us that many young people are using sunbeds. Some mothers are even taking their babies into the booths with them. This is very dangerous, and they are not good mothers. A survey was carried out that revealed a lot of children are using tanning salons because they think a tan makes them look better and slimmer. They have probably been reading magazines with tanned celebrities. These kinds of magazines make children think that being tanned is fashionable, but it is very dangerous. The number of people with skin cancer has doubled in the last 10 years. I think there are going to be even more people getting skin cancer in the future because of tanning. I hope Hayley Barlow from Liverpool will stop tanning and realize that she is beautiful just the way she is.

---

3. Is this an effective summary? Why or why not?

_____

_____

4. Which summary is the best? Why?

_____

_____

C. The article "Children as Young as 11 Use Sunbed Salons" was published in December 2005. However, in 2011, the British government changed the law and banned children and teenagers under the age of 18 from using tanning salons. Do you agree with this change? Why or why not? Discuss your answer with a partner.

D. **WRITING MODEL** A summary and response essay has two sections. After the introduction, there is typically a summary section of one or two paragraphs that summarizes the main ideas of a reading text. Next, there is a response section of anywhere from two to four paragraphs, depending on the number of main ideas that you are responding to. The response section contains your opinions of or personal reaction to the main ideas that you have just summarized. The essay then finishes with a conclusion.

Read the summary and response essay below. Think about your opinion from Activity C. Then answer the questions.

It often seems like many people are unsatisfied with their looks, and one way people can try to change their appearance is by getting a tan. For many, the easiest way to get a tan can be by visiting a tanning salon. However, in the *Guardian* newspaper article "Children as Young as 11 Use Sunbed Salons," Sam Jones points out that children are now starting to use tanning beds. This article raises many important issues: children should not be using tanning salons, the rules regulating tanning salons have to be enforced, and the risks associated with sunbeds need to be better publicized.

In his article, Sam Jones describes how young people were continuing to use tanning salons despite the risks involved. Health advocates wanted to stop children from going to tanning salons because of the large increase in the number of people with skin cancer. If children use tanning salons, they risk developing skin cancer later in life. A survey revealed that young people did not seem to know about the dangers. They did not care about skin damage because they thought having a tan could help clear skin problems. They also felt that a tan helped them look better and thinner. To fight the abuse of tanning salons by young people, local governments began enforcing the laws that did exist and started issuing warnings to salons that weren't obeying the laws. The article ends with the example of a young woman who was addicted to tanning.

In the article, it appears that children were using tanning salons on a regular basis. This is highly dangerous because children are too young to fully comprehend the dangers of using tanning beds, and they will only see the short-term benefits rather than the longer-term dangers. It appears that peer pressure can also influence children and increase their desire to get a tan. The best way to stop children from using sunbeds is by restricting their access to tanning salons.

The article also mentions that local authorities began cracking down on tanning salons that were not following the existing laws at the time of the survey. The rules at the time of the article, such as the requirement to wear goggles, needed to be better enforced. Better enforcement sends a strong message to tanning salon owners that rule-breakers will be punished. Thus, when new rules are put in place, such as the banning of children from tanning salons in 2011, there is a better chance that businesses will follow this law.

Finally, the risks associated with using sunbeds have to be better publicized. As mentioned in the article, many young people did not seem to realize the risks associated with going to a tanning salon. As a result, Jones stated that some children were tanning every day after school, and some young people were not using protective eyewear. There have to be advertisements and public information campaigns to let young people know the dangers, such as skin cancer, involved in using tanning salons. Only then will fewer people seek artificial means to get that sun-kissed look.

All in all, the article by Sam Jones highlights the issues surrounding children and tanning salons such as children's access to tanning salons, enforcement of the laws connected to tanning salons, and the lack of public awareness of the dangers of tanning salons. Children may think that they can improve how they look by tanning, but there are too many dangers involved. Now that children are no longer permitted to use tanning salons, the rules for tanning salons are better enforced, and the public knows more about the risks. It is hoped that the numbers of people diagnosed with skin cancer will start to go down.

Writing Tip

The thesis statement summarizes the main ideas of the essay and is usually found in the first paragraph.

1. What is the thesis statement for this essay? Restate the thesis statement in your own words.

   _____

2. How would you evaluate the summary in this essay? Is it effective? Provide reasons for your evaluation.

   _____

3. What is the first main idea that the essay writer responds to?

   _____

4. What is the essay writer's reaction to the first main idea?

   _____

5. What is the second main idea that the essay writer responds to?

   _____

6. What is the essay writer's reaction to the second main idea?

   _____

7. What is the third main idea that the essay writer responds to?

   _____

8. What is the essay writer's reaction to the third main idea?

   _____

E. Using your own words, write a short summary of the model summary and response essay in Activity D.

F. Go online for more practice with writing a summary and response essay.

In every sentence, the main subject and verb must agree with each other. Singular subjects agree with singular verbs, and plural subjects agree with plural verbs. To avoid errors when writing, identify the main subject of the sentence and the subjects of any clauses and check that they each have a verb that agrees. Prepositional phrases, relative clauses, and noun clauses can be tricky.

Prepositional Phrases: A plural noun at the end of a prepositional phrase modifying a singular subject can cause writers to make subject-verb agreement errors. The subject, not the noun at the end of the prepositional phrase, determines if the verb is singular or plural.

> Sunbed **use** among young people **is** a public health concern.
> prepositional phrase

Subject Relative Clauses: The verb in a subject relative clause agrees in number with the noun that the clause modifies. The main verb of the sentence also agrees with the noun.

> Many **physicians** who **are** against the use of sunbeds **treat** people with cancer.
> subject relative clause

Noun Clauses: A noun clause can be the subject of a sentence. Use a singular verb in these sentences.

> **What personality studies have shown is** that openness to change declines
> noun clause
> with age.

Quantifiers: When quantifiers (see Unit 3, pages 89–90) are used, they usually precede a noun. Look at the noun and check that the main verb agrees with it.

> Almost **every teenager is** open to new experiences. (singular)
> I want to diet because **most of my money is spent** on fast food. (noncount)
> **Most of my friends like** to travel to new places and **experience** new cultures.
> (plural)

A. Underline the main subject in each clause of each sentence. Choose the correct verb.

1. Many people (wants / want) to make big changes in their lives, but most of these attempts never (gets / get) anywhere.

2. Openness (is / are) one of the "Big Five" personality traits, which also (includes / include) extroversion, agreeableness, conscientiousness, and neuroticism.

3. Voters often (votes / vote) for the politicians in an election who (pledges / pledge) change.

4. How much people desire to try new things (declines / decline) as people become older.

5. Not every new college graduate (is / are) impulsive and restless.

6. Recommendations for stronger sunscreen use (was made / were made) by the Canadian Dermatologists' Association.

7. Many patients' prognoses for a complete recovery from cancer (depends / depend) on the type of cancer they (has / have).

B. Read the summary. Underline the twelve subject-verb agreement errors and correct each error.

> The article by Sam Jones, "Children as Young as 11 Use Sunbed Salons,"
> reveal how young people, some as young as 11 or 12, goes to tanning salons.
> Because so many young people in northern England is using tanning salons,
> health campaigners wants stronger rules to control these places. A survey
> about the effects of using sunbeds show that many young people is ignoring
> the risks. They think that tanning in sunbeds improve the way they look. In
> response to the survey, local authorities are making sure tanning salons in
> this part of England is obeying the law. Another thing the survey reveals are
> that some young people are not wearing protective goggles because they want
> to look good. Additionally, the number of people who has skin cancer have
> doubled in the last ten years. As a result, people are asking the government for
> rules that controls the use of tanning salons by young people.

 C. Go online for more practice with subject-verb agreement.

D. Go online for the grammar expansion.

 Write a summary and response essay

 In this assignment, you will write a summary and response essay for Reading 1 or Reading 2. As you prepare your essay, think about the Unit Question, "Why do people want to change who they are?" Use Reading 1, Reading 2, the unit video, and your work in this unit to support your ideas. Refer to the Self-Assessment checklist on page 222.

Go to the Online Writing Tutor for a writing model and alternate Unit Assignments.

PLAN AND WRITE

A. **BRAINSTORM** You may respond to one of the following questions in your summary and response essay: 1) Can people change who they are? or 2) Why do people want to change who they are? Decide which question you will address. Then choose Reading 1 or Reading 2 and complete these tasks.

1. Reread the article you chose and annotate as you read. Use these questions to guide you.
   a. How does the article relate to the question you chose?
   b. What are the main ideas of the article?
   c. What main ideas in the article do you agree or disagree with? Why?
   d. What information in the article supports or disagrees with your point of view?
   e. Do you have any personal experience with or prior knowledge of this topic? What facts and examples support or disprove the main ideas in the article?

2. Discuss your answers with a partner who chose the same article.

B. **PLAN** Follow these steps to plan your summary and response essay.

1. Choose three main ideas from the article and write them below. Write your personal reaction to each one and how each relates to the question you are going to address in the response part of your essay.

   Main idea 1: _____

   _____

   Personal reaction: _____

   _____

   Relation to question: _____

   _____

   Main idea 2: _____

   _____

   Personal reaction: _____

   _____

   Relation to question: _____

   _____

Main idea 3: _____

_____

Personal reaction: _____

_____

Relation to question: _____

_____

 2. Go to the Online Resources to download and complete the outline for your summary and response essay.

 C. WRITE Use your **PLAN** notes to write your summary and response essay. Go to *iQ Online* to use the Online Writing Tutor.

1. Write your summary and response essay.

2. Look at the Self-Assessment checklist to guide your writing.

REVISE AND EDIT

 A. PEER REVIEW Read your partner's summary and response essay. Then go online and use the Peer Review worksheet. Discuss the review with your partner.

B. REWRITE Based on your partner's review, revise and rewrite your summary and response essay.

C. EDIT Complete the Self-Assessment checklist as you prepare to write the final draft of your summary and response essay. Be prepared to hand in your work or discuss it in class.

SELF-ASSESSMENT		
Yes	**No**	
☐	☐	Does the essay build a convincing argument using facts, reasons, and examples?
☐	☐	Has information from Reading 1 or Reading 2 been summarized correctly where appropriate?
☐	☐	Have you made sure there are no subject-verb agreement errors?
☐	☐	Did you use the dictionary to make appropriate word choices?
☐	☐	Does the essay include vocabulary from the unit?
☐	☐	Did you check the essay for punctuation, spelling, and grammar?

D. **REFLECT** Go to the Online Discussion Board to discuss these questions.

1. What is something new you learned in this unit?

2. Look back at the Unit Question—Why do people want to change who they are? Is your answer different now than when you started the unit? If yes, how is it different? Why?

TRACK YOUR SUCCESS

Circle the words and phrases you have learned in this unit.

Nouns	**Verbs**	**Adjectives**
competence	conduct 🔑 AWL	conceivable AWL
consistency AWL	doom	conscientious
dermatology	project 🔑 AWL	impulsive
diagnosis	trigger AWL	olive-toned
incidence AWL	undertake AWL	phenomenal AWL
intention 🔑	urge 🔑	scorching
novelty		sun-kissed

Phrases
lose one's appetite
the jury is still out
with a vengeance

🔑 Oxford 3000™ words
AWL Academic Word List

Check (✓) the skills you learned. If you need more work on a skill, refer to the pages in parentheses.

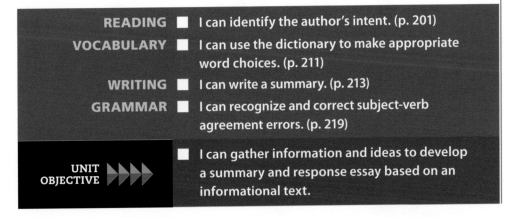

READING ■	I can identify the author's intent. (p. 201)
VOCABULARY ■	I can use the dictionary to make appropriate word choices. (p. 211)
WRITING ■	I can write a summary. (p. 213)
GRAMMAR ■	I can recognize and correct subject-verb agreement errors. (p. 219)
UNIT OBJECTIVE ▶▶▶▶ ■	I can gather information and ideas to develop a summary and response essay based on an informational text.

UNIT **8**

Health Sciences

READING	▶	organizing notes and annotations in a chart
VOCABULARY	▶	adjective/verb + preposition collocations
WRITING	▶	writing a cause and effect essay
GRAMMAR	▶	cause and effect connectors

UNIT QUESTION

What energizes people?

A Discuss these questions with your classmates.

1. When do you have the most energy? Are you a morning person or a night owl?

2. What causes people to suffer from low energy levels?

3. Look at the photo. What are these people doing? How are they energizing themselves? What do you do to energize yourself?

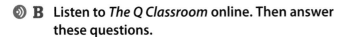
Read an article from *The St. Petersburg Times* and an article from *The New York Times*. Gather information and ideas to prepare a cause and effect essay analyzing two or three methods for boosting energy levels.

B Listen to *The Q Classroom* online. Then answer these questions.

1. What energizes Sophy, Marcus, Yuna, and Felix? Are you energized by the same things? Why or why not?

2. According to Felix, why aren't people getting enough sleep nowadays? What are some other reasons people might not be getting enough sleep in today's society?

iQ ONLINE **C** Go online to watch the video about how different food choices can affect your mood. Then check your comprehension.

cranky *(adj.)* bad-tempered

equation *(n.)* a problem or situation in which several things must be dealt with

serotonin *(n.)* a chemical in the brain that affects how messages are sent from the brain to the body and that also affects how a person feels

turned around *(phr.)* changed, improved

VIDEO VOCABULARY

iQ ONLINE **D** Go to the Online Discussion Board to discuss the Unit Question with your classmates.

E Answer the questionnaire. Check (✓) the methods that you use to feel more energetic.

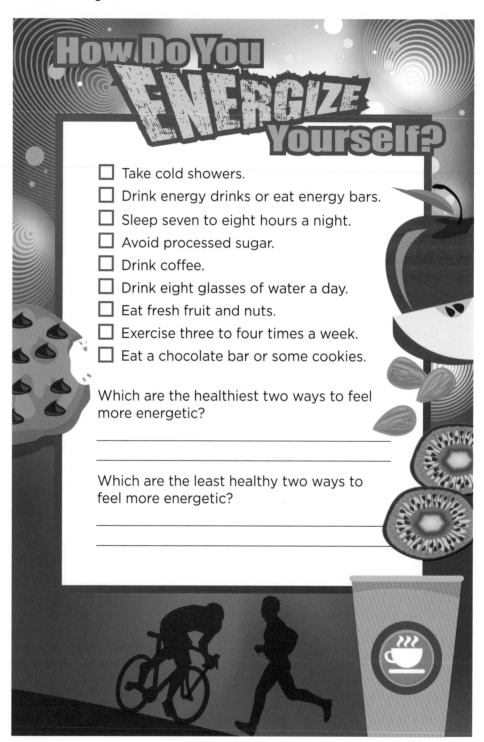

How Do You ENERGIZE Yourself?

- ☐ Take cold showers.
- ☐ Drink energy drinks or eat energy bars.
- ☐ Sleep seven to eight hours a night.
- ☐ Avoid processed sugar.
- ☐ Drink coffee.
- ☐ Drink eight glasses of water a day.
- ☐ Eat fresh fruit and nuts.
- ☐ Exercise three to four times a week.
- ☐ Eat a chocolate bar or some cookies.

Which are the healthiest two ways to feel more energetic?

_____

_____

Which are the least healthy two ways to feel more energetic?

_____

_____

F Work in a group. Compare your results from Activity E. Choose the two best ways to boost energy immediately. Choose the two best ways to boost energy over a longer time period.

READING 1 | A Healthy Lifestyle Can Reduce Fatigue, Boost Energy

 You are going to read a newspaper article from *The St. Petersburg Times* that considers why many people often feel tired and worn out. Use the article to gather information and ideas for your Unit Assignment.

PREVIEW THE READING

A. **PREVIEW** What makes people feel tired and worn out? Check (✓) what you think are the three most common reasons. What else might take away people's energy?

☐ lack of sleep   ☐ financial problems

☐ too much work   ☐ poor diet

☐ too much stress   ☐ too much TV and too many video games

B. **QUICK WRITE** What types of things negatively affect people's energy levels? Write for 5–10 minutes. When you are finished writing, take a couple of minutes to read over your ideas and choose the ones that would go together in the most unified way. Remember to use this section for your Unit Assignment.

C. **VOCABULARY** Work with a partner to find these words in the reading. Circle clues in the text that help you understand the meaning of each word. Then use a dictionary to define any unknown words.

alleviate *(v.)*	fatigue *(n.)*	protein *(n.)*
carbohydrate *(n.)*	hormone *(n.)*	refined *(adj.)*
digest *(v.)*	immune system *(n.)*	restore *(v.)* 🔑
dilemma *(n.)*	metabolism *(n.)*	stamina *(n.)*

🔑 Oxford 3000™ words

 D. Go online to listen and practice your pronunciation.

A. Read the article and gather information about what energizes people.

A Healthy Lifestyle Can Reduce Fatigue, Boost Energy

By David Norrie

Does your energy level crash during the day?

1   Look around you at the gym. Can you be the only one wondering, "How can I get the energy to do this?" And as you get older, it doesn't get any easier. Little wonder we are besieged[1] by commercials for products that promise to boost our energy. Why the obsession with energy? Are we working harder, not taking care of ourselves, or simply expecting more out of each 24-hour day?

Experts generally agree on three culprits: sleep, stress, and diet

2   Quality, uninterrupted sleep is essential in helping the body repair tissue and **restore** itself, especially in people who exercise. Lack of sleep can impede your concentration levels and cause depression. Dr. John Brown, a sleep specialist at the James A. Haley Veterans Hospital, refers to this lack of quality sleep as "sleep debt," comparable, he says, to our society's financial debt.

3   Quality sleep has five stages, with the fifth (rapid eye movement, or REM) commonly associated with a deep sleep or dream state. It is important to get into the later stages of sleep because that is when the body produces growth **hormone**. Growth hormone, secreted[2] by the pituitary gland, affects all aspects of cellular **metabolism**, including **protein** synthesis and breaking down fats. A lack of it lowers metabolism, causing **fatigue** and weight gain.

4   While humans typically need seven to eight hours of sleep each night, "what might be acceptable and tolerable for one might not be for another," Brown says. If you log a normal amount of sleep and continue to experience an abnormal lack of energy during the day, you might want to consult a physician. You might suffer from chronic fatigue syndrome (CFS), which is far more distressful[3] than feeling sluggish[4] in the morning.

5   While CFS can follow a severe illness, abnormal stress, or death in the family, symptoms can also result from sleep apnea. Sleep apnea is characterized by temporary breathing interruptions during sleep, often lasting from 10 to 20 seconds. The pauses in breathing can occur dozens or hundreds of times a night and put a tremendous amount of stress on the respiratory system. Loud snoring, gasping for air

---

[1] **besiege:** to surround somebody or something in large numbers (especially by something unpleasant or annoying)
[2] **secreted:** produced as a liquid substance

[3] **distressful:** causing pain, upsetting
[4] **sluggish:** moving, reacting, or working more slowly than normal and in a way that seems lazy

during sleep, and excessive daytime napping are signs of sleep apnea. Typically a spouse first becomes aware of the situation. Obesity is one major cause of sleep apnea. While obese white males have been studied most thoroughly, the condition can affect anyone.

Stressed out

6   When I was young there was little to worry about other than getting good grades and staying fit. Stress rarely becomes a **dilemma** until we become adults, when work, family, and financial matters expand exponentially. While these common stress factors affect everybody's life, some have a more difficult time coping and the stress manifests itself physically.

7   Stress inhibits the **immune system**, detracts from our focus and often leads us back to the first problem, lack of sleep. Exercise is one good way to **alleviate** stress. But if your mind is cluttered with worries during a weightlifting session or fitness class it becomes difficult to reach your potential and reap the benefits of a successful workout.

8   You've seen ads for weight-loss products that include some derivative of the word *cortisol*. While I do not endorse these products, the hormone cortisol plays a critical part in how the body deals with stress. Cortisol itself, produced in the adrenal cortex, does not pose a threat to the body; its purpose is to help our bodies deal with stress and maintain a healthy immune system. But prolonged stress can induce an overproduction of cortisol, leading to an increase in blood pressure, blood sugar levels, and abdominal fat while suppressing the body's ability to fight cold and infection.

9   Extended anxiety puts the adrenal gland under enormous pressure to try to keep up with the production of cortisol. This can eventually lead to a group of symptoms that some medical practitioners call adrenal fatigue. People with adrenal fatigue typically feel drained[5] in the morning and don't feel fully awake until noon, with lulls in energy all day. Other symptoms include inability to lose weight, difficulty remembering things, colds, and lightheadedness.

Eating yourself to exhaustion

10   As a trainer, the two biggest mistakes I see people make are: 1) going into a good evening workout session having had their last meal around noon, or 2) the reverse, a person who hurried a meal on his way to the gym thinking that would give him proper energy to work out.

11   When and how often you eat are just as important to your energy levels as what you eat. Long periods without food tell our bodies to shut down and conserve energy. That fact has been programmed into our DNA, and it makes perfect sense when you think about it. In the days of Neanderthal Man, food was more scarce. For early man to survive during wintertime or periods of food scarcity, the body's metabolism would slow down dramatically in what you would call "survival mode."

12   To not so great an extent, when we go without food for even five to seven hours, we experience a similar drop in metabolism, a halt in the burning of fuel, and a lull in energy. But eating just before exercise will do nothing but drain your body of its ability to function at an optimum level, as your organs are using energy to process and **digest** food. That is why we feel tired after a large meal.

13   For your body to function as the well-oiled machine it should be, it is better to eat small meals throughout the day, every two to three hours. Consider three basic meals a day with small snacks in between. And by snacks, I mean fruits, nuts, energy bars, etc. Complex **carbohydrates** are the body's preferred source of energy.

14   But perhaps one reason some of us experience fatigue is a diet skewed[6] toward consuming protein

---

[5] **drained**: weaker with less energy

[6] **skewed**: directed toward something in an incorrect way

in large quantities. High-protein meals build muscle and restore our bodies on a cellular level, but a lack of quality carbohydrates makes it much more difficult for our bodies to produce energy. Here's the catch: not all carbohydrates are good for sustained energy. **Refined** sugars, found in sodas and candy bars, give you a quick energy fix but do not provide a good source of long-lasting fuel, typically leaving the body in what's referred to as a "crash" state after they rush through the digestive system.

15 In addition to simple sugars, beware of processed or refined foods, as they are more difficult to break down in digestion. What's more, the foods' molecular structure has changed, robbing them of their true nutrients. Processed and refined foods are higher on the glycemic index, a scale that ranks carbohydrate-rich foods by how much they raise blood glucose levels. Foods high on the index burn quickly and release a rapid shot of energy to the body. Again, this is not good for **stamina** and leaves the body in a crash state. Foods low on the glycemic index release energy more slowly and combat fatigue. Low-index foods are typically lower in calories and fat and higher in fiber.

Vocabulary
Skill Review

In Unit 7, you learned about making appropriate word choices. As you learn new vocabulary, consider the audience you are writing for, the register you should use, and the genre you are working within to decide when to use a word.

B **VOCABULARY** Here are some words from Reading 1. Complete each sentence with a word from the box.

alleviate (v.)	dilemma (n.)	immune system (n.)	refined (adj.)
carbohydrates (n.)	fatigue (n.)	metabolism (n.)	restore (v.)
digest (v.)	hormone (n.)	protein (n.)	stamina (n.)

1. Chicken and beef are two foods that contain a lot of _____.

2. Some runners eat pasta or other foods with a lot of _____ because they believe these foods will give them energy for a big race.

3. Too much caffeine and sugar can affect a person's _____, speeding up nerve activities.

4. You need a lot of _____ to be able to run a marathon.

5. A good diet and plenty of rest can help _____ the symptoms of minor illnesses and make you feel better.

6. After eating, you should allow your body time to _____ the food before you start any exercise.

7. After exercising, you should drink water to _____ the fluids lost during your workout.

8. Severe _____ can be caused by too much exercise or a poor diet, resulting in the desire to sleep all the time.

9. Many adults face a _____ when they must choose whether or not to take time away from work and family in order to exercise.

10. Stress can reduce the effectiveness of your _____ and make it easier for you to become sick.

11. An area of the brain called the pineal gland produces a _____ called melatonin that helps people get the right amount of sleep.

12. Soft drinks and candy bars often contain a lot of _____ sugar, which is not as healthy as the natural sugars in fruits.

iQ ONLINE **C. Go online for more practice with the vocabulary.**

D. Circle the answer that best completes each statement.

1. The main causes of low energy levels are ____.
   a. carbohydrate-rich foods and refined sugars
   b. poor sleep, too much stress, and bad diet
   c. a lack of concentration and depression
   d. working too hard and not taking care of ourselves

2 People need good-quality, uninterrupted sleep in order to ____.
   a. help the body repair tissue and restore itself
   b. digest their food efficiently
   c. stop producing growth hormone
   d. have enough energy to exercise

3. Stress and energy levels are related because ____.
   a. exercise helps to get rid of stress
   b. some people suffer from adrenal fatigue
   c. too much stress has negative physical effects on the body
   d. cortisol is not produced sufficiently when the body is under stress

4. When you eat, how often you eat, and what you eat ____.
   a. affect the glycemic index
   b. are not important for digestion
   c. are programmed into your DNA
   d. have a major effect on your energy level

E. Correct these false statements with information from Reading 1. Write the number of the paragraph in which the correct information is found.

1. It is better to eat large meals three times a day at breakfast, lunch, and dinner. Paragraph: ____

   _____

2. People feel tired and lose weight when they have enough growth hormone. Paragraph: ____

   _____

3. Exercise is a bad way to deal with stress if you are not too worried about things. Paragraph: ____

   _____

4. Food choices high on the glycemic index combat fatigue because they release energy very quickly in the body. Paragraph: ____

   _____

5. Sleep apnea can result from chronic fatigue syndrome. Paragraph: ____

   _____

6. Going without food for several hours results in an increase in metabolism and higher energy levels. Paragraph: ____

   _____

7. Refined sugars provide long-lasting energy. Paragraph: ____

   _____

8. High levels of cortisol have several positive effects on the body. Paragraph: ____

   _____

F. Using your own words, complete these notes based on information found in the reading.

Sleep

1. Good quality sleep is important for _____.

2. Later stages of sleep are when _____.

3. Human growth hormone affects _____.

4. CFS can be caused by _____.

5. Symptoms of sleep apnea include _____.

Stress

1. Adults suffer more from stress because _____.

2. Stress affects _____.

3. Stress can be helped by _____.

4. Cortisol is _____.

5. Symptoms of adrenal fatigue include _____.

Diet

1. The two biggest mistakes people make are _____.

2. What people eat is as important as _____.

3. People feel tired after a large meal because _____.

4. It is better to eat _____.

5. The glycemic index is _____.

G. With a partner, respond to each of the following scenarios using information found in the reading.

1. Sofia is feeling depressed, and she often has difficulty concentrating at work. What would you suggest she do to improve her mood and ability to concentrate?

2. Antwan has recently gained a lot of weight, and he has been feeling very tired. What do you think might be the cause of his problems?

3. Nobuo suffers from increased blood pressure, high blood sugar levels, and weight gain. He also catches a lot of colds. What advice do you have for Nobuo to improve his health?

4. For the past few months, Min Yung has had a lot of difficulty waking up in the morning, and she has been feeling very tired and lightheaded. What do you think could be the cause of her problems?

5. Pei Chen has a lot of energy throughout the day. What kind of eating schedule do you think she might be following?

6. Theodore loves eating candy, but he still feels really tired sometimes. Why might that be happening?

 **H.** Go online to read the magazine interview *Improving Athletic Performance* and check your comprehension.

 # WRITE WHAT YOU THINK

A. Discuss these questions in a group.

1. Are getting enough quality sleep, lowering stress, and eating well realistic ways to boost energy levels for people in today's world? Why or why not?

2. Do you have enough energy to do the things you want to do? What are you doing, or could you be doing, to boost your energy levels?

3. Are most people you know too busy? Do busy people suffer from fatigue and low energy? Why or why not?

B. Choose one question and write a paragraph in response. Look back at your Quick Write on page 227 as you think about what you have learned.

Reading Skill | **Organizing notes and annotations in a chart**

A chart is a useful tool for organizing your notes and annotations from a reading. Creating such a chart makes studying easier. Charts can also make it easier to paraphrase and summarize a text for a report or essay. There are various charts you can use depending on the type of text and the type of writing you plan to do.

Main ideas and details chart

This type of chart helps you identify and understand the relationship between main ideas and details. Record the main ideas in the reading on one side of the chart and the most important details on the other.

Main ideas	Details
Lack of quality sleep decreases energy.	• produce growth hormone when sleeping • sleep apnea causes chronic fatigue syndrome

Cause and effect chart

This type of chart helps you identify and understand the **causes** (the events in a story or the steps in a process) and the **effects** (the results of those events or steps).

Cause	Effect
too much caffeine	nervousness, very alert

Connections to the text chart

This type of chart helps you remember and understand the text in a more meaningful way because you are connecting the text with something you already know.

You can make connections between the reading and:
- things or events in your own life (**text to self**)
- other information you have read (**text to text**)
- issues, events, general knowledge in the world (**text to world**)

Ideas in Reading 1	Connections
One reason some of us experience fatigue is a diet skewed toward consuming protein in large quantities.	**Text to self:** I always feel tired after eating a lot of protein—especially after eating a lot of meat.
	Text to text: I read an online article that said high-protein diets were unhealthy and might cause kidney problems.
	Text to world: High-protein diets are still popular with people who want to lose a lot of weight.

A. Write the number of each corrected statement from Activity E (page 232) next to the main idea that it supports.

Main ideas	Details
a. Good-quality sleep can reduce fatigue and boost energy.	
b. Dealing with stress can reduce fatigue and boost energy.	
c. Having a healthy diet can reduce fatigue and boost energy.	1,

B. Complete this cause and effect chart for Reading 1 with the missing cause or effect.

Cause	Effect
1. quality uninterrupted sleep	body repairs tissue and restores itself
2. lack of sleep	
3.	lower metabolism, fatigue, weight gain
4. sleep apnea	
5.	sleep apnea

Cause	Effect
6. worrying during exercise	
7.	increase in blood pressure, blood sugar, and abdominal fat; harder to fight cold and infection
8. no food for five to seven hours	
9.	fatigue
10. refined sugars	

C. Complete the connections-to-text chart by identifying text-to-self, text-to-text, and text-to-world connections you can make to the information found in Reading 1.

Ideas in Reading 1	Connections
Poor sleep leads to fatigue.	Text to self:
	Text to text:
	Text to world:
High stress levels lead to fatigue.	Text to self:
	Text to text:
	Text to world:
Poor diet leads to fatigue.	Text to self:
	Text to text:
	Text to world:

 D. Go online for more practice organizing notes and annotations in a chart.

You are going to read a newspaper article from *The New York Times* that discusses the growing popularity of energy drinks. Use the article to gather information and ideas for your Unit Assignment.

PREVIEW THE READING

A. **PREVIEW** What do you think the article will say about the caffeine in energy drinks? Check (✓) your answer.

☐ Energy drinks have about the same amount of caffeine as coffee.

☐ Energy drinks have much more caffeine than coffee.

☐ Energy drinks have more caffeine than coffee but less than most sodas.

B. **QUICK WRITE** What types of food and drink boost people's energy levels? Write for 5–10 minutes. Take two minutes to read over what you have written and revise or edit your ideas. Remember to use this section for your Unit Assignment.

C. **VOCABULARY** Check (✓) the words or phrases you know. Then work with a partner to locate each word or phrase in the reading. Use clues to help define the words or phrases you don't know. Check your definitions in the dictionary.

agitated *(adj.)*	**foster** *(v.)*
bar *(v.)* 🔑	**minimal** *(adj.)*
component *(n.)* 🔑	**mystique** *(n.)*
concentration *(n.)* 🔑	**relative to** *(phr.)*
contend *(v.)*	**take issue with** *(phr.)*
disclaimer *(n.)*	**unfounded** *(adj.)*

🔑 Oxford 3000™ words

 D. Go online to listen and practice your pronunciation.

A. Read the article and gather information about what energizes people.

A Jolt of Caffeine, by the Can

By Melanie Warner

1 Every day Tom Cabrera, a 27-year-old auto mechanic who lives in Middletown, Rhode Island, drinks a can of SoBe No Fear energy drink on his way to work. Later in the day, if he goes to the gym, he downs another before his workout.

2 He says he probably could not get through the day without one. "It lifts me up. One minute I'm dragging and then it's like 'Pow!'" he said, widening his eyes.

3 Loyal and enthusiastic customers like Mr. Cabrera have helped propel caffeinated energy drinks into the fastest-growing sector of the $93 billion domestic beverage industry. Sales of energy drinks, which sell for $2 to $3 a can, have grown a torrid[1] 61 percent this year in the United States, according to *Beverage Digest*.

4 But that has scientists and nutritionists worried. Energy drinks have as much sugar and roughly three times the caffeine of soda, and some experts peg their popularity to their addictiveness. And with racy[2] names like Full Throttle and Adrenaline Rush, critics say these drinks are **fostering** caffeine addiction among teenagers.

5 Caffeine can cause hyperactivity and restlessness among children and is known to increase the excretion of calcium, a mineral much needed while bones are still growing.

6 Energy drink manufacturers say they do not market to children and their products have no more caffeine than a typical cup of coffee. But the debate persists. Four countries have **barred** the sale of energy drinks with current levels of caffeine: France, Denmark, Norway, and, two months ago, Argentina.

7 Critics **contend** that much of the skyrocketing growth of energy drinks comes because consumers are getting physically addicted, either by consuming the concoctions[3] daily or guzzling several at a time to elevate their mood.

8 Roland Griffiths, a professor of behavioral biology at Johns Hopkins University School of Medicine, says the amount of caffeine necessary to produce dependency and withdrawal symptoms is about 100 milligrams a day. A can of energy drink has 80 to 160 milligrams, depending on the size, though such information is not listed on any cans. An eight-ounce cup of coffee typically has 100 to 150 milligrams.

9 Some energy brands go so far as to promote their addictiveness as a selling point. "Meet your new addiction! 16 oz of super-charged energy with advanced **components** and a great berry-passion fruit flavor," reads the front page of Pepsi's SoBe No Fear website. Cans of Kronik Energy, made by an Arizona company, warn customers, "Caution: May Be Psychologically Addicting," meant as a daring come-on, not a serious warning.

10 Nutritionists say that while it may be fine for adults to have their dose of caffeine, they worry about children becoming hooked. "I suspect that busy, driven teenagers are grabbing one of these energy drinks instead of eating real food, which I would be concerned about," said Lola O'Rourke, a registered dietitian in Seattle and a spokeswoman for the American Dietetic Association.

---

[1] **torrid:** very hot; (figuratively) fast and strong
[2] **racy:** having a style that is exciting and amusing
[3] **concoction:** a strange or unusual mixture of things, especially a kind of drink or medicine

11 Cans of SoBe, Monster, and others carry a voluntary **disclaimer**, warning that the fizzy liquid inside is "not recommended for children, pregnant women, or people sensitive to caffeine."

12 But the definition of "children" is not always clear. Coke and Pepsi say they aim their products at those older than 20. Rodney C. Sacks, chief executive of the Hansen Natural Corporation, which sells the popular Monster brand, says that his product is appropriate for anyone over 13.

13 In addition to caffeine, other purportedly energy-enhancing ingredients in energy drinks have attracted the attention of European health officials. When France banned Red Bull in 2000, health officials cited uncertainties about the interaction of caffeine, the amino acid taurine, and glucuronolactone, a type of sugar that is produced by human cells and used in metabolism.

14 Beverage companies say energy drinks have been safely consumed around the world for more than a decade and that such concerns are **unfounded**. But they acknowledge that there have been few studies looking at the particular combinations of these compounds. In addition to taurine and glucuronolactone, energy drinks have other unusual ingredients: guarana, a Brazilian herb that contains caffeine; D-Ribose, another sugar used in metabolism; carnitine, arginine, and creatine, three amino acids; and ginseng, an Asian herb said to have antioxidant benefits.

15 Red Bull, the Austrian company that makes the original energy drink, makes ambitious assertions about its particular blend of these ingredients. The company's website boasts that Red Bull "improves performance, especially during times of increased stress or strain," "increases **concentration**," and "stimulates the metabolism."

16 Other manufacturers, however, are more circumspect[4] in their claims. Mary Merrill, group director for sports and energy drinks at Coca-Cola, says the reason taurine, guarana, carnitine, and ginseng are in Full Throttle is because customers want them there.

17 "Energy drinks contain ingredients that consumers have come to expect and want to see," Ms. Merrill said. "We make no claims about any of them. We believe in marketing our brand by focusing on the brand's personality, rather than the ingredients."

18 Mr. Cabrera, the auto mechanic, says he likes it that his can of No Fear has strange-sounding ingredients, listed on the top of the can, but he admits he has no idea what taurine, creatine, and arginine are.

19 Kristi Hinck, a spokeswoman for SoBe beverages, says that if consumers are curious about ingredients, they should do research. "We encourage people to do their homework and look it up," she said. "It's part of the whole **mystique** about energy drinks."

20 Some scientists say this mystique amounts to little more than shrewd marketing of overpriced, caffeinated sugar water. "These are just caffeine delivery systems," said Professor Griffiths at Johns Hopkins. "They're being marketed cleverly to imply they have other ingredients that may be useful to some end."

21 Henk Smit, a researcher in the department of experimental psychology at the University of Bristol in Britain, decided to test the effectiveness of energy drinks. In a study published in the medical journal *Nutritional Neuroscience* last year, Mr. Smit found that energy drinks were effective at improving mood and performance, but he concluded that caffeine was the crucial component.

22 "Any additional benefits of taurine, glucuronolactone, or other ingredients are **minimal** compared to those of caffeine, and from what I know, are speculative at best for most of these ingredients," he wrote in an e-mail message.

[4] **circumspect:** thinking very carefully about something before doing it because there may be risks

23 Mr. Sacks, the Hansen chief executive, **takes issue with** these findings. He says Monster is carefully made to deliver a smoother burst of energy than other forms of caffeine. "When you drink coffee you get jittery, **agitated**, and fidgety," he said. "Our experience is that you don't get the same effect with an energy drink."

24 Mr. Sacks says that if his aim were to simply get customers revved up on caffeine, he would have added more of it. "If I wanted to promote sales, I could have doubled the caffeine," he said. "It's a cheap ingredient **relative** to the others. Why would I spend dollars and dollars per case for these other ingredients when I could just put in 2 more cents and double the caffeine?"

25 It is these other, more expensive ingredients that allow manufacturers to charge $2 to $3 a can when a 20-ounce bottle of soda can be had for $1 to $1.50. And that, says Mr. Pirko of Bevmark, has everything to do with marketing. "You're selling images to people who want to be powerful," he said. "It's a head trip[5]."

[5] **head trip**: a feeling resulting from an action done mostly for your own pleasure

B. **VOCABULARY** Here are some words and phrases from Reading 2. Complete each sentence with a word or phrase from the box. You may need to change the form of the word or phrase to make the sentence grammatically correct.

agitated *(adj.)*	**concentration** *(n.)*	**foster** *(v.)*	**relative to** *(phr.)*
bar *(v.)*	**contend** *(v.)*	**minimal** *(adj.)*	**take issue with** *(phr.)*
component *(n.)*	**disclaimer** *(n.)*	**mystique** *(n.)*	**unfounded** *(adj.)*

1. Some energy drinks contain a large amount of caffeine _____ the amount in coffee and tea.

2. Vitamins are one important _____ of many energy drinks.

3. Energy drink companies create a _____ about their drinks by making the ingredients sound like little-known medicines.

4. People who drink too much coffee can become _____, restless, and nervous.

5. Regular users of energy drinks _____ people who believe the drinks should be banned.

6. Some governments _____ the sale of energy drinks because they want to keep people from using drinks that may be harmful.

7. Some people say that energy drinks improve their _____, so they can pay attention and think better.

8. People who criticize energy drinks _____ that the drinks have too much caffeine in them.

9. Scientists caution that energy drinks can start or _____ an addiction to the caffeine in the drinks.

10. The advertiser made claims that were _____, with no research to support them.

11. For some people the effects are _____, but others suffer severe headaches during caffeine withdrawal.

12. Energy drinks often carry a _____ on their label warning that the drink is not suitable for children or pregnant women.

iQ ONLINE **C. Go online for more practice with the vocabulary.**

D. Read the statements related to the main ideas in Reading 2. Write _T_ (true) or _F_ (false) beside each statement. Correct any false statements.

____ 1. Beverage companies claim that energy drinks are safe and can have a number of benefits.

_____

____ 2. Many scientists consider energy drinks to be a healthy and safe alternative to coffee.

_____

____ 3. There are worries about the negative effects of high levels of caffeine in energy drinks, especially for children.

_____

____ 4. Energy drinks are big business, and their sales are growing fast.

_____

____ 5. The benefits of taurine, glucuronolactone, and other ingredients in energy drinks have been scientifically proven to be much greater than those of caffeine.

_____

____ 6. According to one study, the additional ingredients in energy drinks have few benefits compared to caffeine, the most important ingredient.

_____

_____ 7. Scientists are worried that people who drink energy drinks are becoming addicted because of the high amounts of caffeine.

E. Write the paragraph number in Reading 2 where each detail can be found.

Main idea	Details		Paragraph
1. Energy drinks are very popular.	a.	Some people drink one or two energy drinks every day.	
	b.	Energy drinks are the fastest-growing sector of the beverage industry.	
	c.	Sales grew 61 percent in one year.	
2. Energy drinks contain high levels of caffeine.	d.	Critics say energy drinks encourage caffeine addiction among teenagers.	
	e.	Caffeine causes hyperactivity, restlessness, and loss of calcium in children.	
	f.	France, Denmark, Norway, and Argentina have stopped the sale of energy drinks with current levels of caffeine.	

F. Use this chart to record your notes on the final part of the reading. Remember to write only the most important details.

Main idea	Details
1. Consumers are becoming addicted to energy drinks.	
2. Energy drinks contain other energy-enhancing ingredients.	
3. Scientists say caffeine is the most important ingredient in energy drinks.	
4. Energy drink companies feel the other ingredients are important.	

G. Scan through Reading 2 for statistical information. Answer the questions.

1. How old is Tom Cabrera?

2. How many dollars is the domestic beverage industry worth?

3. How much do energy drinks sell for?

4. How many countries have banned the sale of energy drinks?

5. How much caffeine is necessary to produce dependency and withdrawal symptoms?

6. How much caffeine does a can of energy drink contain?

7. How much caffeine is in an eight-ounce cup of coffee?

8. How large is a can of Pepsi's SoBe No Fear energy drink?

9. According to Coke and Pepsi, to what age group are their products marketed?

10. According to Rodney C. Sacks, what is an appropriate age to start drinking Monster brand energy drinks?

11. In what year did France ban Red Bull?

12. What is the price of a 20-ounce bottle of soda?

H. Based on the information in Reading 2, what answers can you infer to the following questions?

1. Why does Tom Cabrera drink one or two cans of energy drink every day?

2. Why are energy drinks such a fast-growing sector of the beverage industry?

3. Why are scientists and nutritionists worried about the increasing popularity of energy drinks?

4. Why might some companies promote the addictiveness of their energy drinks as a selling point?

5. Why might some companies put voluntary disclaimers on their drinks?

6. Why do energy drink companies add strange-sounding ingredients such as taurine, glucuronolactone, and guarana to their drinks?

7. Why would an energy drink company avoid making claims about the ingredients in its energy drinks and focus on a brand's personality instead?

8. What point is Mr. Sacks trying to make by explaining that caffeine is much cheaper than the other ingredients in energy drinks?

WRITE WHAT YOU THINK

A. Discuss these questions in a group. Look back at your Quick Write on page 237 as you think about what you have learned.

1. Have you ever tried an energy drink? If yes, how did it make you feel? If you haven't tried one, would you?

2. A number of countries do not allow the sale of energy drinks with high levels of caffeine. Do you think the government should step in and control the consumption of these drinks? Why or why not?

3. Is the popularity of energy drinks mainly due to marketing or to their beneficial effects? Explain your opinion.

B. Think about the unit video, Reading 1, and Reading 2 as you discuss these questions. Then choose one question and write a paragraph in response.

1. If people know that a good night's sleep, reducing stress, and eating well are sensible lifestyle choices that help to increase energy levels, why do some people choose to use energy drinks instead?

2. Which method of boosting energy do you prefer: lifestyle changes as in Reading 1 or energy drinks as in Reading 2? Why?

Vocabulary Skill	Adjective/verb + preposition collocations

Some **adjectives and verbs** are often **followed by certain prepositions**. These common word combinations are called **collocations**. Being familiar with these patterns can increase your accuracy as you write and speed up your reading comprehension. These charts show some common collocations found in Readings 1 and 2.

Adjective + preposition

Adjective	Preposition	Example
curious	about	Consumers who are **curious about** the ingredients in energy drinks can do some research.
appropriate	for	The chief executive says the energy drink is **appropriate for** anyone over the age of 13.
aware	of	My spouse first became **aware of** my sleep apnea when I started snoring loudly.
sensitive	to	Some people are **sensitive to** caffeine.

Verb + preposition

Verb	Preposition	Example
worry	about	Many university students **worry about** getting good grades.
focus	on	Some energy drink companies like to **focus on** the brand's personality rather than the ingredients.
refer	to	The tired feeling after a quick sugar rush is **referred to** as a crash state.
deal	with	Cortisol helps our bodies **deal with** stress.

Cause or effect

The collocations *result from* and *be caused by* are used to express cause. *Lead to* and *result in* are used to express effect. They are all common in academic writing.

Low energy levels **result from** people not getting enough exercise.
    effect   cause

Not getting enough exercise **results in** low energy levels.
    cause   effect

A. Complete each sentence with the appropriate preposition. If you need help, look at the Vocabulary Skill Box or scan Readings 1 and 2. Then check (✓) the sentences with collocations used to express cause or effect.

1. Some doctors refer _____ a lack of quality sleep as a sleep debt.

2. Too much stress can result _____ many problems, such as having low energy and not being able to lose weight.

3. Busy people find it difficult to deal _____ making healthy meals on a daily basis.

4. Energy drinks are often marketed _____ young adults who are looking for a quick boost.

5. Sometimes, children's behavioral problems result _____ the effects of too much caffeine.

6. Are consumers curious _____ the strange-sounding ingredients found in energy drinks?

B. Combine the phrases (cause, effect, and collocation) into one sentence. Change the verbs and nouns as necessary to create a grammatical sentence.

1. not get enough quality sleep / feel tired all the time / result from

   <u>Feeling tired all the time results from not getting enough quality sleep.</u>

2. be obese / sleep apnea / can result from

   _____

3. high levels of caffeine / France, Denmark, Norway, and Argentina bar the sale of energy drinks / lead to

   _____

4. eat a large, high-protein meal / feel tired / can be caused by

   _____

5. companies spend a lot of money on marketing them / an increase in sales of energy drinks / may be caused by

   _____

6. drink an energy drink / feel wide awake and alert / can result in

   _____

C. Find five new adjective + preposition or verb + preposition collocations in Reading 1 and Reading 2. Then write a sentence in your own words for each new collocation.

Seven to eight hours of sleep can boost energy.

 D. Go online for more practice with adjective/verb + preposition collocations.

WRITING

At the end of this unit, you will write a cause and effect essay. This essay will include information from the readings, the unit video, and your own ideas.

Writing Skill | Writing a cause and effect essay

People often write to understand the reasons behind something or the results of something: causes and effects. The piece of writing can either focus on the causes of a situation or event or it can focus on the results of a situation or event.

The **causal analysis essay** looks at multiple causes leading to one major result. It usually begins by describing a particular situation and then analyzing all of the causes.

Thesis statement: Poor sleep, high stress, and a bad diet can lead to a lack of energy.

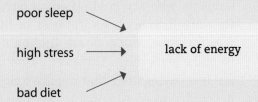

poor sleep

high stress → lack of energy

bad diet

The **effect analysis essay** examines how one major situation has a number of different results. It usually begins by describing a particular situation and then analyzing all of the effects.

Thesis statement: Too much caffeine can result in difficulty sleeping, headaches, and nervousness.

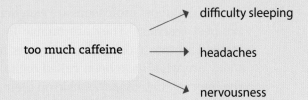

too much caffeine

→ difficulty sleeping

→ headaches

→ nervousness

There are two common problems to watch for in a causal analysis or effect analysis essay.

1. The relationships between cause and effect must exist and be logical. Avoid mistaken causal relationships—jumping to conclusions without first checking the logic of your argument.

   ✗ Drinking the right energy drink leads to happiness.
   ✗ Eating a large meal with too much protein immediately results in illness.

2. The causal relationships must be supportable with details such as facts, examples, statistics, quotations, and anecdotes.

A. **WRITING MODEL** Read the model essay written in response to an English composition class assignment. Then answer the questions with a partner.

English Composition 101 Midterm Essay Assignment:

Why do some students have very low energy and difficulty concentrating? Write an essay analyzing why some students have trouble staying awake during class.

Class Time Is Often Sleepy Time

1   There is a serious problem that is growing on university campuses. In ever greater numbers, undergraduate students are finding it difficult to stay focused in class. It is routine to see students closing their eyes during lectures or staring out the window. While some students hide behind their books, other students move around in their chairs, trying to keep alert. Why are students struggling to make the most of their class time? The reasons for this struggle to stay awake lie in student jobs and university classes.

2   One culprit for this lack of focus in class is the increasing number of students who are holding down part-time or even full-time jobs while they are in school. As the cost of living continues to rise and tuition fees increase, students are finding it necessary to have a job in order to make ends meet. However, often the only jobs available to students are low-paying ones that require long hours in order to make the money necessary to go to school. The long hours cut into study time, forcing students to study later and later into the night. It is not rare for a student to arrive home from a part-time job at 9 p.m. and then to be faced with another four or five hours of homework. It is hard to imagine being bright and energetic for an early morning class after that.

3   Another explanation for why students are not focusing in class is that classes can often be boring affairs that students must endure. One reason may be that most professors are excellent researchers, but not necessarily the best teachers. They are unable to engage students in learning and instead lecture from prepared notes in a traditional manner. Students today are what have been called digital natives, used to multitasking on the Internet, listening to music on their smartphones, and watching TV in a 500-channel universe. To suddenly ask them to listen to lectures read aloud in a monotone voice leads to wandering minds.

4   Schedules packed with work and study, along with classes that do not engage students' attention, lead to difficulties focusing in class. Something must change if university students are going to get the most possible out of their programs of study. Students need to make a commitment to work fewer hours, and universities need to make a commitment to improve classroom lectures.

---

1. What type of essay is this?

   ☐ causal analysis essay   ☐ effect analysis essay

2. What is the thesis statement for this essay? Underline it.

3. What is the first topic sentence? Underline it twice.

4. Note the first major cause and its effect in the margin.

5. What is the second topic sentence? Underline it twice.

6. Note the second major cause and its effect in the margin.

7. What is the concluding statement? Underline it.

B. **Complete this cause and effect chart for each main body paragraph of the essay in Activity A.**

Working part-time or full-time jobs is making students tired and unable to focus.	
Cause	**Effect**
1. rising cost of living	
2.	students need a job
3. usually have low-paying jobs	
4.	have to study late at night
5. study late at night	
6.	
7.	
8.	
9.	
10.	

Critical Thinking **Tip**

In Activity C, you will create a cause and effect chart. Organizing information in this way can help you remember material better and use it more effectively to express your own ideas.

C. **Imagine you have been assigned to write an essay based on one of the readings in this unit. Choose Reading 1 or Reading 2 and create a cause and effect chart in answer to one of these essay questions.**

1. What are some reasons why people feel tired during the day?

2. What can people do to boost their energy?

3. What are some effects of consuming energy drinks?

4. Why are energy drinks becoming so popular?

D. WRITING MODEL Read the model cause and effect essay. Then fill in the diagram that follows with the major effect in the rectangle, the main causes in the ovals, and the associated important details on the lines. Some of the information has been completed for you.

Tips for Graduate Students to Keep up Their Energy

In recent years, the multiple demands put onto graduate students seem to be getting heavier and heavier. These demands, such as the pressure to pass exams, the requirement to write a thesis or dissertation, and the need to have a part-time job, can drain students of their energy. Some students may even feel trapped in an exhaustion from which there is no escape. However, there are measures that students can take to beat that feeling of being tired all the time. Namely, getting lots of exercise, sleeping well, enjoying healthy drinks, and staying positive all help maintain the high levels of energy that students need on a daily basis.

Exercise is known to boost energy levels. While students may find it hard to carve out the time to exercise, thirty minutes of exercise three times a week is enough to keep fatigue at bay. A great time to get mobile is early in the morning. Students can try a light jog or a brisk walk before breakfast. This exercise will get their blood flowing and carry oxygen to the brain, helping them to feel bright and alert for the rest of the day. Another tip is to not stay sedentary all day. When studying for long periods of time, students should get up and walk around. For example, after every hour of studying, students should stand up and go for a five-minute walk before hitting the books again. Finally, stretching before bed is another way for students to keep themselves in top form. It can help tired muscles get the oxygen they need to support an active lifestyle.

Along with exercising, getting enough good quality sleep is very important for students who are feeling tired all the time. The key to getting good quality sleep is having a comfortable mattress. A lumpy, secondhand futon or a twelve-year-old mattress from home might be the culprit preventing a good night's sleep. It is important for students to speak with a sleep expert and find the right mattress for their sleeping style. In addition, students should avoid using electronics before going to bed. It might be fun watching YouTube videos before bed, but the glowing blue light from the screen has been known to have a negative effect on sleep quality. Lastly, a regular sleeping schedule is vital for maintaining normal energy levels. Most people need at least eight hours of sleep a night. Thus, pulling an all-nighter one night and then sleeping for twelve hours straight the next night is not a good idea. The best plan is to go to bed every night at 10:30 p.m. and wake up at 6:30 the next morning, fresh and ready to start the day.

Good hydration is another factor that can help maintain energy levels. The first and best choice is plenty of water. To avoid feeling sluggish and dehydrated, students should aim to drink at least eight glasses of water a day. Another good drink for a quick pick-me-up is green tea. Green tea is rich in antioxidants, and it has less caffeine than coffee. Being sugar free, it is also a much better choice than soda pop or energy drinks, and students can avoid the sugar crash that comes with consuming those types of sweetened beverages. Finally, a good investment for students is a good quality juicer. Having enough vitamins and minerals is key to staying energetic, but many students are not able to eat the recommended seven to eight servings of fruits and vegetables. However, with a juicer, students can drink their vitamins and minerals and find the energy they need for studying.

Finally, having a positive mental attitude is the most important factor contributing to staying energetic. There are many challenges to being a student, but it can help if problems are seen as opportunities for learning. By seeing setbacks as learning experiences, students are less likely to feel depressed and drained. For example, when students fail tests, they can analyze those tests so that they can do better next time. Another tip to help keep students' energy up is to remember to smile. It may seem silly at first, but it is hard to feel depressed and tired if you are smiling. Finally, it is important to see the good in people. The professor may seem like an enemy at times, but there may be a reason behind what he or she is doing. For example, those early morning quizzes might be to ensure that students make it to class on time, thus helping them learn more in the end. Holding people in a positive light will help students stay in a good mood, thus helping them not feel drained and exhausted.

All in all, graduate students can keep up their energy levels with plenty of exercise, good quality sleep, healthy drinks, and positive attitudes. It might be hard at first, but putting these four pieces of advice into practice is sure to boost energy levels. Once the benefits of having high energy levels start to be enjoyed, living a healthy lifestyle will be natural.

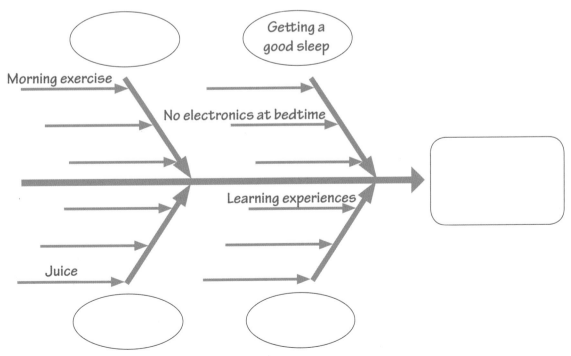

 E. Go online for more practice with writing a cause and effect essay.

Grammar   Cause and effect connectors

Tip for Success

In order to sound fluent, use connectors only when you need to demonstrate a clear relationship between ideas.

Cause and effect connectors show the exact relationship between your ideas and give your writing coherence.

The **coordinating conjunction** *so* follows the cause and is connected to the effect in a sentence. It does not usually start a sentence in formal academic writing.

> People do not get enough exercise, **so** they suffer from low energy levels.

The **subordinators** *because*, *due to the fact that*, and *since* connect to the cause in a sentence. They are used in dependent (adverbial) clauses. Notice the use of the comma when the dependent clause comes first.

> Some people have low energy **because** they do not get enough exercise.
> I have low energy levels **due to the fact that** I don't eat enough complex carbohydrates.
> **Since** you feel so tired, you should stay home and rest.

The **transitions** *as a consequence*, *as a result*, *because of this*, *consequently*, *for this (that) reason*, and *therefore* all follow the cause and are connected to the effect.

> People do not get enough exercise. **Consequently**, they suffer from low energy.
> People do not get enough exercise; **for this reason**, they suffer from low energy.

A. Underline the cause once and the effect twice.

1. Jody says his high energy level is **due to the fact that** he drinks an energy drink every morning.

2. France, Denmark, Norway, and Argentina banned the sale of some energy drinks **because** they contain high levels of caffeine.

3. Many customers like strange-sounding ingredients. **Consequently**, energy drink companies add ingredients like guarana, D-Ribose, and carnitine to their beverages.

4. Energy drinks contain caffeine. One study noted that **because of this**, these drinks can improve mood and performance.

5. Energy drinks have a loyal, enthusiastic customer base. **For this reason**, sales of energy drinks have grown quickly.

B. Draw an arrow from each cause to its effect.

Cause and Effect		
1. She feels tired every day.	←	She's not getting enough sleep.
2. I feel energetic while I work.		I drink coffee in the morning.
3. People eat too many processed and refined food items.		People suffer from low energy levels and fatigue.
4. There is a lot of caffeine in energy drinks.		People are becoming addicted to energy drinks.
5. Energy drinks can give a boost of energy.		People working long shifts buy energy drinks.
6. He has symptoms of chronic fatigue syndrome.		He has sleep apnea.
7. People need quality, uninterrupted sleep.		The body repairs tissue and restores itself during sleep.

C. Rewrite the sentences in Activity B using these connectors. Change nouns to pronouns as needed to make your sentences sound natural.

1. for this reason

2. because

3. as

4. due to the fact that

5. because of this

6. as a consequence

7. since

 D. Go online for more practice with cause and effect connectors.

E. Go online for the grammar expansion.

Unit Assignment   Write a cause and effect essay

 In this assignment, you will write a cause and effect essay that examines the best methods for boosting energy levels. As you prepare your essay, think about the Unit Question, "What energizes people?" Use information from Reading 1, Reading 2, the unit video, and your work in this unit to support your ideas. Refer to the Self-Assessment checklist on page 254.

 Go to the Online Writing Tutor for a writing model and alternate Unit Assignments.

PLAN AND WRITE

A. `BRAINSTORM` **Brainstorm a list of all the different ways of increasing energy that you read about in this unit. Then complete the activities.**

1. List the positive and negative effects that each energy booster has on people.

2. Review each energy booster and decide whether the positive effects outweigh the negative effects. Then decide which energy boosters are best.

B. `PLAN` **Follow these steps to plan your cause and effect essay.**

1. Choose two or three energy boosters to examine in your essay. Think of some reasons for using these methods. Then think of their positive effects.

 2. Go to the Online Resources to download and complete the graphic organizer and the outline for your cause and effect essay.

 C. `WRITE` **Use your** `PLAN` **notes to write your essay. Go to** *iQ Online* **to use the Online Writing Tutor.**

1. Write a cause and effect essay on the best methods for boosting energy levels.

2. Look at the Self-Assessment checklist to guide your writing.

REVISE AND EDIT

 A. `PEER REVIEW` **Read your partner's essay. Then go online and use the Peer Review worksheet. Discuss the review with your partner.**

B. `REWRITE` **Based on your partner's review, revise and rewrite your essay.**

C. `EDIT` **Complete the Self-Assessment checklist as you prepare to write the final draft of your essay. Be prepared to hand in your work or discuss it in class.**

SELF-ASSESSMENT		
Yes	No	
☐	☐	Does the essay build a convincing argument using facts, statistics, reasons, anecdotes, quotations, and examples?
☐	☐	Does the essay use cause and effect connectors effectively?
☐	☐	Are collocations with prepositions used correctly?
☐	☐	Does the essay include vocabulary from the unit?
☐	☐	Did you check the essay for punctuation, spelling, and grammar?

D. **REFLECT** Go to the Online Discussion Board to discuss these questions.

1. What is something new you learned in this unit?

2. Look back at the Unit Question—What energizes people? Is your answer different now than when you started the unit? If yes, how is it different? Why?

TRACK YOUR SUCCESS

Circle the words and phrases you have learned in this unit.

Nouns		**Adjectives**
carbohydrate	mystique	agitated
component 🔑 AWL	protein	minimal AWL
concentration 🔑 AWL	stamina	refined AWL
dilemma	**Verbs**	unfounded AWL
disclaimer	alleviate	
fatigue	bar 🔑	**Phrases**
hormone	contend	relative to
immune system	digest	take issue with
metabolism	foster	
	restore 🔑 AWL	

🔑 Oxford 3000™ words
AWL Academic Word List

Check (✓) the skills you learned. If you need more work on a skill, refer to the page(s) in parentheses.

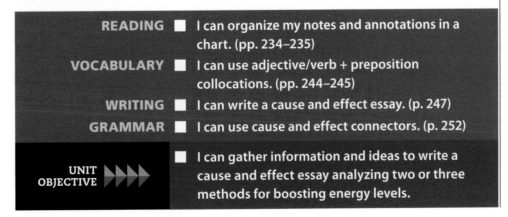

READING	☐	I can organize my notes and annotations in a chart. (pp. 234–235)
VOCABULARY	☐	I can use adjective/verb + preposition collocations. (pp. 244–245)
WRITING	☐	I can write a cause and effect essay. (p. 247)
GRAMMAR	☐	I can use cause and effect connectors. (p. 252)
UNIT OBJECTIVE ▶▶▶	☐	I can gather information and ideas to write a cause and effect essay analyzing two or three methods for boosting energy levels.

AUTHORS AND CONSULTANTS

Authors

Nigel A. Caplan is an assistant professor at the University of Delaware English Language Institute. He holds an M.S.Ed. in TESOL from the University of Pennsylvania and is a doctoral candidate in Education at the University of Delaware. He has taught in several US universities as well as in the UK, France, and Germany. His research and professional interests include genre-based writing pedagogies and teaching grammar as part of academic writing. He is also co-author of two books in the *Inside Writing* series.

Scott Roy Douglas is an assistant professor in the Faculty of Education at the University of British Columbia's Okanagan campus. He holds a Ph.D. in Education from the University of Calgary with a specialization in Teaching English as a Second Language. Over the years, he has had the privilege of working with additional language learners throughout the world, from the Middle East to Asia. His current research interests include novice academic writing, language assessment, vocabulary acquisition, and English for Academic Purposes curriculum and materials design.

Series Consultants

ONLINE INTEGRATION

Chantal Hemmi holds an Ed.D. TEFL and is a Japan-based teacher trainer and curriculum designer. Since leaving her position as Academic Director of the British Council in Tokyo, she has been teaching at the Center for Language Education and Research at Sophia University on an EAP/CLIL program offered for undergraduates. She delivers lectures and teacher trainings throughout Japan, Indonesia, and Malaysia.

COMMUNICATIVE GRAMMAR

Nancy Schoenfeld holds an M.A. in TESOL from Biola University in La Mirada, California, and has been an English language instructor since 2000. She has taught ESL in California and Hawaii, and EFL in Thailand and Kuwait. She has also trained teachers in the United States and Indonesia. Her interests include teaching vocabulary, extensive reading, and student motivation. She is currently an English Language Instructor at Kuwait University.

WRITING

Marguerite Ann Snow holds a Ph.D. in Applied Linguistics from UCLA. She teaches in the TESOL M.A. program in the Charter College of Education at California State University, Los Angeles. She was a Fulbright scholar in Hong Kong and Cyprus. In 2006, she received the President's Distinguished Professor award at Cal State, LA. She has trained EFL teachers in Algeria, Argentina, Brazil, Egypt, Libya, Morocco, Pakistan, Peru, Spain, and Turkey. She is the author/editor of publications in the areas of integrated content, English for academic purposes, and standards for English teaching and learning. She recently served as a co-editor of *Teaching English as a Second or Foreign Language* (4th ed.).

VOCABULARY

Cheryl Boyd Zimmerman is a Professor at California State University, Fullerton. She specializes in second-language vocabulary acquisition, an area in which she is widely published. She teaches graduate courses on second-language acquisition, culture, vocabulary, and the fundamentals of TESOL and is a frequent invited speaker on topics related to vocabulary teaching and learning. She is the author of *Word Knowledge: A Vocabulary Teacher's Handbook* and Series Director of *Inside Reading, Inside Writing,* and *Inside Listening and Speaking,* all published by Oxford University Press.

ASSESSMENT

Lawrence J. Zwier holds an M.A. in TESL from the University of Minnesota. He is currently the Associate Director for Curriculum Development at the English Language Center at Michigan State University in East Lansing. He has taught ESL/EFL in the United States, Saudi Arabia, Malaysia, Japan, and Singapore.

AUDIO TRACK LIST

🔊 Q: *Skills for Success Second Edition* audio can be found in the Media Center.

Follow these steps:

Step 1: Go to iQOnlinePractice.com.

Step 2: Click on the Media Center icon. 🔘

Step 3: Choose to stream or download ⬇ the audio file you select. Not all audio files are available for download.

Class Audio

Unit	Page	Listen	Download
Unit 1			
1	3	The Q Classroom	⬇
1	6	Work With the Reading	⬇
1	13	Work With the Reading	⬇
Unit 2			
2	28	The Q Classroom	⬇
2	32	Work With the Reading	⬇
2	38	Work With the Reading	⬇
Unit 3			
3	55	The Q Classroom	⬇
3	58	Work With the Reading	⬇
3	65	Work With the Reading	

Back

Unit	Activity	Track File Name
Unit 1	The Q Classroom, p. 3	Q2e_05_RW_U01_ Q_Classroom.mp3
	Work With the Reading, p. 6	Q2e_05_RW_U01_ Reading1.mp3
	Work With the Reading, p. 16	Q2e_05_RW_U01_Reading2.mp3
Unit 2	The Q Classroom, p. 35	Q2e_05_RW_U02_Q_Classroom.mp3
	Work With the Reading, p. 38	Q2e_05_RW_U02_Reading1.mp3
	Work With the Reading, p. 47	Q2e_05_RW_U02_Reading2.mp3
Unit 3	The Q Classroom, p. 64	Q2e_05_RW_U03_Q_Classroom.mp3
	Work With the Reading, p. 69	Q2e_05_RW_U03_Reading1.mp3
	Work With the Reading, p. 76	Q2e_05_RW_U03_Reading2.mp3
Unit 4	The Q Classroom, p. 95	Q2e_05_RW_U04_Q_Classroom.mp3
	Work With the Reading, p. 98	Q2e_05_RW_U04_Reading1.mp3
	Work With the Reading, p. 107	Q2e_05_RW_U04_Reading2.mp3
Unit 5	The Q Classroom, p. 126	Q2e_05_RW_U05_Q_Classroom.mp3
	Work With the Reading, p. 132	Q2e_05_RW_U05_Reading1.mp3
	Work With the Reading, p. 140	Q2e_05_RW_U05_Reading2.mp3
Unit 6	The Q Classroom, p. 158	Q2e_05_RW_U06_Q_Classroom.mp3
	Work With the Reading, p. 163	Q2e_05_RW_U06_Reading1.mp3
	Work With the Reading, p. 171	Q2e_05_RW_U06_Reading2.mp3
Unit 7	The Q Classroom, p. 190	Q2e_05_RW_U07_Q_Classroom.mp3
	Work With the Reading, p. 194	Q2e_05_RW_U07_Reading1.mp3
	Work With the Reading, p. 204	Q2e_05_RW_U07_Reading2.mp3
Unit 8	The Q Classroom, p. 225	Q2e_05_RW_U08_Q_Classroom.mp3
	Work With the Reading, p. 228	Q2e_05_RW_U08_Reading1.mp3
	Work With the Reading, p. 238	Q2e_05_RW_U08_Reading2.mp3

iQ ONLINE extends your learning beyond the classroom. This online content is specifically designed for you! *iQ Online* gives you flexible access to essential content.

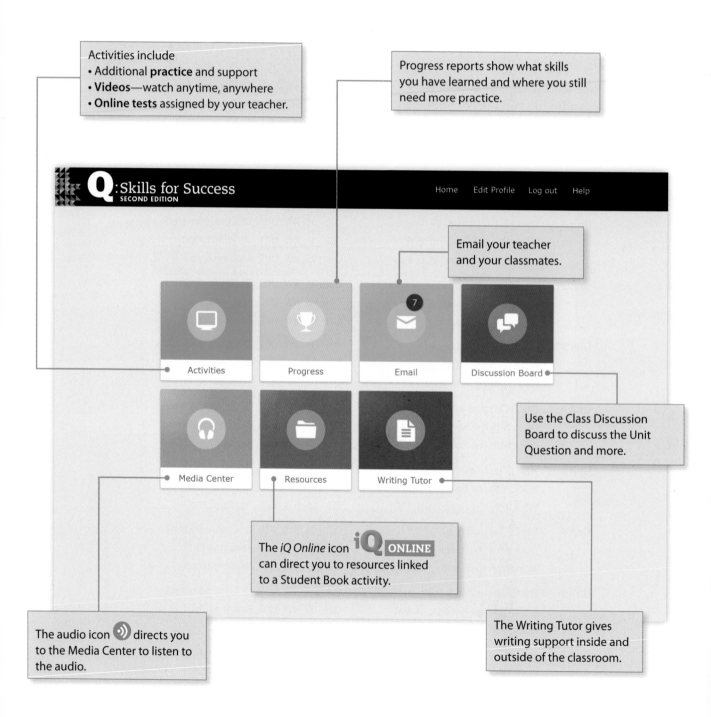

Activities include
- Additional **practice** and support
- **Videos**—watch anytime, anywhere
- **Online tests** assigned by your teacher.

Progress reports show what skills you have learned and where you still need more practice.

Q:Skills for Success
SECOND EDITION

Home   Edit Profile   Log out   Help

Email your teacher and your classmates.

Activities   Progress   Email   Discussion Board

Media Center   Resources   Writing Tutor

Use the Class Discussion Board to discuss the Unit Question and more.

The *iQ Online* icon **iQ ONLINE** can direct you to resources linked to a Student Book activity.

The audio icon directs you to the Media Center to listen to the audio.

The Writing Tutor gives writing support inside and outside of the classroom.

SEE THE INSIDE FRONT COVER FOR HOW TO REGISTER FOR *iQ ONLINE* FOR THE FIRST TIME.

Take Control of Your Learning

You have the choice of where and how you complete the activities. Access your activities and view your progress at any time.

Your teacher may

- assign *iQ Online* as homework,
- do the activities with you in class, or
- let you complete the activities at a pace that is right for you.

iQ Online makes it easy to access everything you need.

Set Clear Goals

STEP 1 If it is your first time, look through the site. See what learning opportunities are available.

STEP 2 The Student Book provides the framework and purpose for each online activity. Before going online, notice the goal of the exercises you are going to do.

STEP 3 Stay on top of your work, following the teacher's instructions.

STEP 4 Use *iQ Online* for review. You can use the materials any time. It is easy for you to do follow-up activities when you have missed a class or want to review.

Manage Your Progress

The activities in *iQ Online* are designed for you to work independently. You can become a confident learner by monitoring your progress and reviewing the activities at your own pace. You may already be used to working online, but if you are not, go to your teacher for guidance.

Check 'View Reports' to monitor your progress. The reports let you track your own progress at a glance. Think about your own performance and set new goals that are right for you, following the teacher's instructions.

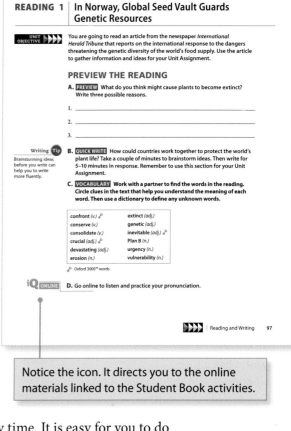

Notice the icon. It directs you to the online materials linked to the Student Book activities.

iQ Online is a research-based solution specifically designed for English language learners that extends learning beyond the classroom. I hope these steps help you make the most of this essential content.

Chantal Hemmi, EdD TEFL
Center for Language Education and Research
Sophia University, Japan

VOCABULARY LIST AND CEFR CORRELATION

🔑 The keywords of the **Oxford 3000**™ have been carefully selected by a group of language experts and experienced teachers as the words which should receive priority in vocabulary study because of their importance and usefulness.

AWL **The Academic Word List** is the most principled and widely accepted list of academic words. Averil Coxhead gathered information from academic materials across the academic disciplines to create this word list.

The Common European Framework of Reference for Languages (CEFR) provides a basic description of what language learners have to do to use language effectively. The system contains 6 reference levels: **A1, A2, B1, B2, C1, C2.** CEFR leveling provided by the Word Family Framework, created by Richard West and published by the British Council. http://www.learenglish.org.uk/wff/

UNIT 1

abandon *(v.)* 🔑 AWL, **B1**
assimilate *(v.)*, **C2**
confine *(v.)* AWL, **B1**
cure *(n.)* 🔑, **B1**
divorced from *(phr.)*, **B2**
ethnicity *(n.)* AWL, **C1**
exploit *(v.)* AWL, **B1**
habitat *(n.)*, **C1**
indigenous *(adj.)*, **C1**
initiative *(n.)* 🔑 AWL, **B2**
in jeopardy *(phr.)*, **C2**
in the face of *(phr.)*, **C2**
integral *(adj.)* AWL, **C1**
oblige *(v.)*, **B2**
persist *(v.)* AWL, **B2**
predominant *(adj.)* AWL, **C2**
retain *(v.)* 🔑 AWL, **B1**
revival *(n.)*, **C1**
scenario *(n.)* AWL, **C1**
shift *(n.)* 🔑 AWL, **A2**
substitute *(v.)* 🔑 AWL, **B1**
suppress *(v.)*, **C1**
target *(v.)* 🔑 AWL, **B2**
wake-up call *(n. phr.)*, **C2**

UNIT 2

boom *(n.)*, **B1**
boost *(v.)*, **B2**
consensus *(n.)* AWL, **B2**
devotion *(n.)* AWL, **C2**
emerge *(v.)* 🔑 AWL, **A1**
engage in *(phr. v.)*, **B1**
estimate *(v.)* 🔑 AWL, **A2**

evolve *(v.)* AWL, **B1**
execute *(v.)*, **B2**
gray area *(phr.)*, **B1**
incentive *(n.)* AWL, **B1**
it dawned on me *(phr.)*, **C2**
labor *(n.)* 🔑 AWL, **A1**
leisure *(n.)*, **B1**
menial *(adj.)*, **C2**
pass your prime *(phr.)*, **C1**
regard as *(phr. v.)* 🔑, **B2**
respectively *(adv.)*, **B2**
rhythm *(n.)* 🔑, **B2**
sophisticated *(adj.)*, **B1**
strategy *(n.)* 🔑 AWL, **A1**
the going rate *(phr.)*, **C1**
the odds are *(phr.)*, **B2**
thriving *(adj.)*, **C1**

UNIT 3

alteration *(n.)* AWL, **B2**
bias *(n.)* AWL, **B2**
campaign *(n.)* 🔑, **A2**
concoct *(v.)*, **C2**
credible *(adj.)*, **C1**
distort *(v.)* AWL, **C1**
document *(v.)* 🔑 AWL, **C1**
error-prone *(adj.)*, **C1**
ethical *(adj.)* AWL, **C1**
inherent *(adj.)* AWL, **C1**
left in the dark *(phr.)*, **C2**
legitimate *(adj.)*, **B2**
manipulate *(v.)* AWL, **B2**
misleading *(adj.)*, **C2**
prominent *(adj.)*, **B2**

provoke *(v.)*, **B2**
scale *(n.)* 🔑, **B2**
scrutinize *(v.)*, **C2**
skyrocket *(v.)*, **C2**
take...with a grain of salt *(phr.)*, **B2**
tempting *(adj.)*, **C1**
transformation *(n.)* AWL, **B2**
unprecedented *(adj.)* AWL, **C1**
visualize *(v.)* AWL, **C2**

UNIT 4

confront *(v.)* 🔑, **B1**
conserve *(v.)*, **C2**
consolidate *(v.)*, **C1**
crucial *(adj.)* 🔑 AWL, **B1**
daunting *(adj.)*, **C2**
devastating *(adj.)*, **C1**
devote *(v.)* 🔑 AWL, **B1**
dominate *(v.)* 🔑 AWL, **B1**
dubious *(adj.)*, **C2**
erosion *(n.)* AWL, **C1**
extinct *(adj.)*, **C2**
genetic *(adj.)*, **B1**
inevitable *(adj.)* 🔑 AWL, **B1**
inhabit *(v.)*, **B2**
intensively *(adv.)* AWL, **C2**
mediator *(n.)*, **C2**
mission *(n.)*, **B1**
mundane *(adj.)*, **C1**
navigate *(v.)*, **C2**
orbit *(n.)*, **B2**
Plan B *(n.)*, **B2**
quarantine *(v.)*, **C1**

reassemble *(v.)*, **C1**
urgency *(n.)*, **C1**
vulnerability *(n.)*, **C2**

UNIT 5

accommodate *(v.)* AWL, **B2**
anticipate *(v.)* 🔑 AWL, **B1**
appealing *(adj.)* 🔑, **C2**
concede *(v.)*, **B2**
controversy *(n.)* AWL, **B1**
counterintuitive *(adj.)*, **C2**
criteria *(n.)* 🔑 AWL, **B1**
division *(n.)* 🔑, **C2**
encounter *(v.)* 🔑 AWL, **B1**
fatal *(adj.)*, **C1**
form bonds *(phr.)*, **C2**
hybrid *(adj.)*, **C2**
in decline *(phr.)*, **C2**
intentionally *(adv.)*, **C2**
isolated *(adj.)* AWL, **B1**
mingle *(v.)*, **C1**
negotiate *(v.)*, **B1**
neutral *(adj.)* AWL, **B2**
nomadic *(adj.)*, **C2**
pop up *(phr. v.)*, **B2**
proponent *(n.)*, **C2**
regulated *(adj.)* AWL, **C2**
reinforce *(v.)* AWL, **B1**
specialized *(adj.)*, **C1**

UNIT 6

abundant *(adj.)*, **C1**
adjust *(v.)* 🔑 AWL, **B1**
anticipate *(v.)* 🔑 AWL, **B1**
appliance *(n.)*, **C1**
aptitude *(n.)*, **C2**
concept *(n.)* 🔑 AWL, **A1**
consequence *(n.)* 🔑 AWL, **A2**
conservation *(n.)*, **B1**
constraint *(n.)* AWL, **C1**
contaminated *(adj.)*, **C2**
convene *(v.)* AWL, **C2**
craftsmanship *(n.)*, **C2**
device *(n.)* 🔑 AWL, **A2**
disposal *(n.)* AWL, **B2**

dubious *(adj.)*, **C2**
elimination *(n.)* AWL, **C2**
founder *(n.)* AWL, **B2**
incinerate *(v.)*, **C2**
obsolete *(adj.)*, **C1**
participant *(n.)* AWL, **B1**
permeate *(v.)*, **C2**
sustainable *(adj.)* AWL, **C2**
thrive *(v.)*, **C1**
tinker *(v.)*, **C1**

UNIT 7

competence *(n.)*, **B2**
conceivable *(adj.)* AWL, **C2**
conduct *(v.)* 🔑 AWL, **A2**
conscientious *(adj.)*, **C2**
consistency *(n.)* AWL, **C1**
dermatology *(n.)*, **C2**
diagnosis *(n.)*, **B2**
doom *(v.)*, **C1**
impulsive *(adj.)*, **C1**
incidence *(n.)* AWL, **B2**
intention *(n.)* 🔑, **A2**
lose one's appetite *(phr.)*, **C1**
novelty *(n.)*, **C2**
olive-toned *(adj.)*, **C2**
phenomenal *(adj.)* AWL, **C2**
project *(v.)* 🔑 AWL, **C2**
scorching *(adj.)*, **C2**
sun-kissed *(adj.)*, **C2**
the jury is still out *(phr.)*, **C2**
trigger *(v.)* AWL, **C1**
undertake *(v.)* AWL, **B1**
urge *(v.)* 🔑, **B1**
with a vengeance *(phr.)*, **C2**

UNIT 8

agitated *(adj.)*, **C2**
alleviate *(v.)*, **C2**
bar *(v.)* 🔑, **C1**
carbohydrate *(n.)*, **C1**
component *(n.)* 🔑 AWL, **A2**
concentration *(n.)* 🔑 AWL, **C2**
contend *(v.)*, **C1**
digest *(v.)*, **C2**

dilemma *(n.)*, **B2**
disclaimer *(n.)*, **C2**
fatigue *(n.)*, **C1**
foster *(v.)*, **C1**
hormone *(n.)*, **C1**
immune system *(n.)*, **C2**
metabolism *(n.)*, **C2**
minimal *(adj.)* AWL, **B2**
mystique *(n.)*, **C2**
protein *(n.)*, **B1**
refined *(adj.)* AWL, **C1**
relative to *(phr.)*, **C2**
restore *(v.)* 🔑 AWL, **C2**
stamina *(n.)*, **C2**
take issue with *(phr.)*, **C2**
unfounded *(adj.)* AWL, **C2**